# Mary of CANADA

*Joan Skogan*

# Mary of CANADA

THE BANFF CENTRE
PRESS

*The Virgin Mary in Canadian Culture,
Spirituality, History, and Geography*

Copyright ©2003 by Joan Skogan

All rights reserved. No part of this book may be reproduced, stored in a retrieval system or transmitted in any form or by any means without prior written permission from the publisher or, in the case of photocopying or other reprographic copying, a licence from Access Copyright (The Canadian Copyright Licensing Agency), 1 Yonge Street, Suite 1900, Toronto, ON M5E 1E5.

NATIONAL LIBRARY OF CANADA CATALOGUING IN PUBLICATION DATA

Skogan, Joan, 1945–
    Mary of Canada: the Virgin Mary in Canadian culture, spirituality, history, and geography / Joan Skogan.

    Includes bibliographical references.
    ISBN 1–894773–03–9

    1. Mary, Blessed Virgin, Saint—Devotion to—Canada. I. Title.

BT652.C3S56 2003     232.91'0971
C2003-906106-X

This book was published with the help of The Writers' Trust of Canada.

Other versions of parts of the work were published in *Voyages: At Sea with Strangers* (HarperCollins Publishers Ltd., 1992) and in the "Mary of Canada" essay edited by Barbara Moon at the Banff Centre's Creative Non-fiction and Cultural Journalism program. The essay appeared in *Taking Risks: Literary Journalism from the Edge* (Banff Centre Press, 1998), and, in shorter form, edited by Zsuzsi Gartner, in *Saturday Night* (December 1998). Hecate Strait and Dixon entrance are also the waters of transformation in *The Good Companion* (Orca Book Publishers, 1998). The Chimney Coulee section of the book was shortlisted for the 2002 CBC Literary Award for travel literature, and was published as a Long Grain of Truth prizewinner in *Grain*, Fall 2003.

*Cover and book design by Alan Brownoff*
*Edited by Kim Echlin*
*Copyediting by Maureen Nicholson*
*Proofreading by Lesley Cameron*
*Printed and bound in Canada by Houghton Boston Printers*
*Cover sculpture by Ted Bellis, photo courtesy of Joy La Fortune*

The Banff Centre Press gratefully acknowledges the Canada Council for the Arts for its support of our publishing program.

THE BANFF CENTRE
FOR THE ARTS

BANFF CENTRE PRESS
Box 1020
Banff, Alberta
T1L 1H5
www.banffcentre.ca/press

*For L. D. Cunningham, and in remembrance of Mary Kelly, Lawn, Newfoundland*

✶ CONTENTS ✶

  XI  *Acknowledgements*

  XV  *Introduction*

    I  CHAPTER 1 ✶ At Sea

  23  CHAPTER 2 ✶ Map-Making

  57  CHAPTER 3 ✶ Mary in Canada

109  CHAPTER 4 ✶ Eastern Settings

125  CHAPTER 5 ✶ Northern Blessings

159  CHAPTER 6 ✶ In the West

217  CHAPTER 7 ✶ Roads

265  CHAPTER 8 ✶ Common Ground

285  *Sources*

*... to Mary*

*the silent one*

   *compassionate*

   *and loving*

   *who is not afraid to*

   *say "Yes" to Love.*

Jean Vanier, dedication, *Be Not Afraid* [1]

*One hazy morning on the highway at 90 miles an hour, H. E. saw the Virgin Mary appear in a bush. A few days later, overflowing with a newfound faith, he realized, in the morning light, that it was only the hull of a pale blue rowboat leaning against a tree.*

Carol Dallaire, *Les Lieux Communs / Commonplaces* [2]

✻ ACKNOWLEDGEMENTS ✻

I AM THANKFUL for the sharp intelligence and love given to the text, and to me, by my editor, Kim Echlin. Cheryl Cohen suggested the order of the journeys in an earlier version of the book. My aunts Joan McMonnies and Muriel Ross encouraged me through the work, as did Joe and Oley Skogan, as well as Adelaide Ambers and her mother Marie Leo, Jeannine Anstee, Sharon Butala, Myra Davies, Christine Fitzpatrick, Erling Friis-Baastad, Vanessa Grant, Margaret Horsfield, Theresa Kishkan, Myrna Kostash, Patricia Robertson, Jean Rysstad, and Sister Sheila Gairns, r.c. of the Cenacle Order. Early in the project, Bishop Remi de Roo, retired, Catholic Diocese of Victoria; Father Donald Dodman, retired, St. James Anglican, Vancouver; and Father Kevin Wiseman (dec.), who said mass at Our Lady of Victory on Gabriola Island, trusted the idea of an ecumenical Virgin Mary in Canada. Carol Mark and Edward Klimuszko at Novalis Press were kind enough to find me a copy of Leonard St. John's briefly out-of-print *The Novalis Guide to Canadian Shrines* when my own copy went missing. The *Guide* is now back in print. I am particularly grateful to The Writers' Trust of Canada's

Woodcock Fund. When completion of the book was delayed, they gave me the money that allowed the work to continue.

Research help was generously provided by Father Leo Casey, retired, Oblates of Mary Immaculate; Michael Clark at the Emily Carr Institute of Art & Design; Kenlyn Collins, librarian, Winnipeg Art Gallery; Raymonde Cyrenne, Canadian Literature Research Service, National Library of Canada; John Donlan, reference librarian, Vancouver Public Library; Andrew Geggie, Geographical Names of Canada, Natural Resources Canada; Terry Glavin; Patricia Molesky, Glenbow Archives; Rev. James Hanrahan, principal, St. Mark's College, University of British Columbia; Laurie Rolland; Rod Sharmon; Liliane Theriault, s.m., archivist, Misericordia Sisters, Montreal; Sylvie Thivierge, Musée de la Civilisation, Quebec City; Father Andrew Takach, Oblates of Mary Immaculate; Margaret Wittich, Catholic Diocese of Thunder Bay; and the Vancouver Maritime Museum.

The publisher would like to thank Dick Bellis for permission to use the cover artwork, titled *St. Mary*. Ted Bellis, the artist, was a carver and a logger in British Columbia.

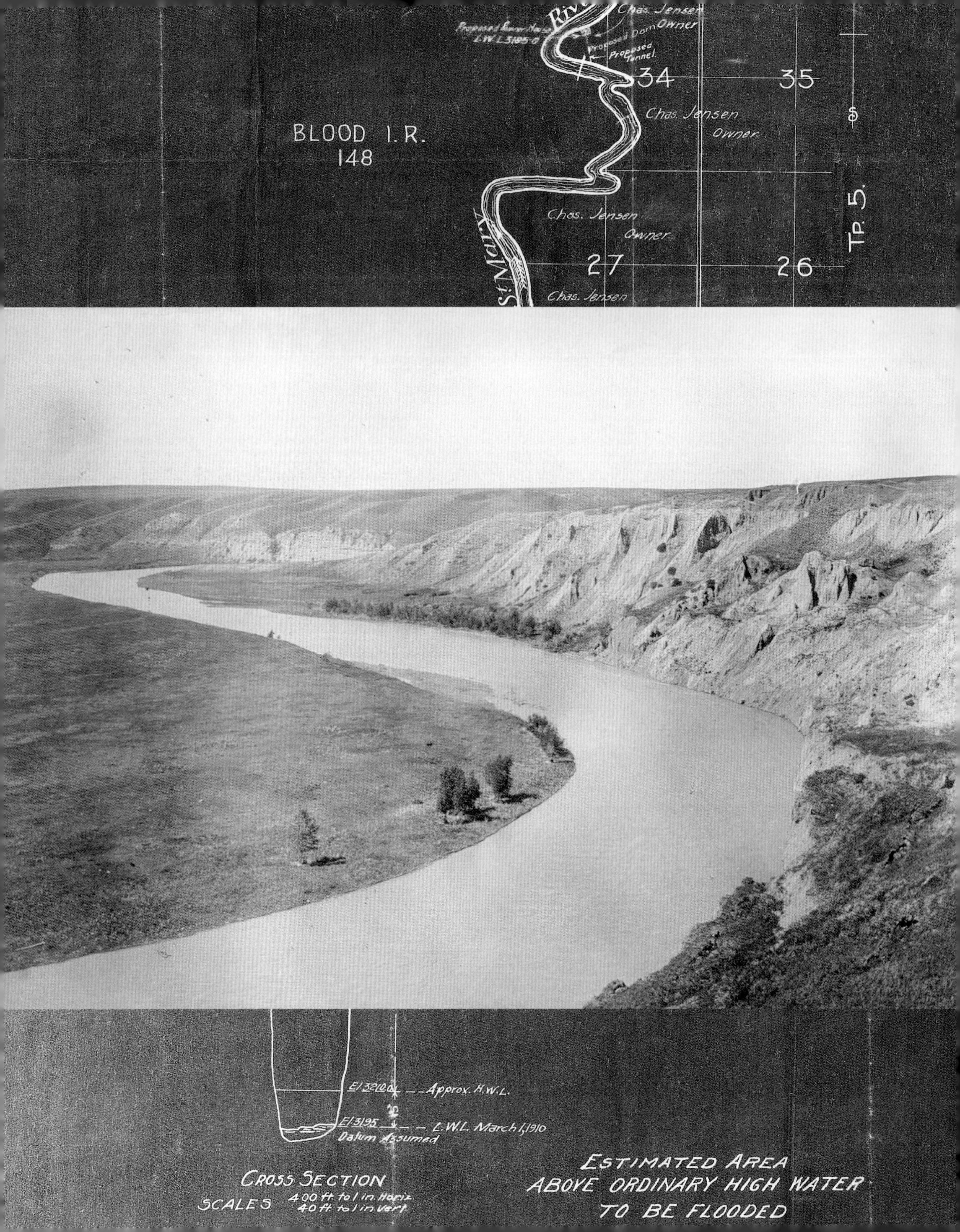

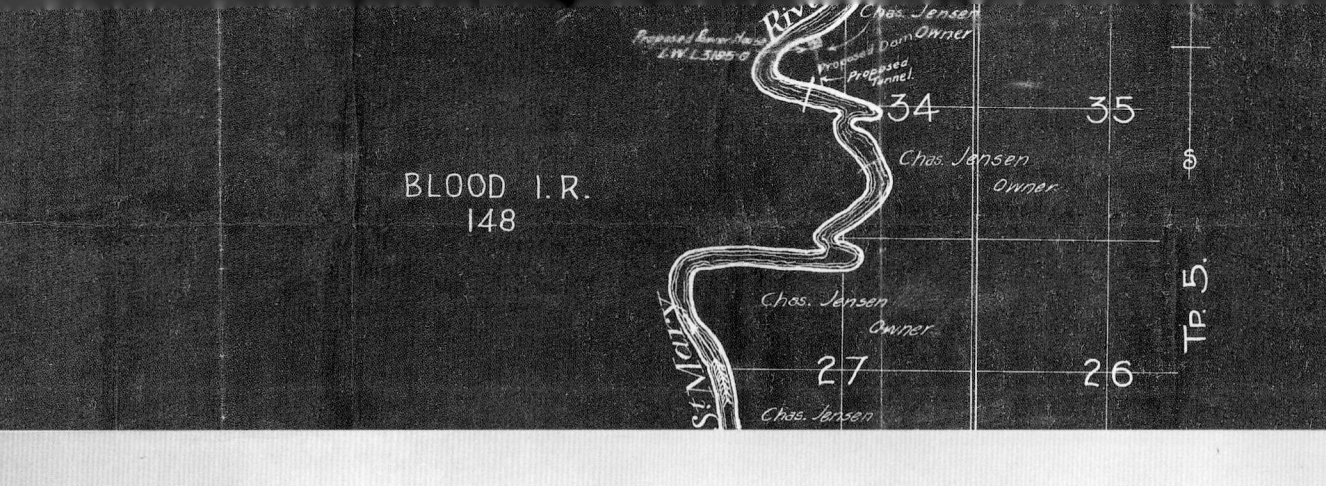

CROSS SECTION
SCALES  400 ft. to 1 in Horiz
40 ft. to 1 in Vert

ESTIMATED AREA
ABOVE ORDINARY HIGH WATER
TO BE FLOODED

KIM ECHLIN

# Introduction

JOAN SKOGAN MAKES A PILGRIMAGE THROUGH OUR CULTURE AND HISTORY IN THIS QUEST FOR THE VIRGIN MARY IN CANADA. WE MAY HAVE BEEN UNAWARE OF THE VIRGIN'S PRESENCE IN OUR MIDST BUT SKOGAN SHOWS US HOW THOROUGHLY MARY'S NAME IS THREADED THROUGH OUR GEOGRAPHY AND OUR STORIES. WITH AN HISTORIAN'S ATTENTION TO RESEARCH AND A PILGRIM'S RECEPTIVITY, SHE FINDS OUR CANADIAN VIRGIN MARY IN BOTH UNEXPECTED AND TRADITIONAL PLACES: GAZING FROM A RENAISSANCE PAINTING AT THE ART GALLERY OF ONTARIO; WAITING IN A ROADSIDE SHRINE IN VEGREVILLE, ALBERTA; PERCHED ON THE DASHBOARD OF A CAR THAT HAS RUN OUT OF GAS ON A NORTHERN HIGHWAY.

*Mary of Canada: The Virgin Mary in Canadian Culture, Spirituality, History, and Geography* is a work of non-fiction, but like art, it has the capacity to teach us to see anew what has always been before our eyes. We learn how the Canadian Mary has lived among our ancestors, and how she embraces our current disillusion and aloneness and need for love — a need as urgent as our need for sleep or water. It is Skogan's particular genius that has also discovered in Mary of Canada a deep fondness for irony and a joyous laughter at the antic human spirit.

A pilgrimage used to be thought of as the course of a mortal life enacted as a journey. Joan Skogan has spent much of her life at sea where she worked as a fisheries observer. She first discovered the Virgin Mary on her beloved Pacific waters while walking rolling decks with the hard-scrabble fishermen she respected. Skogan was unwillingly forced to abandon the sea; we feel her fathomless longing for that life in her wandering, as if for the first time, on the dry, still land. Ashore she looks for compassion, and remembers the Virgin Mary she first encountered on a ship. I like to think of the whole of an individual life as a kind of pilgrimage and if this is so, Skogan's quest for Mary in Canada began long before she was obliged to leave her beloved ocean.

Mary persistently transforms herself to become recognizable in different times and places. In *Mary of Canada* we see how the Virgin has travelled the oceans to come to this new land, and adapted to northern snow and ice and blackflies. Our Canadian Mary has coursed over the freshwater rivers with the Indians, walked our northern expanses with the earliest *courier de bois*, and ridden in the backpacks of settlers. She has inspired contemporary artists and comforted city wanderers who have no place to lay their heads. She appears in movies and the landscape with ready grace. She has lent her helping hand to small-town girls who need a potent mixture of spunk and suffering to get where they are going. Skogan's quest for Mary shows us how the Virgin's spirit nods with hope over our individual lives and reminds us of a compassion that is eternal.

A single pilgrimage is short; Mary's journey, even in Canada, has been long. Skogan digs so deep into her research on dry land — in history, art, and storytelling — that she discovers Mary even in the northern constellations.

I have a theory about how women quest. A male hero strides away from home, battles his monsters and enemies, and returns back to the home he left. We know this story to our bones. But a female quester carries her home within. She can never go back to the place she left. When she returns, her home is renewed by the abundant and idiosyncratic energies that took her journeying in the first place. Skogan first encounters Mary at sea but she recognizes her in the landscape of Canada in this surprising search. There is a feeling that when one works hard to break out of old structures, one risks disorder and getting lost; there is also a feeling of the infinite to this quest. We learn in this book that Mary is probably on, or at the end of, nearly every Canadian road.

*Mary of Canada* is about a quest for an ever-changing order that will allow the universe to embrace us with unexpected compassion. It is about human need set against the final incomprehensibility of war, illness, suffering, and in the end, death. It is also about finding comfort in unfamiliar places, frequently with strangers, always in a moment of transcendent mystery. Mary is a traveller who walks with compassion on one side and ironic and joyous laughter on the other.

I am intrigued and delighted by Joan Skogan's prose style, so wonderfully matched to her unfurling search. She spins her stories and connects them by a repeated phrase or an allusive image. Her imagination leaps at resonances, both visual and verbal, in all things concerning Mary. I find in her style a fitting, bottomless language for the Virgin. It is a language of holding tensions and paradox that suits the yearning and ironic quest of a twenty-first century searcher. I think it is about new order, found in association and detail, an order — if we are receptive — that brings the sea a little closer to the land and the compassion of Mary to a northern soul.

## CHAPTER 1

# *At Sea*

I USED TO THINK MARY WAS EASIER TO RECOGNIZE AT SEA. SHE WAS NEAR AT HAND THERE. SHE AND THE PLAYMATES PINNED TO THE BULKHEADS WERE USUALLY THE ONLY OTHER WOMEN ON BOARD WHEN I WORKED AS AN OFFSHORE FISHERIES OBSERVER ON THE CANADIAN WEST COAST. ON THE JOINT-VENTURE HAKE FISHERY IN THE DEEP WATERS OFF VANCOUVER ISLAND, THE RUSSIAN TRAWL FISHERMEN KEPT HER BELOW DECKS IN THEIR SHARED CABINS AND TEA CORNERS, IN COLOUR MAGAZINE CLIPPINGS OF SIXTEENTH-CENTURY ORTHODOX ICONS, PICTURES WITH SOFTENED EDGES IN WHICH THE GRAVE, GOLD-HALOED HEAD WAS FINGERED THIN.

*eiparthenos (Ever-Virgin)* ✱ *Ark of the Covenant* ✱ *A Mercy for the Worlds* ✱ *Cause of Our Joy* ✱ *Comforter of the Afflicted Consolatrix Afflictorum* ✱ *Domina* ✱ *Gate of Heaven* ✱

On board Polish fishing ships, the Byzantine Black Madonna of Czestochowa, as painted by Saint Luke himself on a plank from Mary's cedar wood kitchen table, kept watch in the captain's cabin and the crew's mess. On one ship, she also hung over my bunk, guarding my well-being at the captain's insistence after the hawser line snapped when the fishermen and I were on the stern. Under her jewelled crown, the Madonna of Czestochowa's sword-scarred right cheek and straight-edged, sombre face seemed not unlike the look of the trawl bosun or the winch man or even me, some nights, when we hauled in the rain and dark.

In my Low Anglican childhood, the most memorable Mary appeared onstage in the blue-gowned co-star role usually played by blond girls in the nativity scene. Christmas allowed a pregnant Protestant Mary to be important, but only briefly. Thirty years later, at sea, where Mary seemed to come to my attention more than she ever had on land, my interest in her stirred. The ocean and the offshore vessels carried her closer to me. She came nearest of all on *Lana Janine*, a Canadian black cod boat fishing the twelve-hundred-fathom grounds at the western edge of Canada's sea limit. *Lana*, formerly *Mary Lou*, first rigged for tuna in the Gulf of Mexico more than forty years before — 36.58 metres; 255.41 gross tons; stem: raked; stern: fantail; build: caravel — and I were the same age. Neither of us had ever stopped working for long, though *Lana* lay underwater some while at an upcoast dock after her Bering Sea halibut voyages. Like Stan Rogers's hard-aground *Mary Ellen Carter*, the boat who had saved her crew through so many Atlantic gales, *Lana Janine* was raised. Changing my name to Mary Ellen Carter occurs to me sometimes, here on land. The need for a rise-again daydream never surfaced offshore, even when I was the only woman among ninety-man crews on Polish stern trawling ships — some Russian vessels carried a few women — and on Canadian draggers. In storms blowing vessel crews' fury with Canadian fishing regulations, or gusts of my own sometime loneliness, or sixty-knot winds across the deep-water grounds, the ocean and the possibility of Mary must have held me up more than I knew.

Left on board by the long-ago Mexican crew, the Virgin Mary lived in a locker on *Lana Janine*'s top deck. The door by the wheelhouse ladder was inset with a blue glass cross. In the locker, beyond the potato sacks, past the cases of root beer and Coke, stood an altar. On the altar, a hardwood arch. Under the arch, Mary of the Black Cod Grounds on the Bowie Seamount—thirty-two hours running time west-northwest of Nahwitti Bar.

Mary and the captain, the cook, the engineer, the deckhands, and I climbed forever up one side of *Lana Janine*'s slanted decks, then braced ourselves for the steep-angled descent down the opposite edge of the roll. The boat's heavy main mast had been taken to make more deckroom for black cod traps, so she rolled on a following sea, and when she was headed into swells. She rolled, wallowing in the waves' trough and riding high in the spray. *Lana Janine* rolled when her main engines were running and when they were shut down for a few hours after midnight, so we could drift, asleep on the Pacific. She rolled on both rising and falling seas, and on no sea at all, on calm water. Only one of the men spoke against her for this. "Roll, then, you bloody whore," he would say. Roll your guts out. But she could not help herself. Even the latches on all her port and starboard doors were loosened from the strain of leaning.

In bunks built abeam, the men and I slid through the short nights, suffusing our heads with blood on one roll, jamming our feet into the bulkheads on the next. If the chapel door banged into my sleep on blowing nights, I would skitter across the slanted deck in bare feet to catch it before we heeled back. Against the shadowed bulkhead at the back of the locker, the Madonna's white plaster face was dark enough to make her Mexico's Indian Virgin of Guadalupe. When *Lana Janine* lunged alone on the ocean at night, the figure of the woman with the rusted rosary swinging wildly on the portside lean seemed to be the boat herself, Our Lady of the North Pacific. She would bear us home, I thought, despite the desperate motion of her hull, and the long curve of the sea before the land would rise before us again. On those nights, I put my shoulder to her sanctuary door, pushed hard to secure the catch, then returned to my

bunk to surrender again to the head-to-foot sliding which slowly turned to sleep.

At sea, Mary was, like the rest of us on board, both familiar and foreign. The crew and I were our landselves until, out of sight of land, with nothing to count on but the boat and the sea, with no one to help us but ourselves, and maybe Mary, we became something other than we had been on land. Our vision lengthened across limitless ocean, reached deep undersea to the dolphins playing fathoms below the keel in the clear water two hundred sea miles off the coastal headlands, then retracted to the fish under our boots and the next meal. Silent, shared exhaustion passed for intimacy, until the gift of some small, unasked-for kindness, like dry gloves or a clean cup, caused us to know we could read each other's minds. Or until someone's impromptu imitation of a hake or a black cod or a captain made us laugh. I laughed so hard on *Lana Janine* I once almost went over the deck rail on one of her lunges, when the freeboard was lower than ever as the hatches began to fill. Out there, we complained less about hard days and, in time, were more tender and nearer to one another than we might have been working together on land.

Mary, too, was both known — of and with the ocean, and the boat and us — and new — exotic, far-knowing, and, for me, always from another country. She came from Russia or Poland or Mexico, and from somewhere else beyond those places. Offshore, she was necessary and inescapable, like the sea.

On shore, she was harder to find. When I staggered inside the fear that I had lost my real home because I couldn't work on boats and ships anymore, I looked around for Mary on land. I missed her, or perhaps I only missed the sea. At first, she seemed to live only in churches where her cheeks were too pink, and she would not look me in the eye. I read about other Marys: Egyptian *Mer*, whose name meant both "waters" and "mother-love"; *Aphrodite-Mari*, born in the seafoam off Cyprus; Slavic *Marzanna*, Mari-Anna who ensured the harvest; Saxon *Wudu-Maer*, Wood-Mary, goddess of the groves.

I knew Mary must have been outside church doors in Canada sometime, though. She must have stepped ashore here with other sailors.

MORE THAN A THOUSAND YEARS AGO, Mary took ship with the first Old World sailors and fishermen to see the inshore waters and headlands that would become part of Canada.

At the Strait of Belle Isle's northern entrance, the Old Norse saga of Erik the Red keeps company with archaeological finds from L'Anse aux Meadows, Newfoundland, to tell the story of North America's first Christian experience. A slate hearth; a cooking pot; an anvil and signs of a forge; a small, perfect spindle whorl, and remains of turf walls for seven buildings — including a Viking-style great hall — have been excavated near a stream running through lush meadows edging a sheltered bay. Narratives of several expeditions from Iceland and Greenland to the place Erik's son, Leif the Lucky, had named Vinland the Good survive in the long saga.

Newly Christian Viking colonists, perhaps 135 men, including two priests, and fifteen women, likely built L'Anse aux Meadows as a base for coasting voyages as far south as New Brunswick to load valuable lumber, furs, grapes, and butternuts, probably shipped regularly, and profitably, back to Greenland.

The home place on the bay would have been crowded warm with bodies when sailors, hunters, and everyone else gathered at Christmas time. Smoke from cooking fires and candles would have drifted through the scent rising from fire-warmed walls made of earth, seagrass, and saltwater-soaked wood to mingle with the smell of slow-roasted venison and the faint sweetness of dried, amber-coloured berries called cloudberries or bakeapples. The Mary carried in Viking hearts could have been part of the Celtic "Mary Mother of joy … corn of the land … treasury of the sea … wished-for visitant of the homes of the world"[1] from Gaelic invoca-

*At Sea*   5

tions and blessings known to the Scottish sailors on Viking crews. A hermit in the Scilly Isles off the British coast had converted Olaf Tryggvason, Norway's tenth-century ruler, to Christianity. His successor, Olaf the Holy, was the king who had banished Erik the Red to Iceland for murder.

The first Virgin Mary to come ashore in Norse imagination and memory as a newcomers' form for Mary of Canada might have borne a Byzantine Madonna's sombre features. The Vikings had long absorbed cultural images from the lands they raided as far south as the Mediterranean. Byzantine Madonnas would eventually grace Russian, Bulgarian, Romanian, Greek, and Serbian Orthodox Churches, and traditionally Russian "beautiful corners" — the icon places — in homes across a country not yet imagined.

In the L'Anse aux Meadows homes, Mary the Mother of Christ probably abided in Viking settler hearts alongside Norse mother goddesses Frey and Frigg. Newly Christian Icelanders and Greenlanders would also have known the old god Odin's chosen sacrifice: he hung nine days on the Tree of the World to gain the gift of a drink from the holy water of inspiration and foreknowledge in the spring at the root of the tree.

A tree of life grows deep in the mythic ground of many cultures. The rose and fruit-bearing tree in the Virgin Mary's garden iconography shares some of its root system with the Bountiful Trees in the Dead Sea scrolls, the Tree of Life in Genesis's Garden of Eden, and the olive and fig trees who went forth with the vine and the bramble to appoint a king in the Old Testament Book of Judges. Trees of which their earthly groves and forests were only symbols held up parts of the Babylonian and Celtic spiritual worlds, and other places nearer to us. Canada's west coast is still supported by a huge hemlock pole because the strongest man from the Tsimshian village in Metlakatla Pass went down into the earth on a cedar bark rope ladder to brace it against his shoulder. The Toronto Italian community's *Festa di Maria Santissima degli Angeli di Quasani* — Festival of the Most

Holy Virgin of the Angels of the Village of Quasano — includes the Tree of Cockaigne, a high pole hung with treats for the climbers.

The L'Anse aux Meadows colonists skirmished with, and were eventually outnumbered by, native peoples they called *Skraelings*. Maritime Archaic Indians (whose seventy-five-hundred-year-old ritual burial place on the Atlantic shore is the world's oldest similarly-made grave site), Dorset Inuit, and later Beothuk Indian people all treasured the Labrador and Newfoundland coastal places the *Vinland Sagas* described as nearly paradise: "no lack of salmon in the river or the lake, bigger salmon than they had ever seen. The country seemed to them so kind that no winter fodder would be needed for livestock ... In this country, night or day were of more even length than in either Greenland or Iceland."[2]

During the Vikings' twenty years or so in the kind country, two Skraeling babies were baptized, undoubtedly without the informed consent of their parents, and a Viking child, the first non-native North American, was born. The infant boy, Snorrie, returned to Greenland with his parents and the others around 1023. About two hundred years later, another Snorrie, the brilliant Icelandic poet and historian, Snorrie Sturluson, set down the recited myths and sagas of earlier times.

Mary's story as a new Canadian had begun with the Vikings, though Icelanders would not return to Canada for almost nine hundred years.

BASQUE FISHERMEN from the mountain lands behind the southeast edge of the Bay of Biscay between France and Spain were probably fishing east coast cod stocks in small boats before the fifteenth century. The long, rocking sea passages made by these men linked Basque Virgins standing steady in the faraway churches of Our Lady of Yrun Urancu and Our Lady of Aranzazu to the ocean within which they swayed with the fishermen and their boats as a layer of spiritual belief in lives infused

*At Sea* 7

with other certainties. The men fishing off the coast of a place they knew as *Terra Nova* were as sure of their eternal connection with the bear stars above them as they were of their astonishingly accurate means of calculating ocean and land distance. From a sturdy, perhaps Iron Age, oral inheritance, Basque people knew how to measure the world by extending the patterns of stones set in lines within circles that still lie in the mountain pastures above the Bay of Biscay. Basque fishing voyages continued all the while explorers with other minds, and other Marys, were making their way by sea to the New World.

Several Marys, including one dressed in a new Marian colour signifying extravagance as well as a heavenly goddess connection, likely accompanied Giovanni (Zuan) Caboto, sometimes known as John Cabot, when he made landfall somewhere on the southern coast of Newfoundland in June 1497. In the five-hundred-year-old cherished Newfoundland inheritance of English sailors' stories, John Cabot's *Matthew* sailed into St. John's harbour in the tender calm of early evening on St. John the Baptist's Day, June 24, 1497. Cabot set foot ashore to claim the land for King Henry VII of England at a place where trees stood behind a shelter made by unseen people.

Cabot was a citizen of Venice, the gleaming city-state built on sea trade, where the words *Desponsamus te, Mare* — We wed thee, O sea — were declaimed as a state ceremony in Venice's Adriatic Sea harbour every Ascension Day. He would have known both the delicate austerity of Gothic Virgin Marys similar to the figure painted in Simone Martini's 1333 *The Annunciation,* and the seemingly sweet nature of the gentle, fair-faced Renaissance Madonnas like Pietro Perugino's late-fifteenth-century *Virgin and Child with Saints,* often painted in robes coloured the new powdered lapis-lazuli blue, more precious than gold leaf, that appeared in fifteenth-century Italian churches and palaces.

John Cabot would also have seen gold-leafed, haloed, centuries-old Marian images plundered from eastern ports to adorn Venice's huge St. Mark's Basilica, and Orthodox Virgin icons treasured by Greek scholars, artists, and merchants living in the city. Probably, he also knew the Virgins of early Byzantine mosaics and frescoes in waterfront churches along the eastern Mediterranean Levant where Captain Caboto, merchant seaman, had sailed cargo galleons in the spice trade, years before he followed his overseas dreams.

But the Mary image dearest to John Cabot and his crew might well have been the more simply made *Nuestra Señora de la Esperanza*, the Spanish Virgin of Hope who protects all seafarers from drowning and shipwreck. Her wooden image is still borne through Seville streets every year as part of a Holy Week penitential procession. Cabot had sailed to Spain more than once to try to interest the Spanish in funding his New World voyage from Seville.

Nuestra Señora de la Esperanza made her way onto a Canadian chart in waters the width of a continent plus forty sea miles west of Cabot's landfall. On the coast that would become British Columbia, she lives in Esperanza Inlet, named while eighteenth-century Spanish ships dispatched from Spain's naval base at San Blas, Mexico, were charting Pacific waters for the King of Spain.

Under my desk, where all of Canada's Pacific passages, inlets, bays, channels, reaches, gulfs, and straits are not only dried, flattened, and depth-marked, but also rolled and hidden so as not to flood the too-still land with longing, the same Canadian Hydrographic Services marine chart — Juan de Fuca Strait to Dixon Entrance Loran C 3000 — marks

*orning Star* ✳ *Mystical Rose* ✳ *Mater Dolorosa* ✳ *Notre Dame du Portage* ✳ *Notre Dame de Bon Secours* ✳ *Our Lady of Good Help* ✳ *Our Lady of Good Hope* ✳ *Our Lady of the H*

the waters on which another form of the Virgin, shaped from very different hopes, once moved on the winds and tides here with Spanish explorers. The conquistadores' *Nuestra Señora de los Remedios*, Spain's version of Mary designated as Virgin of Victory in war since the European Holy League victory at the 1571 Battle of Lepanto against the Turks was dispatched from Mexico with Juan Bodega y Quadra on the well-made vessel named for her, but usually, fondly, known as the *Favorita*.

The Favorita in modern Mexico, and in some Canadian communities, is the Indian Virgin of Guadalupe who appeared at the Aztec moon goddess Tonantzin's hill at Tepeyac in 1531, and who became Mary of Mexico's revolution. Pope Pius XII declared her Patroness of all the Americas in 1946. John Paul II calls upon her as Mother of the Americas.

Alberto Ruy Sánchez, the Mexican writer and publisher, says:

> This virgin is so powerful that each one can accommodate her to their needs. These religious phenomena are much more famous and powerful when they are several things at the same time, when they mean different things to different people and solve different needs for people.
> This Virgin of Guadalupe becomes the virgin of Mexico because she had the qualities of racial mixture that were right for a big mixture of indigenous people. Being *mestizo*, her image was enough of a product of a mixture for all of them.
> For those who were trying to build a nation at that moment, this virgin became a key factor, much more important than the flag and its symbols. Since the independence of Mexico, she has been absolutely popular, and she cannot stop being popular. The day of her celebration, December 12 in Mexico City, the

population of her pilgrims is calculated at more than four million people. Imagine that. It's immense. It transforms the whole city.

There are believers of the Virgin of Guadalupe in other religions. Of course, in Mexico many indigenous people have their own religion, many times they don't believe in Christ or accept him but even those who don't accept the Catholic Church as it is organized from the big cathedral in Mexico City, or in Rome, even those accept the Virgin of Guadalupe.[3]

In Canada, the Virgin of Guadalupe is treasured by many First Nations people, as well as by Canadians who first knew her in Mexico or Central America or South America. *La Morenita's* — the little dark one's — arms enclose the Americas from Nunavut to Cape Horn, and their coastal waters.

SAILORS AND FISHERMEN at sea for long enough always find a way to make a prayer. "Hail, Queen of heav'n, star of the sea, pray for the wand'rer, pray for me," from the old hymn for sailors, or other offerings. When the Polish fishing ships found fair weather to transship tonnes of frozen hake onto a Poland-owned mother ship offshore, the vessels lay at peace out of the shipping lanes, swaying together, for hours. Some off-loading days, alcohol from the freighter's sea stores came back on the cargo slings: rectified spirits, beer, a little vodka. Once, a bottle of warm Russian champagne for me. That champagne had searched oceans, my bosun said, looking for a woman to be surprised by its appearance, and smile, holding the bottle in her arms before the youngest fisherman pulled the cork with his teeth.

In time, in this brief *balagan* — party — time before the winds changed, before we took up trawling and hauling again, the deck bosun always flung his whistle, sometimes his watch, and the fishing crew their shirts, into the sea. Seven weeks outbound from England in 1583, the men on two of Sir Humphrey Gilbert's three Newfoundland colony expedition ships did the same when the *Swallow* and the *Golden Hinde* found each other in thick fog at Conception Bay. Edward Haies, commander of the *Golden Hinde*, the only one of these vessels to reach England again, recorded, "for joy and congratulation of our meeting, they spared not to cast up into the air and overboard their caps and hats in good plenty."[4]

IN THE SUMMER OF 1497, when Atlantic seafarer John Cabot and the *Matthew* again made port in England, Mary of Canada may have been mildly pleased with Captain Cabot's report to King Henry VII, confirming masses of fish heaving heavy and bright in the seas off the coast of England's new colony. (King Henry gave Cabot £10, which Mary of Canada, Our Lady of Good Help herself, would gladly double today to get the cod stocks back.) The Bristol cod merchants who had financed the voyage were greatly cheered. Mary may have practised her endless patience with human wishful thinking and greed concerning Cabot's certainty that he had found the edge of the country belonging to the Great Khan. She might have shaken her head over the fuel he added to a four-hundred-year-long fire for glory that would consume hope, ships, and men on all three Canadian coasts in a persistent European treasure hunt set on the glittering prize of a northwest passage to Orient riches.

Next year, John Cabot made way on the same course to the New World, searching for the island where all spices and jewels were said to be born. No one saw him or his crew again. With every jar that hit the bar in the waterfront taverns of European ports, sailors muttered about Cabot's new land, otherwise known as the sand and rocks at the bottom of the sea.

✸

IN SUMMER 1501, Portuguese brothers Gaspar and Miguel Corte-Real meandered along the Labrador coast aboard tiny, smooth-planked caravels meant for the Mediterranean trade. Our Lady of the Navigators, present at the wheel of all Portuguese and Spanish ships entering uncharted waters, was sailing with them. Somewhere on the Labrador coast, Gaspar Corte-Real traded bits of his gear for some glittering objects the Beothuk people had found: one gilt shard from a broken sword of Italian workmanship; two Venetian-style silver earrings.

Our Lady's response to the Corte-Reals' capture of fifty-seven Beothuk or Mi'kmaq people was not recorded in any logbooks. The New World people, who were sold in Lisbon after Miguel Corte-Real's return, soon died in captivity. Gaspar Corte-Real's ship, perhaps also carrying a slave cargo, had disappeared in an Atlantic storm on the homeward voyage. His brother searched for him the following summer, and he was also lost.

The Corte-Reals left a name for the rocky coast bordering a seemingly limitless potential cod harvest, calling it *Lavradore* after the Portuguese word for landowner or farmer. And they left an opening for the Portuguese "White Fleet" fishboats, with the Virgin Mary in the wheelhouse, to feed Europe from the Grand Banks cod stocks for centuries.

WHILE MONARCHS, merchants, and sea dogs on the other side of the Atlantic were organizing Northwest Passage dreams into ocean expeditions, the Basques were fishing cod from April to July every year on grounds they already knew well. By 1520, their big, slow whaling ships were bound for the Strait of Belle Isle, where bowhead and right whales travelled off Newfoundland and Labrador. Along with heavy fishing gear and Basque forms of Mary connected to the sea, their vessels brought a cultural legacy from one of earth's oldest homelands to find ancient linkages here.

*Euskara Batua*, Standard Basque, is distinct from all other European languages. A few linguistic roots are shared with the Gaelic and Old Irish speech that is the transformed remnant of ancient Celtic languages. Similar slender word filaments may connect Euskara Batua with some Caucasus languages from the other side of the Zagros Mountains.

The Basques met Mi'kmaq people onshore while cod was being salted and whale oil rendered in more or less permanent seasonal beach shelters. Five hundred years later, European blood-group tests would show that the two peoples shared an old inheritance before they ever met. A high frequency of type O blood occurs across the Basque population, similar to the high type O levels in Canada's aboriginal people. Contemporary archaeological and anthropological investigations theorize that Basque people came together in a discrete population around the Mediterranean as a mix of Mesolithic hunter-gatherers and the first farmers in the Neolithic period.

Every man in the Basque cemetery on Saddle Island in Red Bay, Labrador, lies with his head turned west. Bone-bound, empty eye sockets look toward the oldest human longing for earthly paradise in the place where the sun disappears. The Basque dead are turned to the Hebrew Garden of Delight, earthly paradise from which humans were exiled to lands "east of Eden"[5] (Genesis 4:16); to the mythic western Isles of the Blessed, and King Arthur's last resting place in Avalon, the Celtic "Apple Isle" across the western sea. West is Mary's way. The Rose Windows around the Madonna's face or figure at Chartres and other European cathedrals are set into the west walls.

WEST, more than five thousand kilometres west of Red Bay, Labrador, out on the Pacific coast, *Ensenada de Nuestra Señora del Rosario la Marinara* was the name Spanish naval officer Francisco Eliza gave to the waters his expedition explored in 1791. The British Columbia gulf and strait first called after the protective Virgin of the Sailor's Rosary would eventually settle for "Georgia," courtesy of Captain George Vancouver.

The Spanish Virgin who protects sailors would have been on watch for Canadian seafarers one February night in 1881 near Cedros Island off the Mexican Baja California coast. Fearing pirates, the Mexican cargo schooner captain was reluctant to put a line on the small open boat drifting off his stern. But two of his crewmen, uncertain, too, yet determined to see if mercy was needed, rowed back with a small water cask, just in case. They found Captain and Mrs. MacArthur, their surviving children, and two crewmen, near death from thirst and hunger. They had been forty-six days in the lifeboat, 2,619 sea miles on the northeast trades, since Captain MacArthur's full-rigged *Milton*, out of Maitland, Nova Scotia, burned and sank north of the equator when the coal in her holds caught fire.

Nuestra Señora de la Esperanza keeps care of Nova Scotia sailors, even when they're privateers — legalized pirates roving in the interest of saving Nova Scotia's West Indies sea trade, then stifled by the Napoleonic wars — and even when they capture her ship, *Nuestra Señora del Carmen* — Our Lady of Mount Carmel — off the Venezuelan coast with a cargo of salt. The Nova Scotia brigantine *Rover* brilliantly outgunned and outmanoeuvred four or five Spanish coastguard schooners. And benefited from a lucky breeze or two. "*Misericordia* — Mercy," the Spanish marines and sailors at last asked the captain of the *Rover*. Mercy was given, and rewarded by fair winds home to Nova Scotia for the *Rover* and her crew, as well as the salt-cargo profits.

IN CANADA, the Virgin Mary of the sea, and of the explorers and fishermen who returned to Europe, would be changed by the needs of

ual Vessel ✷ Stella Maris, Star of the Sea ✷ Theotokos (God Giver) ✷ Vessel of Honour ✷ Virgin Most Faithful ✷ Virgin Most Prudent ✷ Virgin Most Venerable ✷ Virgin Most Renown

newcomers who stayed here, and by the first peoples, who already knew this place to be a world infused with a sacred presence that was, like Mary, always and forever becoming. As the Virgin Mary was becoming "of Canada," so the physical matter of the country became part of her.

When another Viking-borne Mary arrived in late-nineteenth-century Canada, she was travelling with Lutheran Icelandic immigrants. The Mary whom Martin Luther had described as "God's workshop" lived deep inland with Norse people this time, enduring smallpox and flood waters with the Icelanders until their Lake Winnipeg west shore settlement took hold. The Virgin known to the new Lutheran settlers was also living across Lake Winnipeg and in other northwestern places as Mary of Canada by then, in a shape that joined the bodies of the country's animals and beautiful Cree embroidery with an open, generous spiritual presence.

Writer W. D. Valgardson grew up in the Icelandic community at Gimli (the great hall of heaven in Norse mythology), Manitoba, where he set his picture book *Sarah and the People of Sand River*. The story begins before Sarah was born at an Icelandic farm on Lake Winnipeg, when a Cree woman from Sand River on the other side of the lake "took a pendant of Mary and the Christ child from around her neck and gave it to Sarah's grandmother, who had cared for Cree people dying of smallpox. The Madonna pendant was made of brightly coloured beads stitched on deer hide. 'It is all I have,' the woman said. 'But always wear it. If any of my people see it, they will know you are a friend.'"[6]

✳

IN 1905, Mary of Canada, made from the elemental material as well as the spirit of her northern home, honoured John Cabot and the people of Newfoundland and Labrador by appearing, surreal and serene, enclosed in an iceberg floating in St. John's harbour on the 408th anniversary of Cabot's arrival.

SEABORNE EXPLORERS accompanied by the Virgin of an older world are gone, but seafarers still sometimes step ashore in Canada with the form of Mary most familiar to them. Thousands of Portuguese fishermen who had come to consider St. John's, Newfoundland, their second homeport marched from the waterfront through the city in 1955, bearing a statue of Portugal's Our Lady of Fatima as a gift for the Basilica of St. John. The White Fleet fishing crews and Newfoundland finally remembered Gaspar Corte-Real in 1965, and they put him up in bronze beside the Confederation Building.

Every day in Canadian ports, merchant mariners from many countries still disembark from cargo ships to ask for help from Mary Star of the Sea and her assistants at *Stella Maris* seafarers' dockside missions in Vancouver, British Columbia; Saint John, New Brunswick; Harbour Grace, Newfoundland; Halifax and Herring Cove, Nova Scotia; Sarnia, Scarborough, Thunder Bay, Hamilton, and Toronto, Ontario; Baie Comeau, Montreal, Quebec City, Trois-Rivières, and Sept-Iles, Quebec.

*Ste. Marie Sur Mer No. 37*, *Star of the Sea III*, *Santana Maria*, and many forms of *Stella Maris* are still registered Canadian fishing vessel names, though the Mary-named schooners, brigantines, and packets sea-trading here until the early twentieth century are gone. The *Lady of Lourdes* served Fort Providence, and other Mackenzie River and Great Slave Lake communities, through the 1920s.

The sea and the vessels she supports are still female in English. Even when the vessels are battle cruisers or aircraft carriers, or named for a man, like the old west coast wooden seiner *Snow Prince*, or the new Canada Steamship Lines cargo ship *Honourable Paul Martin*, they become female forms at sea, containers of human beings entrusted to the ways of a life-giving, life-bearing, life-taking natural force always associated with female divinity.

In some minute, transmuted measure, Canada's oceans contain the same ageless salt water that soaked the prairies in Cretaceous geologic times: evaporated and returned, diluted and freshened in billions of years' rain and groundwater; frozen, diminished, melted, deepened, and likely washed offshore out to the two-hundred-mile sea limit. On current and earlier marine charts, in Canadian and trading vessel names, in maritime and fishing traditions, and in faith, Mary, too, is diffused in Canadian Atlantic, Pacific, and Arctic waters.

❋

AND A BASQUE FISHERMAN'S TOMBSTONE at Placentia, Newfoundland, still hints at a faint, perhaps slightly, strangely familiar, impossible to name, fragrance from the far past: "Here lies, having died on May 1, 1676, John de Sale Cesana, Son of the House of Sweetest Odour." The reverberative meaning of a sweetly scented ten-thousand-year-old Basque culture — fishermen's bones yearning west; red roof tiles shipped outbound as ballast, then left by the Red Bay graves in Labrador;

and the Virgin Marys of lamp-lit shrines in an ancient homeland — made a long, inland, western drift in Canada.

✷

ON *LANA JANINE*, when the swells were climbing in God's country twelve hundred fathoms deep around the Bowie Seamount, the engineer spoke of the other captain, the man who took the boat every second thirty- to thirty-five-day trip, saying how he was fond of ordering the Norwegian wheel turn — six hours on, and stay on — and how he would chuck sugar into the sea when the wind picked up out here. She wants something sweet, the other captain would say.

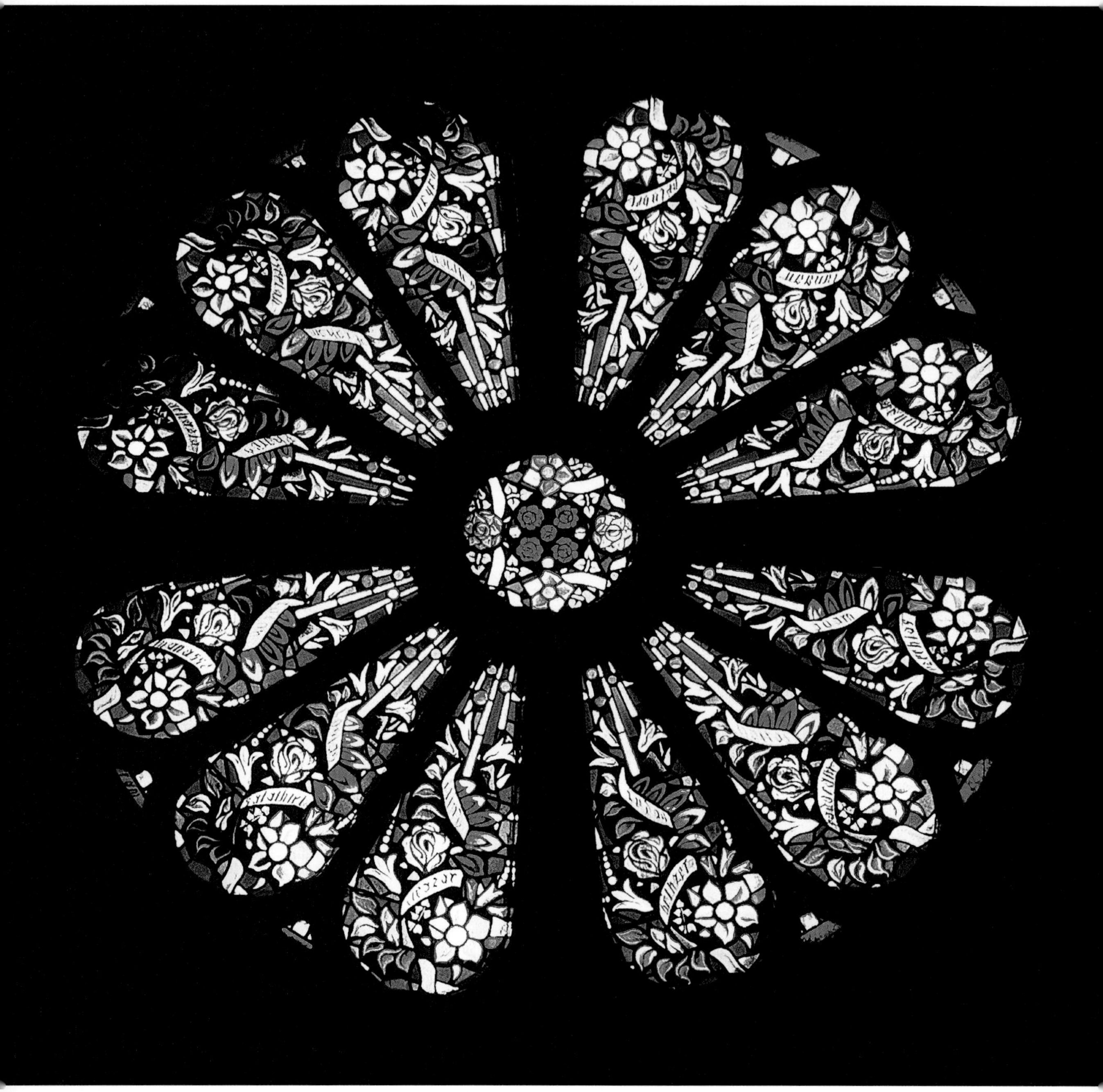

✳ CHAPTER 2 ✳

# Map-Making

AFTER THE SEA, I SEARCHED FOR A WAY TO LIVE ON LAND, AND FOUND ONLY MY RESTLESSNESS AND UNEASE; THE MEMORY OF SOLACE FROM MARY OF MERCY ON THE OCEAN WAS COMFORT I NEEDED TO HOLD HARD. BUT MY CLENCHED GRIP ON AN ELUSIVE AWARENESS THAT HAD ALWAYS BEEN MORE AN INTUITION OF GRACE WITHIN THE FAMILIAR SWAY OF THE SEA THAN A CLEAR IDEA ABOUT MARY CAUSED HER TO FLOW FROM MY GRASP.

From the back row in the Yukon, Toronto, and Gabriola Island churches named for Mary, there seemed to be only a text-edged definition of the Mother of God, and me, who had no right to be present because I hadn't risked Christianity as love or unfaltering belief, or worshipped anywhere much except in Huck Finn's parish past the edge of places I already knew too well.

I have never been good with borders set on the past or on my imagination or around my own safety, or much else that has always seemed more diffused to me, spilling into some other possibility, or time, or hope. I can't even draw and colour a conventional curved mandala for myself. My mandala circle is always a world where the colours in watery shapes wash into one another.

Nor was I any good at staying still on dry land. If I could not be at sea, I could be overseas, on the move. I was better, I thought then, at being in the rowdy *Rus* bazaar in Trebizond, Turkey, before catching the night boat across the Black Sea to Georgia. Still, a glint of gold, tesserae-angled into the mosaic eyes given the Madonna who had glanced at me while I stood at her church door in a flowered field above the port, came back to me on the crossing. Midway, when water on deck caused the crew to lock passengers into a hot darkness heaped with exhausted, or passed-out, or seasick bodies, I saw golden eyes again as a man who looked to be from the Caucasus mountains climbed the baggage hills around me to fire a wooden match on his belt buckle so he could find his pregnant wife to trickle water into her mouth. He must have seen my own eyes pit-lamped in his small flame before it died, must have shared some wordless knowing of a need for mercy as well as a blink of gold with the Trebizond Virgin because he stretched himself across one more ridge of bags to reach my mouth with the last swallow in his tin cup.

Another restless year, I was better at teaching high-school English in Warsaw, Poland, and visiting Muzeum Etnograficznego Virgins, who had sometimes flowed in Polish rivers or appeared in trees in their first forms, than at seeing the need to map a way toward Mary in Canada, or staying put on Gabriola Island in British Columbia. I was better yet at finding passage on a Polish cargo ship bound for the Levant ports out of Gydnia on the Baltic when the school year was done. On the freighter making way in Atlantic and Mediterranean waters, the Black Madonna of Czestochowa was present, framed and facing the bow as she had been on Polish trawlers working the ocean on the other side of the world. If the steady-eyed Byzantine Madonna pointing to the gleaming Christ Child in her lap had not been made by Saint Luke himself on Mary's own kitchen table, she was most likely painted from the fifth-century Constantinople Virgin called Hodegetria, the one who points the way. Because she is the harbour pilot's Virgin, I saw her near the waterfront in Alexandria, Egypt, too, working in a small church and a dockers' café.

In the mountains behind Syria's port at Latakia, I passed an afternoon in a huge fortress poked into the sky eight hundred years ago, wondering if the Tigris River–born Kurdish gentleman who had come to own it in that time might have seen some of the original Byzantine Madonnas in his travels. Since childhood, since reading with a flashlight under the covers, I've known the name of this man who loved honour, poetry, and scholarship as much as his battle plans, and who paid his soldiers a ransom for Holy Land Crusaders captured under his command so he could send the Christians home. Saladin's — Salah Al-Din's — name was given to me by the man I trusted most when I was eight and nine years old. And Robin Hood heard Saladin's name from Good King Richard himself on Sherwood Forest short leave from the Crusade to win Jerusalem from heathen hands. Robin and Richard were Our Lady Mary's men, and Salah Al-Din, who gave all his own worldly goods in acts of mercy even after he had conquered Cairo, would have known Maryam of the Koran, into whom Allah had breathed his spirit as a mercy for the world.

I had time to go down to the crumbled Byzantine and Crusader churches outside the castle entrance, while the chief engineer and the motormen from the ship unloading containers back in Latakia were still measuring arrow slits in the stone towers Salah Al-Din had captured from European knights and soldiers. In the churches' sun- and shadow-patched ruins, I sat awhile with British scholar Marina Warner's *Alone of All Her Sex: The Myth and the Cult of the Virgin Mary* to learn how Robin Hood and King Richard's Virgin Mary had been, as ever, transformed and expanded in Syria and other eastern places.

 The book I had carried across the world was stained with Pacific Ocean fish blood, probably ling cod, and dotted with offshore fishery notes made on some Polish ship: "Tow #107: 22 metric tons hake, 600 kilo. dogfish? @ 400 kilo. yellowtail. Check Loran. Test Line #4. (Rybitwa = sea bird)." I had left the sea to live on land, and if I had not learned how to be at peace with myself in one, still place, at least I knew by then that the Mary who had murmured in my salt water wondering was contained in the Virgin Mary who has shape-shifted her response to our need for a recognizable Holy Mother through two thousand years of differing traditional forms.

✳

THE POTENTIAL for Mary's passionate involvement in daily human lives was enriched by the intensely personal mysticism Roman Catholic Crusaders, and the Holy Land pilgrims from every country in Europe who followed them, found in Eastern — Orthodox, Coptic, Maronite — churches. Soldiers and pilgrims carried Mary as Mater Dolorosa, Mother of Sorrows, into western Christianity, and the fourteenth-century Black Death made sure of her permanent presence. Crusader armies equipped with the Virgin Mary's name as well as their swords also reinforced powerful possibilities in the idea of Mary as Our Lady of Victory in war.

✳

ON THE EDGE of a twentieth-century war a year or so after the freighter voyage, the Madonnas in Slovenia's national gallery in

Ljubljana were the only mothers I had seen at peace for months. Grouped together like friends, some of the oldest among them offered still faintly gilded apples or pears to the Christ Child sprawled on their knees. One Holy Mother in weathered stone held a pomegranate for her little boy to admire. I don't know anymore if I understood then, or later, that the pomegranate as a sweet-fleshed emblem for women and fertility once belonged to other heavenly queens named Hera or Juno. I know the Ljubljana Madonnas, almost smiling, sat or stood at relaxed ease, at home here on earth.

In time, if I could not manage feeling entirely at home on Gabriola Island, at least I was there, making a one-line, soon lost, pencilled note that Mary had appeared more frequently in the last two decades than in the previous four hundred years. But I was leaning out my upstairs window pretending I was looking for the far, smudged line of the coast range while quotidian Hail Marys and other Marian prayers in millions were rising to heaven in dozens of languages from a world where more girls seem to be named for Mary than for anyone else.

From the window on the west coast of Canada, I was trying to believe I could see the Prokletije Mountains between Kosovo and Albania. And see myself, wandering away from the fourteenth-century Serbian church at Decani there, the year before, swaying along the footbridge across the river pouring through the high, rocky pass, then thinking about Celtic Ilyrian tales still known in Albania while I searched for violets and ate chocolate instead of climbing the rocks on the slopes of the Prokletije Mountains to find the high cave named the Hermitage of the Mother of God in Belaya.

But I knew the mountains between Kosovo and Albania could never be seen from my upstairs window. Or the grassy track to Decani church, or the footbridge, mountain trails, and passes that had become escape routes for Kosovo Albanian people fleeing Serb shelling that year in the surrounding countryside. I knew there was no going back to the rocky trails on the other side of the river in the mountains at Decani, willing,

*"What are those flowers?" said Aguilar. "Where did you get these? Roses blooming at this time of year? That's very odd."*

*He started to remove the roses from Pitoque's arms, and instantly they sprang from his grasp, transforming themselves into birds of scarlet plumage. They took wing...*

*Aguilar let out a low whistle and turned back to attend to Pitoque. At once, he let out a cry.*

*"Holy Mother of God." He fell to his knees onto a floor mat of woven palm, "Dear Mother Mary."*

*Pitoque gazed at the Spaniard... He was staring at Pitoque's chest. It seemed there was something extraordinary there. Pitoque looked down and saw what it was — where the roses had been pressed against his robe, where a considerable quantity of his blood had run, now there was an astonishing sight. The blood had dried into the likeness of a woman's profile.*

*Aguilar let out a moan. "Sweet Name of Mary."*

From *The Dark Virgin: A Novel of Mexico*, by Oakland Ross

this time, to set down the violets, the chocolates, and my unwillingness to ever ask for mercy, or grant it to myself, to search for the quiet Mother of God living in cave shadows.

After a while, when I also knew that my willingness to be aware of Mary only at sea or in other countries was formed in my own shallow waters, I began, slowly, to look for her on Canadian ground. No ordnance map was marked with directions to the Virgin Mary. I needed to stake my survey peg in our land, then stretch the map lines from there to discover Mary of Canada.

I looked outside my back door on Gabriola Island first, not on garden ground, because gardening doesn't occur to a hunter-gatherer like me, even if the hunting and gathering only happens in my mind, but beside the logging slash, where a faint, cinnamon-sweet scent floated in the air and wild roses flourished, as they do in unbroken earth across the country. *Rosa nutkana* (Nootka rose), along with *Rosa woodsi lindl* (prairie rose), *Rubus odoratus* (rose raspberry), and *Rosa acicularis* (prickly rose) are some of Mary's wild roses in Canada.

✷

THE ROSE HAS BEEN MARY'S FLOWER since she inherited the Romans' Flower of Venus, Aphrodite's Mysteries of the Rose, and a Gnostic Gospel belief that roses had sprung from the first menstrual blood of Psyche, the virgin soul, when she fell in love with Cupid as Eros. In brilliant dew, fragrant *rosas de Castilla* filled Juan Diego's cape when the Virgin of Guadalupe appeared to him in 1531 at Tepeyac, Mexico. In the medieval cathedrals of Europe, Mary was often addressed as the Rose, Mystic Rose, or Queen of Roses. Chartres Cathedral's Virgin Mary window on the west wall is the Rose of France.

Mary's roses or mandala-rose stained-glass windows also show up, often unrecognized, in Canadian Protestant (as well as Catholic) churches. A red rose in full bloom is set beneath the words, "The Beauty of God's Grace" on the May 2001 cover of *Crossroads Compass*, the magazine of *100 Huntley Street*, Canada's national daily Protestant evangelical Christian TV program broadcast from Burlington, Ontario.

The 100 Huntley Street rose might be one of Agriculture Canada's winter-hardy Explorer roses. Mary of Canada, Queen of Roses, is more than pleased with the Morden, Manitoba Research Station for developing roses able to survive −35°C. With only snow as protection, the disease-resistant, repeat-blooming, minimal-pruning Champlain (velvety dark red, outstanding for continuous flowering); Simon Fraser (medium pink, low shrub); Louis Jolliet (medium pink, spicy fragrance); John Cabot (medium red, a climber); William Baffin (medium red, a climber and rambler); Alexander MacKenzie (deep red, vigorous); Martin

Frobisher (soft pink, hardy rugosa); and other Explorers will bloom here every year.

Wild roses, though, were the flowers first used to make rose beads. Petals from wild roses in warmer places were ground smooth, then rolled into spheres to be dried and strung as rosary beads that would scent the air with each turn of the fingers warming them. Rosary beads for counting the recital of Marian prayers are an ancient devotion. Beads or knots marking meditative chants and prayers used in Hindu, Buddhist, and Islamic traditions suggest that medieval crusaders, Holy Land pilgrims, and sea traders may have carried the practice to western Christianity.

Prime Minister Jean Chrétien's desperate grandmother recited three rosaries every day during the 1896 federal election campaign. The extra rosaries were needed because her Liberal party organizer husband had been refused confession and absolution for giving alcohol to prospective voters. Jean Chrétien explains in his 1985 autobiography *Straight from the Heart*: "It was a common practice; my grandfather's father-in-law, Laforme, had done the same thing for the Tories. It was also a sin. The priest, however, gave absolution to my Tory great-grandfather but not to my Liberal grandfather ... only the Bishop of Trois-Rivières could absolve someone of such a terrible sin." François Chrétien declined to confess to the bishop whom his grandson describes as "an ardent Conservative who used to emphasize in his sermons that Heaven is blue and Hell is red, *rouge*."[1] Madame Chrétien's rosary prayers were answered when the bishop eventually sent a Franciscan priest to confess François Chrétien.

Although Canada's oldest rosary may be the beads found in the Basque graves on Saddle Island in Red Bay, Labrador, and in the burned ruins of the Jesuits' seventeenth-century Sainte-Marie-aux-Hurons mission. Mary's beads have also attended NHL games in New York Rangers' coach Fred Shero's non-Catholic pocket as well as with other coaches and players, all the while Phil Esposito was speeding through Hail Mary and the Lord's Prayer on ice before the game-opening

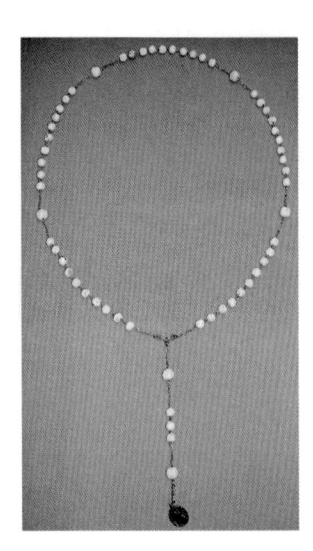

Morning Star ✳ Mystical Rose ✳ Mater Dolorosa ✳ Notre Dame du Portage ✳ Notre Dame de Bon Secours ✳ Our Lady of Good Help ✳ Our Lady of Good Hope ✳ Our Lady of the

*Remember — to prevent rain on your wedding day in Canada, pin a rosary to the clothesline the night before.*

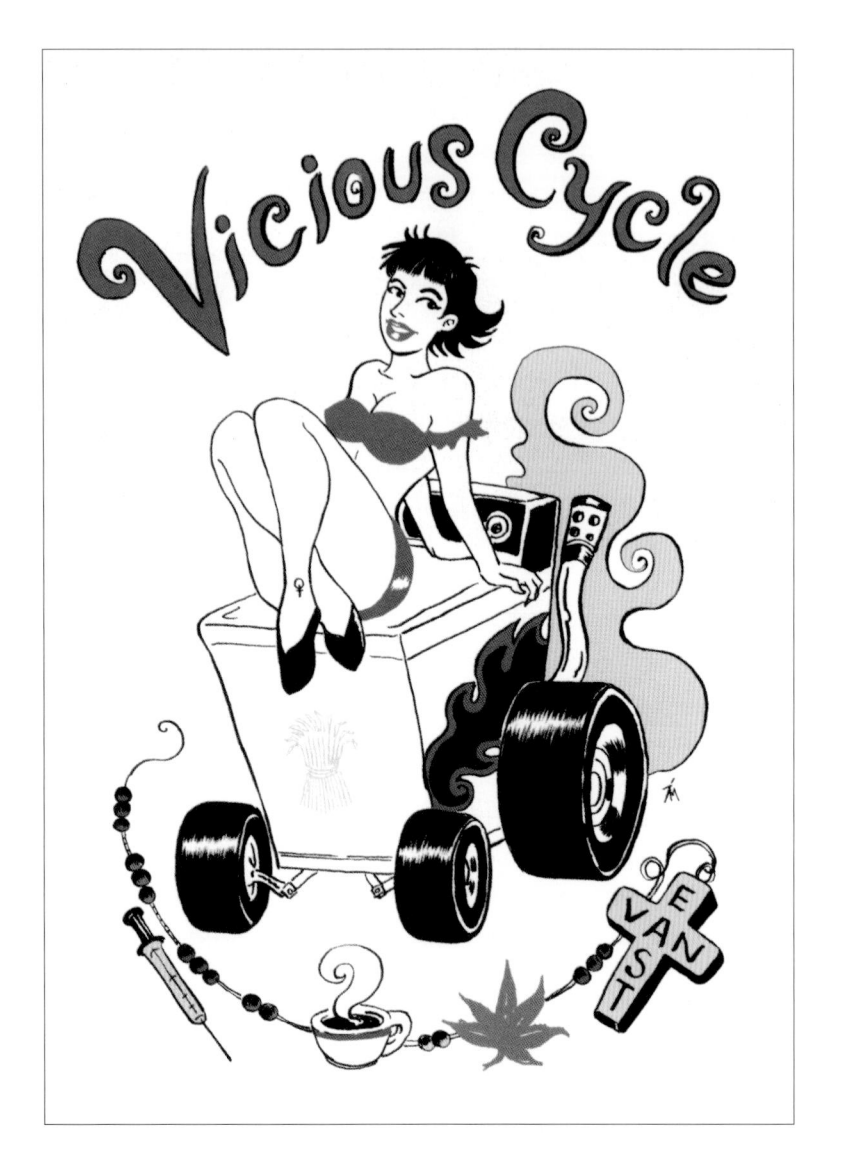

32 MARY OF CANADA

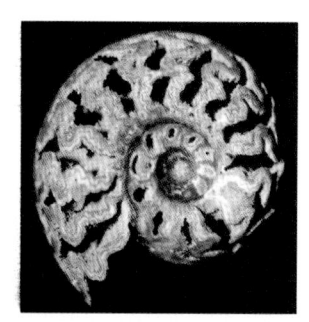

national anthem ended. The rosary adorned with a marijuana leaf and a coffee cup on the logo for Rebecca Freeland's Vicious Cycle Laundromat on Commercial Drive in East Vancouver rises from other holy rituals.

Rituals joining roses and Mary to some of human culture's oldest sacred matters, and to the sea, are still performed in Canada. In some Canadian churches, the rose that descended to Mary from Aphrodite's six-petalled flower is the centre of the pilgrim's labyrinth patterned after the walkway at Chartres Cathedral. In need of a symbolic journey to replace dangerous Jerusalem pilgrimages, medieval Christian churches adopted the spiral walkway that had always meant mystical entry into the womb of the earth, and rebirth in a return to the world along the same narrow road. A universally found coiled-snake pattern at the entrance to caves or hillside temples led Neolithic ceremonial walkers into the earth. Minoan culture on Crete, where the *labrys,* a double-bitted axe, was used to sacrifice bulls to the moon goddess, named the path that circles in on itself.

Chartres Cathedral's twelfth-century inlaid stone whorl is the model for Nanaimo, British Columbia's Bethlehem Retreat Centre labyrinth. The Benedictine sisters at the Centre's House of Bread monastery say the popular, eight-thousand-stone, grass-edged, spiral path can be "a meditation tool ... used by anyone from any tradition." A downtown Vancouver Anglican church offers a portable version of the Chartres labyrinth to St. Paul's Hospital cancer patients undergoing chemotherapy and radiation.

Like the Russians who tossed roses and other flowers into the sea on the site where the *Kursk* submarine sank in the Barents Sea with 118 of their sons, lovers, husbands, and brothers on August 12, 2000, Nova Scotia fishermen throw wreaths of roses into the Atlantic at the Lunenburg Fishermen's Memorial Service. Their ritual connecting roses to Mary of the ocean drifts into the reflected self-images seen by viewers of *Aporia*, Toronto artist Giselle Amantea's installation of flower-framed mirrors etched with references to "Roses," American artist Marsden Hartley's painted elegy for the drowned sons of a Nova Scotia family with whom he had stayed in the 1940s. Brilliant pink against the dark water around them, Hartley's rounded blooms and their burden of sorrow will be borne by the waves a while, then absorbed into the sea.

Roses awash with salt water, or carved in white pine for a nineteenth-century Quebec Virgin Crowned with Roses, or described in almost every setting of Marian Engel's *The Glassy Sea*, even the Eglantine convent in London, Ontario, where the Anglican sisters were "seldom mystical and were above all cautious of Mariolatry,"[2] are some of the riches created from the vast cargo of cultural meanings the Virgin Mary of the Old World brought with her to Canada.

Her store of the world's treasure included not only the sea, moon, and stars, along with springs, flowing water, roses, apples, grain, and other earthly blessings, but also a constellation alight with her images in art.

✶

FROM THE FIRST CENTURY C.E., human beings have drawn, painted, sculpted, carved, touched, carried, described, and dreamed the

Virgin Mary as a holy mother who is always a changing woman. Her ongoing shape-shifting and expanding attributes and titles are born in prayers. Two thousand years of petitions to the mother of all, formally recited, or muttered under the breath, gasped between sobs, or kept unspoken, were — are — formed in the certainty that Mary knows human need in each prayer-maker's time and place. The visual images first made in early church frescoes, gold-leafed icons, and magnificent statues and paintings held many Marys and meanings long before modern mass production multiplied them in kitchen calendar pictures, and the plaster or plastic figures keeping house in shrines on dusty roadsides or in home corners.

In *Reading Pictures: A History of Love and Hate*, Canadian writer Alberto Manguel chooses the fifteenth-century *The Virgin and Child Before a Firescreen*, sometimes attributed to Robert Campin and to other artists, to display the coded secrets in a painting set in recognizable, probably Netherland, domestic reality. The straw-coloured, woven hemp fire screen haloes (via the Roman Empire's rays around Apollo, the sun god, inherited by the early Christian church) long-haired, well-kept Mary as a young wife in her well-appointed home. She offers her breast, full with the milk of mercy and love (commercially remembered in Liebfraumilch wine!) to her child, and to the painting's beholders. Manguel writes, "The first image of the Virgin and Child that has come down to us dates from the third century. It was painted on one of the walls of the catacombs of St. Priscilla in Rome and shows ... a veiled mother holding a child on her knees, the child's face turned toward us, His left hand on her breast, while another figure, perhaps an angel, points to a star above them.

"The depiction of the nursing goddess is ancient and universal: Ishtar in Mesopotamia, *Pacha Mama* among the Aztecs, *Dewaki* nursing Krishna in India, Isis in Egypt and many more."[3]

Almost every detail of *The Virgin and Child Before a Firescreen* — the nondescript three-legged wooden stool in the corner, the lick of flame still visible over the firescreen, and more — holds another level of the artist's

**Portraits of a Lady**

*Our lady was forbidding, her babe, grim. Even their clothes hung rigid and absolute until Cimabue and Giotto allowed air in. Then,*

*robes billowed to fall in gentle waves. Campin invited us to hold the child — as if it were our own — and we grew nearly filial with*

*the mom. But the boy became a man and died and she, after a proper interval, danced off to vanish in the wild. Boucher thought*

*he spied her there, bathing with a friend. Later, Renoir may have glimpsed her, naked at a bath. Manet claimed to have found her*

*naked too, dining in some park with two clothed men. This proved a hoax. Pollock splashed through chaos on his hopeless quest. Rothko sought*

*her. He disappeared and left us staring at an empty field. We're abandoned to our loss, victims who celebrate an orphanhood. We do have that,*

*at least: a small meal, if not a feast, a final bit of nourishment before we stagger home (gullible, slack-jawed, almost dumb) to beg the absolute to take us in.*

From "Portraits of a Lady," *The Exile House*, by Erling Friis-Baastad

Map-Making   35

intention. Some of the secrets have only been revealed by contemporary means. X-ray inspections show the Christ Child's uncircumcised penis, painted over by a later, more prudish artist. The two octagonal tiles at the edge of Mary's dress, which otherwise falls to a satisfyingly modern-looking black-and-white tiled floor, mean that the eighth day after birth, the day of circumcision and naming in Jewish law, has not yet arrived.

Other secrets concealed in Mary's images by venerable international custom occasionally appear in Canada. In East York, Ontario, tears rolled down a colour print of a 750-year-old icon of the Mother of God at the Greek Orthodox Church of Mother Portaitissa, Saints Raphael, Nikolaos and Irene in September 1996. Church donations were encouraged, but Tsar Peter the Great's response to Marian sorrow involving money would have been more helpful to parishioners and miracle seekers. In 1720, Peter quit inspecting progress on his beloved Ladoga shipping canal to travel through the night for a long, hard look at the Virgin Mary icon weeping high above the crowds in a St. Petersburg church.

At the original, wood-built Winter Palace on the Neva River, surrounded by Orthodox priests and state officials as witnesses, Peter removed the icon's fabric backing, found the eye cavities where congealed oil had been inserted, then lit candles to melt the oil and cause the Virgin to weep. In East York, Ontario, the priest, half a million dollars, and the Virgin's tears vanished, much as the signs of grief that had drawn thousands of visitors to a Montreal man's Mary statue in 1986 had melted away in bacon fat.

History, social conditions, fashion, and church doctrine are the more usual transformers of the Virgin Mary's outward appearance. The heavenly queen who shimmered in a sweet-grained, layered matrix made from the Gospels, later apocrypha narratives, and Middle Eastern, Greek, and Roman cultures rich in starry goddess mothers became a delicate, richly robed Renaissance Madonna, then a milder, humbler Holy Mother who seemed closer to earthly families in some centuries.

The ordinary intimacy of Mary's place in daily life outside church walls shows up in traditions like the very old "Lullaby to the Infant Mary" — *Dormi, dormi blandula / Caeli gaudium puella / Dormi, dormi blandula /* Sleep my sweet, sleep my pretty / Little girl who is heaven's joy / Sleep, sleep, my little shining child — and in flower's names and customs. Lavender gained its fresh, lasting scent when the mother of Christ dried his baby clothes over its bushy growth. Even the lady slippers in the lane are Mary's flowers, first named Our Lady's slippers. Dandelions are Mary's Bitter Sorrow on the testimony of every child, including me, who ever tasted the milk in their stems. But the queen of Mary's blooms is still the rose.

Giselle Amantea's installation infused with references to the Marsden Hartley Nova Scotia roses, along with an 1876 Ontario Mennonite embroidery showing the Virgin Mary in the Rose Bower, the rose images in Canadian church windows and architecture, and the herb-garden roses contradicting a less natural, less beautiful form of Mary in the 1998 film *The Hanging Garden* — all root Mary in Canada in one of the oldest Marian traditions in the world.

On the rural Nova Scotia ground filmed in *The Hanging Garden*, her roses grow far away from the porcelain statue of a remote-faced Blessed Virgin Mary who represents "the eyes of God in the house,"[4] according to aged Nana, who sets the watchkeeper virgin on a shelf beside her bed. This Virgin observes Nana's son, Poppy, brutalizing his mother, his wife, and his children, wounding everything he touches except his beloved garden, where roses thrive among lad's love, aphrodite, and other folk-named herbs and flowers. Porcelain Mary shatters in the chaotic rage Nana creates when she sees her teenaged grandson, William, caressing another boy in the rose garden one night.

✳

MORE THAN VISUAL IMAGES, rose traditions, and other culturally inherited customs came ashore with Mary in Canada. Her Old World freight included religious history and theological debate. *The Hanging Garden*'s remote, brittle Mary is an image of the Roman Catholic Blessed Virgin Mary who is set apart from human beings by her Immaculate Conception, the belief that she was conceived and born exempt from sin (proclaimed as dogma by Pope Pius IX, 1854), and by her bodily Assumption into heaven (proclaimed as dogma by Pope Pius XII, 1950). Hundreds of years earlier, this Mary without the softening, hope-filled light of the Christ Child in her arms, carrying only European theological and translation arguments about her birth and death that would continue for centuries, arrived in Canada with the Jesuits and Ursulines from France.

The widow Marie Martin, a baker's daughter running her brother-in-law's cartage business in Tours, France, about 1625, wore a shirt of knots and thorns, lashed herself with nettles, and ate wormwood. Joyce Marshall, translator and editor of *Word from New France: The Selected Letters of Marie de l'Incarnation*, writes, "These actions must be considered within the context of the times. They were recognized spiritual practices. By suffering pain, one shared to a small extent Christ's sufferings on the cross; by degrading the body, one demonstrated one's lack of worth, and only by a demonstration of one's worthlessness before God could one win such spiritual favours as Marie Martin longed for — the actual presence of Christ, the interpenetration of her being by his being."[5] (Not to mention that wormwood is now known to be the key, mind-jittering ingredient in nineteenth-century absinthe.)

On a night in late December 1633, Marie Martin, now Marie de l'Incarnation of the cloistered Ursuline teaching order in France, had a dream she described in a letter probably written in May 1635 to Dom Raymond de Saint-Bernard, the Feuillant priest who had been her spiritual director from 1625 until 1633. In Marie de l'Incarnation's dream, she and another woman were walking, hand in hand, on a difficult journey to reach their dwelling place. At last they came upon a solitary man who admitted them to "a large and spacious place that had no roof but the sky. The pavement was white as alabaster but spotted all over with vermeil. There was a wonderful silence there."[6]

In one corner of the dream landscape stood a miniature white marble house, "Upon its roof there was an embrasure in the form of a seat and on this the Blessed Virgin was sitting, holding the little Jesus in her arms." A church appeared so far below the Virgin's house that only the summit of its roof, enveloped in mist, could be seen. "There was a road to go down into these great vast spaces, but it was exceedingly dangerous because of having terrible rocks on one side and awful and unguarded precipices on the other. In addition, it was so straight and narrow that it was frightening even to look upon it." In the dream, the Blessed Virgin, tiny enough, marble house and all, to be enclosed in Marie de l'Incarnation's arms, kissed her, and turned three times to whisper to the child Jesus.[7]

When the Ursuline Mother Superior arranged for Marie de l'Incarnation to meet a member of the Jesuit order, and Jacques Dinet, Jesuit Superior, became her spiritual director, he told her the steep, fog-bound dream country with the white ground was undoubtedly Canada. Jesuit policy concerning Mary's place on earth as well as heaven is included in Marina Warner's *Alone of All Her Sex*: "The Jesuits, founded in 1534, applied themselves with the fierce militancy of their order to spread the belief in Mary's Immaculate Conception, for it was one of the special Catholic ideas that roused the Reformers' tempers, and therefore proclaimed Rome's defiance and fearlessness."[8]

In 1639, Marie de l'Incarnation and two other Ursuline sisters sailed for New France to share missionary responsibilities in the colony with the Jesuits who were also their spiritual directors. The Virgin Mary who stood apart from humanity attended both Jesuit missions on northern lakes and rivers, and the Ursulines' convent and school in seventeenth-century Quebec.

In *Virgin Trails, A Secular Pilgrimage* (2002), sharp-eyed, open-hearted Canadian Robert Ward, who walked far and long (and sometimes lined up longer) to reach Europe's Marian shrines, writes about Mary's Immaculate Conception: "Even within the Catholic Church it always aroused controversy. Aquinas, the supreme philosopher of the Christian Middle Ages, rejected it, as did even Mary's greatest eulogizer, Saint Bernard of Clairvaux. After the Reformation, the Jesuits warned their flock that anyone who denied the Immaculate Conception was well on his way to hell, even as the Dominicans in the church next door preached the opposite … the Church officially steered the middle course: Catholics could believe in the doctrine or not as their conscience dictated … Then in 1854, Rome changed tack. The doctrine of the Immaculate Conception was declared dogma."[9] Ward, another non-Catholic pilgrim in thrall to Mary's endurance and beauty, traces much of the reason and timing for the 1854 declaration to the Catholic Church's fear of the oncoming rush of modernity, and of the new Italian republic in the making.

This more remote mid-nineteenth- and twentieth-century Mary Immaculate form of the Roman Catholic Blessed Virgin Mary was hard for me to know. Marina Warner, whose Marian scholarship was in part inspired by the loss of her own joyous, young devotion to Mary, a love dissolved by sorrow and disillusion in the realization that no human girl or woman, however shamed by Church authority, can emulate this Virgin's moral and physical purity, writes, "Soaring above the men and women who pray to her, the Virgin conceived without sin underscores rather than alleviates pain and anxiety."[10]

I own a portion of pain and anxiety, but I was an adult and a wanderer through books and across countries and oceans when I set out to look for a way to know Mary. It was too late for me to be intimidated by the demands imposed on so many Canadian women and girls in the name of the Virgin once used to inspire Toronto singer and playwright Marie-Lynn Hammond to endure a Lenten dental appointment without anaesthetic. Only because I was free to be an awkward, itinerant pilgrim to the idea of Mary who still resonates with the staying power of older, wilder, divine mothers while she moves and changes in the world was she within reach of my hopes.

Mary Immaculate would become part of the Virgin who is, as ever, mysteriously and simultaneously, all of her forms, aspects, titles, times, and always becoming. The Mary who had been painted as *Maria Regina* in the sixth century while the early church struggled for, and with, state power in Rome and Byzantium-Constantinople had also become the sweetheart of medieval troubadours, and the militant hope for soldiers all the while she had been moving nearer to earthly homes as a mother of sweetness and humility.

Thirteenth-century Italian Saint Francis of Assisi's gentle compassion for all living creatures inspired his creation of the first Christmas crèche as a scene showing a family struggling with all-too-human earthly poverty and homelessness as well as being touched by divinity. Mary gradually came to represent milder, more passive virtues such as obedience and humility. Saint Joseph, who had been quietly resting in the background for fifteen centuries, became more important.

alupe ✳ Argentina: *Our Lady of Lujan* ✳ Bolivia: *Our Lady of Copacabana* ✳ Brazil: *Our Lady of Aparacida* ✳ Chile: *Our Lady of Carmel of the Maipu* ✳ Columbia: *Our Lady of Ch*

42   MARY OF CANADA

In the 1600s, the form of the Virgin Mary who sailed to New France from the mother country was affected by European wars, endless theological arguments, and the faint, disturbing possibilities of a middle class that would surely require women to keep quiet at home, as well as by the heightened emotions of the Catholic Counter-Reformation.

Let alone the seventeenth-century miracle baby who would become Louis XIV of France. After twenty-three years of childless marriage, and many pilgrimages to Mary's shrines and to the wonder-working bones of her mother, Saint Anne, at Apt, the Queen of France gave birth to a boy in 1638. Anne of Austria, passionately involved with the Catholic Counter-Reformation, was regent while the future king was still a child, and sustained a strong presence in Canada through her connections with both the Jesuits and the Ursulines. She sent letters to Marie de l'Incarnation, who often requested donations of funds and goods from the ladies of the French court. Queen Anne appears as France herself in the Ursulines' c. 1670 painting, *France Bringing the Faith to the Indians of New France*, attributed to Récollet order artist Frère Luc, a.k.a. Claude François. The Virgin Mary in Frère Luc's *Immaculate Conception* was painted in 1672 for the Trois-Rivières church of the same name served by the Récollets.

The Immaculate Conception (less interesting than the possibility of being the child of the devil, writes Percy Turner, describing her childhood in an e-mail sent from her forest-fire watchtower in Pearl Luke's northern Alberta novel *Burning Ground*) has occupied the minds, and sometimes the metaphors, of more than a few Canadian writers. Northrop Frye did not take kindly to the usage in his 1951 review of Anne Wilkinson's *Counterpoint to Sleep*: "There is some unsuccessful fantasy, and even the wit of 'Winter Sketch' does not conceal the fact that it is bad metaphysical poetry to speak of a snowfall as 'Immaculate conception in a cloud / Made big by polar ghost.'"[11]

*The Immaculate Conception Photography Gallery*, Katherine Govier's 1994 short story collection, holds two I. C. tales. In the title story, the photographer who only absent-mindedly named his shop at 1816 St. Clair

Avenue West, Toronto, after the parish church in his Italian home village becomes all too involved in the conception of photographs made immaculate by the airbrushed, negative-snipped removal, or insertion, of various individuals. Once you have the immaculate conception of photographs, and memories, you have existentialism, and, eventually, you have a man who eliminates his shop from a photograph of St. Clair Street, sticks the altered image in the window, shuts the shop door for the last time, and walks ... west.

Govier's "The Immaculate Conception Baby Shower" does include a real baby girl conceived by a real man. Physically. Conveniently. In Calgary. But the place where her mother's hopes for herself were conceived years before, and left behind, and where she imagines her daughter will find beauty and joy in 2012 or so, is Dawson City, the Yukon, and its "insistent clear skies, still light at eleven o'clock at night, the feeling of possibility they lend to a day. She will love the individual boreal forest, where the tree roots knit together in the shallow ground and the tops shoot up for light, thin and close as the teeth of a comb."[12]

Mary Immaculate's distance from ordinary women is fiercely documented by Canadian playwrights. In Deborah Porter's play *No More Medea*, Mary (who shops at the Toronto Holt Renfrew's) responds to Medea's accusation of "a particularly sanguine legacy. Immaculate conception. Virgin birth." She says, "The lies of legend. Don't you think I see it? Live with it?"[13]

In the author's foreword to her *Sacred Hearts* script, playwright Colleen Curran notes, "My cousin had a record based on the movie *The Song of Bernadette*. I traded her a Beatles 45 for it and whenever we wanted to put on a 'serious' show we played the record and lip-synced the story with actions for family and friends we had forced to be our audience. I think that we all secretly wished we could be Bernadette or the little children of Fatima and be the recipients of a miracle — a divine message. But we never thought of the consequences."[14] Curran's play reveals the Canadian small-town consequences when Mary spins on her stone pedestal to prove she *is* responding to an ordinary woman's failure and confusion, and to her prayer for hope.

Denise Boucher's *Les Fées ont soif* — *The Fairies Are Thirsty* — casts three Marys. Marie is the housewife who sings, to the tune of "I'se the Bye That Builds the Boat,"

> I'se the gal that scrubs the wash
> And irons every Monday
> He's the bye that makes the dirt
> And kicks my ass on Sunday.[15]

The Madeleine character is a hooker in the good girl–bad girl theatre of the Madonna, a whore who could be played by an actress with hair red enough to match the bright mop supposedly flaunted by Mary Magdalene, a.k.a. Sainte Marie-Madeleine. In the play, round-heeled Madeleine is afraid of getting fat and being alone. She wishes she were a mother, or a virgin again.

The third Mary is the Statue, holding a chain instead of a rosary between her fingers, while she recites, "As for me, I am an image. I am a portrait / My two feet stuck fast in plaster," to begin the litany of her distance from human beings as "she who has no body."

The three Marys of Boucher's play sing, "Have mercy upon us. Have mercy on you,"[16] to introduce the frequent switching and eventual transformation of their stereotypes. (I believe you, Mary. You can see how earthly girls and women exhaust themselves trying to live up to the perfect-female version of you.)

A not particularly merciful Virgin of Our Lady of Fatima's Mary Immaculate — Virgin alone — time period is present in Toronto writer Erika de Vasconcelos's novel *My Darling Dead Ones*. When a baby girl is born in Beira, Portugal, "She will bear her mother's name, Helena, with

Maria in front of it. They will call her *Leninha*, little Helena, from now on. And Maria is a name that *Leninha* will not care for, later, with its connotations of goodness, and worse, virginity. There is a picture of her, the real Maria, hanging in the dining room, whose green eyes follow *Leninha* no matter which end of the room she is in. For the next twenty years this Virgin in her immutable blue dress will seem quite real to *Leninha*, though not a benevolent presence. An accusatory one. A third mother."[17]

As the novel moves between Portugal, Toronto, and Montreal, older ideas of Mary as Mother, rooted in earth and immersed in sea, surge beneath the surface of women's lives interwoven with gardens, children, lovers, and husbands in both countries, and with Portuguese poems, songs, and medieval legends.

The passionate, intuitive ways of the women in *My Darling Dead Ones*, even those who have "exchanged their vanity for pairs of Sorel boots and inelegant, down-filled coats,"[18] would have been familiar to Portuguese explorers Gaspar and Miguel Corte-Real, if not to an English sea dog of their time who was cruising the Pacific coast, packing his own portion of the religious matters that would affect Canada. In 1579, Francis Drake, a man of occasionally proselytizing Calvinist Puritan beliefs and a few contradictory pillaged-Spanish-gold-personal-place-setting habits, dropped anchor and astonished native people, probably on the west coast of Haida Gwaii, Queen Charlotte Islands. Drake sailed on as far north as the Stikine River mouth at 56°46′ latitude, marked the position of his certain discovery of the Northwest Passage, then turned south to claim Vancouver Island and everything else he had seen as New Albion on behalf of Queen Elizabeth I.

In a time when British Puritanism was evolving into Presbyterian and other Reformed Churches, Drake's *Golden Hinde* off the west coast of Canada was carrying twenty-six tonnes of gold taken from Chile, Peru, and Mexico's Spanish ports and cargo galleons; a Puritan chaplain; and a copy of Reformist John Foxe's *Book of Martyrs*. The Virgin Mary was hiding below decks in the form of a small, tooth-marked figure. One of Drake's bosuns had wrenched her away from a Spaniard being taken hostage in the Mexican seaport of Guatulco, and he had bitten down hard to be sure she was gold.

The Virgin Mary became a Presbyterian, though. Question 37 of the Presbyterian Church of Canada's *Westminster Larger Catechism*, asks, "How did Christ, being the Son of God, become man?" Answer: "Christ the Son of God became man by taking to himself a true body, and a reasonable soul, being conceived by the power of the Holy Ghost in the womb of the Virgin Mary, of her substance, and born of her, yet without sin."[19]

Don Gillmor, who searched for his Scottish Canadian ancestors in *The Desire of Every Living Thing* (1999), turned thoughtful when I asked him about Presbyterian Mary. Then he said, "She would probably have to wear a thick, brown hand-knitted sweater covering her entire body." *The Desire of Every Living Thing* describes Gillmor's Winnipeg grandmother, "My grandmother, Georgina Maitland, had been raised in the Free Presbyterian Church, which had taken its doctrine from Calvin, who believed that human beings were fundamentally corrupt and deserved to be damned. The Free Presbyterians disapproved of organ music and hymn singing and talking on Sunday. They disapproved of most things. It was a stark, wintry religion and was conducted in bleak brown churches, the antithesis of Rome's magnificent, frivolous cathedrals ... Her family came to Canada in 1905, when Georgina was six."[20]

✶

A PRESBYTERIAN WHO APPROVED OF MANY THINGS, and who worked on a Nicola Valley, British Columbia ranch some years before the Maitlands came to Canada put the heart back into me, though, when the Mary map was so dotted with research trails I couldn't see the road. George Edwards was well loved in the Nicola Valley for his gentle, kindly ways and his generosity. His ranch-country neighbours all benefited from his horse and cattle skills, as well as his shoe-cobbling, fiddle-playing, and fine preaching when the Presbyterian minister couldn't make it. Edwards's history holds no mention of his feelings about Mary, but at least one of the children for whom he made skating rinks, or shoes, or taught Sunday school, or funded an education, remembered all her life that he told her, "Never be a bigot, little 'un, never interfere with a man's religion … If he prays, be thankful that he prays."[21]

As much or more than George Edwards's Presbyterian connection, *Lana Janine*'s galley stove burning through one of my desperate, deskbound daydreams may have brought him to mind. The stove with two temperatures — cold and forging steel — had done duty in the old British Columbia Penitentiary in New Westminster before it had been assigned black cod hard time, the cook said one day when the offshore marine weather report's wind, wave, and swell height were flowing into the galley on a following sea while he was frying slanted eggs. Not that George Edwards, a.k.a. Bill Miner, was long in escaping from the penitentiary, where he had been registered as a guest regarding the Cariboo gold dust long gone from the CPR passenger train in Canada's first train robbery in September 1904, as well as the mail train robbery in May 1906.

Bill Miner, still missed in the Nicola Valley, and at this desk, is said to have died in a Georgia prison around 1911. George Edwards, Presbyterian, is thought, is hoped, to have made it down to Mexico and maybe South America with one or two former colleagues from an earlier stagecoach business venture. There, he would have come under the care of the Virgin of Guadalupe who also minds prisoners in some of the cells at British Columbia's Nanaimo Regional Correctional Centre, and in other Canadian jails, or the Mary of Mercy who favoured Robin Hood and other more or less repentant bandits of the Middle Ages.

✶

CANADIAN PRESBYTERIANS (along with poet Alden Nowlan's "First Lesson in Theology" grandmother who always knew God was a Baptist —

"John the Baptist baptized him / so what else could he be be?"[22]) and everyone else in the country have been questioned about religion in each decennial census since 1871. Our answers are "an important source of information on the ethnocultural profile of all Canadians," according to Statistics Canada.

The 2001 census records about 43 per cent of Canada's almost 32 million people as Catholic of both Western (Roman) and Eastern (Byzantine — Ukrainian, Slovak, and Greek — and Antiochean or Maronite) Rites.

Statistics Canada reports, "The proportion of Protestants, the second largest group, declined from 35% of the population to 29% or about 8.7 million people."

Two per cent of the population is Muslim.

Orthodox Christians — Armenian, Coptic Orthodox, Greek, Russian, Serbian, and others — make up about 1.6 per cent.

About 1.1 per cent of Canadians are Jewish.

Fewer still are of Hindu, Sikh, Buddhist, or other Eastern faiths.

The census form has categories, and small percentages of Canadians, for "para-religious groups" — "Aboriginal or First Nations spirituality, Kabalarian, New Age, New Thought-Unity-Metaphysical, Scientology" and "other religions."[23] About 16 per cent of Canadians say they have no religious affiliation.

✸

SOME WAY ACROSS MY MARY MAP, marked with research trails and my footsteps, an earlier census offered me a way to form questions about how Mary of the old, richly cultured, traditional, fractiously religious world might be faring in her very new country. In the 1871 Ontario census records, I saw something of myself, too.

PART OF MY FAMILY lived in the loop of Ontario census entries, as well as in photocopies of handwritten notes scratched under blurred photographs by some one-sixty-fourth or so blood-connected hand. In the notes and the census lists, great-great-grandparents, disappeared uncles and aunties, second and third cousins, died-in-childbirth first wives, and the stepmother's niece who became someone's wife all showed me their changes of mind, heart, and style about churches: Presbyterian, both Scottish and Canadian; Anglican; Christian Science; and Primitive Methodist, out of France, where an eighteenth-century devoutly Catholic mother, a dissolute priest, and the French Revolution created a Protestant Huguenot connection. The Dutch American great-grandmother whose mother's family may have come to New Amsterdam (New York) with Peter Stuyvesant's colonists did not (would not?) record religious affiliation.

Maybe she was a Gypsy. Rearranging census entries to fit imaginary forebears is irresistable when you can't find ancestral threads suitable for stitching yourself into the past. The 1871 census offered seven same-first-and-last-named men as possibilities for my family's first Scottish immigrants to Canada in the 1840s. One man bearing the sturdy Scottish names with the closest birthdates appealed to me because I imagined him as tough and capable of transformation. He isn't a likely blood relative: "Roman Catholic. Ethnic Origin: African, unknown code. Labourer."[24] A younger, impossible ancestor with the same surname but Irish origin, and Wesleyan Methodist family, had the best first name: Rebel.

If the Ontario census couldn't supply unchanging spiritual certainty, neither could the handwritten notes about this Scottish root. At the top of the page is a slanted line of words, added last, in haste perhaps: "slipper makers to Mary, Queen of Scots." Presbyterianism was likely a safer choice after the elegant Catholic queen was beheaded in 1587 by Queen Elizabeth I.

✳ *Our Lady of Grace* ✳ *Our Lady of the Assumption* ✳ *Our Lady of Good Counsel* ✳ *Our Lady of the Navigators* ✳ *Our Lady of the Sacred Heart* ✳ *Our Lady of Victory* ✳ *Our Mo*

Fantasizing images of the slippers, let alone their makers, required a shoe-history reference book and an act of will. The slippers could have been brocade, perhaps cream coloured or gold, trimmed with silk ribbon or lace. They may have been heeled with smallish, hardwood forms covered by soft, stretched smooth leather. Maybe they were flat-heeled, cut and laced to fit a long, narrow foot in black glove leather, made for a queen walking narrow, silent prison spaces. The slipper-makers' tiny, precise hand motions, and their ability to craft a vision into being with the measure of sympathy for which my hopes insist, are diffused by distance.

Even my imagination can't make sixteenth-century slipper possibilities stand in for a spiritual legacy. But slippers were all I could take to heart from the census and other family records, except for the immediately vanished perception that threads of air scented with earth, damp wood, and salt water rose from the names, odours not unfamiliar to me, and which I would still like to believe were real.

Imagination and possibility have been used as sometime means of transport in this journey toward Mary of Canada, in the prayer that their streams might be as much an approach to her as were the rivers and roads I followed, and the expeditions made into forests of archives and texts. Bear with me.

Mary lives in Canada, I know now. The Holy Virgin of Old World religious traditions softens the December 24 front page of a national newspaper as the Montreal United Church stained-glass Madonna, then appears both as the 2003 glowing Virgin Mary sightings on frosted windows in isolated northern Saskatchewan communities, and as Dashboard Mary on a Canadian blues CD.

In Canada, Mary the Mother of Christ, the surviving western link in a line of goddesses that began with the earth itself, changes her ways and forms to meet all of us in our need for tenderness. She finds herself in Lutheran and other Protestant liturgies, and in devotion to the Catholic Blessed Virgin Mary, patron saint of all humanity, the same Mary who

*Map-Making* 51

*O thornless rose of ineffable beauty,
thou didst bud forth on the border
	of paradise.
For through thine unopened gate, the
	gate was opened
and through thy sacred icon
thou dost call the Canadian people
	to enter in,
proclaiming thyself to be their
	protectress
and defence against the enemy.*

*Wherefore we cry unto thee:
Rejoice joy of Canada.
Rejoice, fragrant blossom of Paradise,
Rejoice, vine that bore the fruit of life,
Rejoice, gate of Paradise,
Rejoice, ladder from heaven to earth,*

*Rejoice, restoration of Eve,
Rejoice, mother of the New Adam,
Rejoice, mother of Him who bruised
	satan's head,
Rejoice, Joy of Canada.*

From "Akathist Hymn for the Theotokos Joy of Canada Pilgrimage," Archbishop Lazar Puhalo, Monastery of All Saints of North America

has her place in Cree sacred pipe rituals and in the dance for the ancestors at Fox Lake in Alberta's Little Red River area. Mary of Canada abides in the Orthodox Church's Mother of God of Canada icon, and in the Alberta wheat crop irrigation system flowing from St. Mary's River. As the Mexican Indian Virgin, Our Lady of Guadalupe, Mary is the Catholic Patroness of all the Americas, and she often keeps company with Canada's First Nations and Latino people. She's our NAFTA Madonna.

She lives on the west side of the mihrab — prayer niche — set to show the direction to Mecca in every mosque; in a few Biblical references to a young Jewish girl whose neighbours probably knew her as Miriam of Nazareth (who gives birth to Yeshua in Alexandria in Nino Ricci's *Testament*), and in a jack pine in Thoreau MacDonald's *Pine Tree Madonna*.

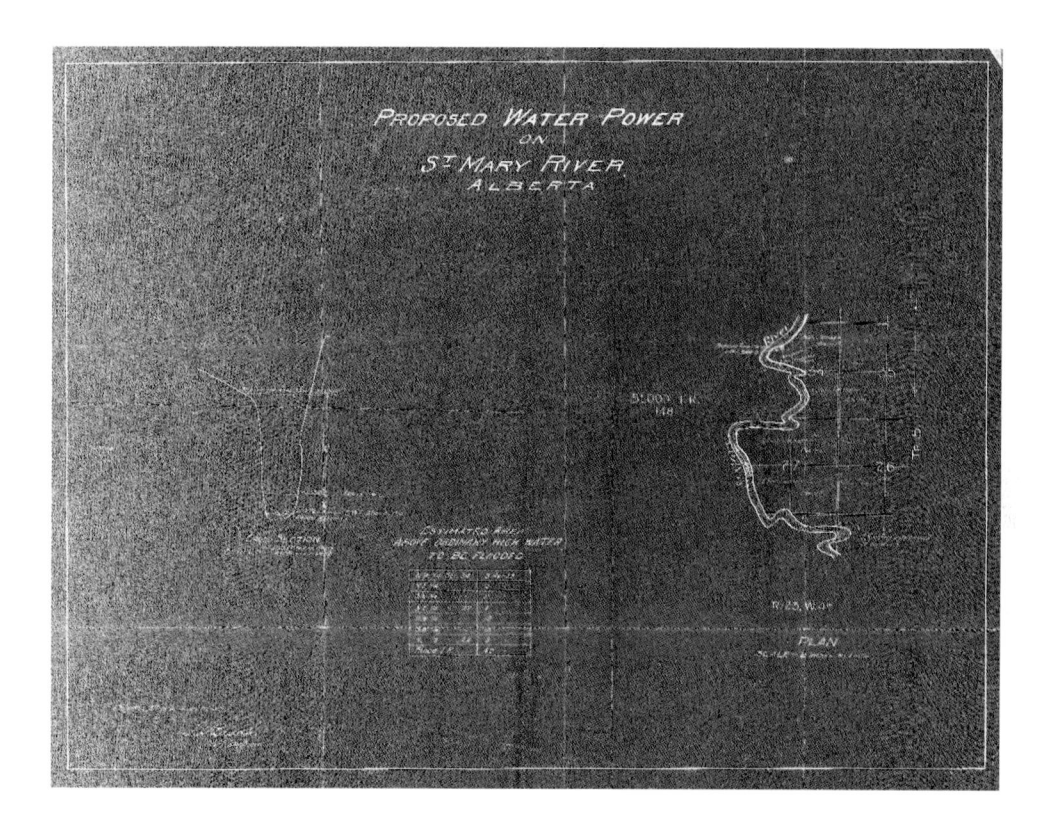

Her Canadian-made forms have been shaped by habitant carvers, loggers with chainsaws, and trappers with hunting knives, as well as by traditional and contemporary artists (and tattooists).

The country starred with Madonna images contains both Winnipeg artist Richard Williams's modern Annunciation portraits showing a short-haired, often naked or vulnerable Mary in a torn cloak, and the older comfort that was sustained when the outline of a robed Madonna holding the infant Christ appeared as an eight-centimetre pentimento image leaking through fresh blue paint on the wall of a Mi'kmaq reserve home at Indian Brook, Nova Scotia, in April 2001. Always, Mary holds some measure of Our Lady of Mercy, Notre Dame de Misericorde.

*Refuge of Sinners* ✳ *Saint Mary the Virgin* ✳ *Saint Mary of the Angels* ✳ *Settena Maryam, Our Lady Mary, Arabic* ✳ *Singular Vessel of Devotion* ✳ *Tower of David* ✳ *Tower of Ivory*

Alone in a scarlet dress, Madonna della Misericordia stood three times taller than the kneeling human figures under her dark cloak when her images first appeared in Europe. She was responding to desperate need by sheltering plague victims five hundred years before Montreal's Les Sœurs de Misericorde, the Sisters of Mercy, bought a warehouse to use as Misericordia Hospital in Edmonton in 1900. In 1965, when I thought *misericordia* meant the misery of dancing to Sam Cooke's soul songs with a tumour-fattened right knee, I didn't pay much attention to the sisters' Lady of Mercy standing in the hospital chapel with her head bent over the child she held to her shoulder. Mercy and token-cost bone surgery were given to me at Misericordia Hospital, anyway.

Today, the Madonna of Mercy at Edmonton's new Misericordia Community Hospital is a modern sculpture with soft lines offering her openness to approach. Misericordia came to mean mercy from the Latin words *miser* (wretched), *miserere* (to have pity), and *cord* (heart).

Spread misere, solitaire for the player who deals himself only miserable cards, was "the solo game"[25] Dangerous Dan McGrew was playing in back of the bar that bad night in the Malamute Saloon. Neither the need for mercy, nor Mary's capacity to give it, has changed much since Robert Service wrote "The Shooting of Dan McGrew" up in Yukon Territory some while after the Klondike's first gold strike in 1896. The lady known as Lou wasn't the only gal in Dawson City the night Dan was shot. Mary of Canada was in town, too, over at the tiny new hospital named for her, helping the Sisters of St. Anne cool fevers and hand out vitamin-C mercy to gold miners down with scurvy and typhoid.

Wherever Mary of Canada finds herself in the country, her merciful lack of surprise at any human deed, thought, or failure, and her encompassing tenderness for all creation transcends religious labels, money, status, background, geography, and all else that divides us. Our Lady of Perpetual Help (with hypothermia and all else) acts fast in Margaret Atwood's novel *Cat's Eye*, paying no mind to the nominally Protestant background of an eight-year-old girl who has fallen through creek ice in a Toronto ravine. The child grows up to become an artist, and a mother, who paints the Mary she needs, "in blue, with the usual white veil, but with the head of a lioness ... If Christ is a lion, as he is in traditional iconography, why wouldn't the Virgin Mary be a lioness?"[26] The *Cat's Eye* heroine's next Virgin Mary portrait shows the Mother of God wearing a winter coat over her blue robe, carrying grocery bags, and looking tired as she descends to snow-covered earth.

Mary who walks snow-covered earth with Canadians also works NHL dressing rooms, Kingston prison, and the street, as well as 170-plus Catholic shrines, and any number of private altars. Hundreds of Canadians — friends, strangers, priests, truck drivers, scholars, and many writers and artists — helped to map the ways to Mary of Canada. Their advice, along with reference books, sacred texts, and my own faith in all journeys, could only be the means to break trail toward Mary's patient presence. Every side road into distraction or blank despair of meaning in the search, and back, I had to cut for myself. I have come to believe it's a lucky thing for me and other drifters of all kinds that Mary, at heart, is of no fixed address. Across the country then, with a map made on the go, following signs left by a tender Virgin of much Canadian experience.

*According to the* Vancouver Sun, *a number of Canadians recall going to schools they would have sworn were named after Our Lady of Perpetual Health. A few of the other kids thought they were attending Our Lady of Professional Help. A Canadian grown-up wrote a school walkathon support cheque to Our Lady of Perpetual Motion.*

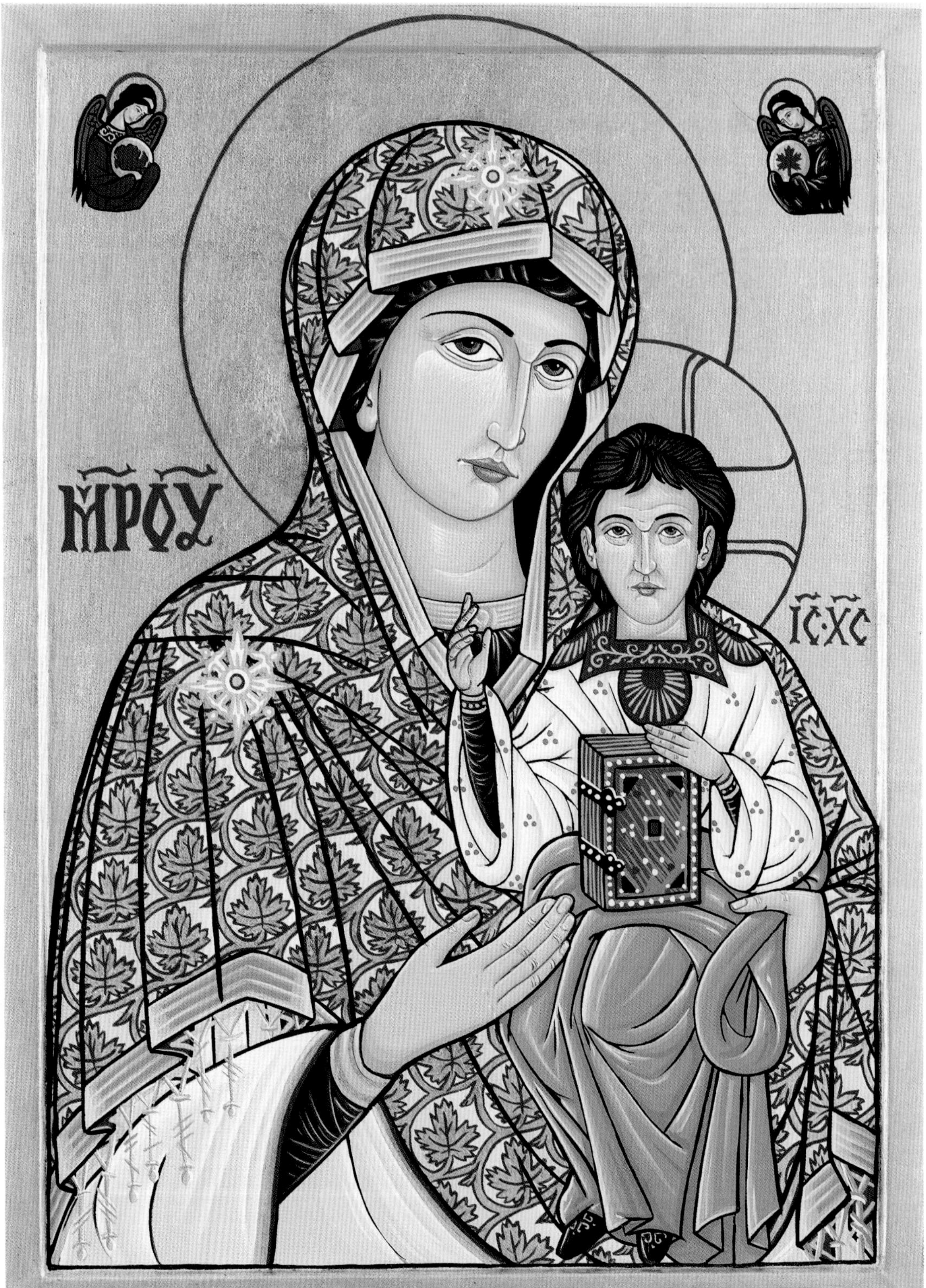

MP ΘY
IC XC

* CHAPTER 3 *

# *Mary in Canada*

THE VIRGIN MARY HAS BEEN A PERMANENT PRESENCE ABSORBING CANADA'S WIDE, WILD GEOGRAPHY AND HUMAN RESPONSES TO THE LAND FOR ALMOST FIVE HUNDRED YEARS. HER MERCIES WERE INHERENT IN THE GROUND AT CHIMNEY COULEE, I THOUGHT ONE WINTER IN SASKATCHEWAN'S CYPRESS HILLS, FORMED WITHOUT LINES, YET SEPARATED ONE FROM ANOTHER, LYING INTERLEAFED IN THE PRAIRIE EARTH UNDER MY BOOTS IN THE SNOW THE WAY MEMORIES LIE IN THE MIND, THEIR OVERLAPPING FOLDS THINNING AS THEIR SETTING DEEPENS.

*iparthenos (Ever-Virgin)* ✳ *Ark of the Covenant* ✳ *A Mercy for the Worlds* ✳ *Cause of Our Joy* ✳ *Comforter of the Afflicted Consolatrix Afflictorum* ✳ *Domina* ✳ *Gate of Heaven* ✳

*Canada — The nursing mother of half a continent.*
— Toronto Globe, December 10, 1861

From *The Dictionary of Canadian Quotations and Phrases*

*Perhaps we are a country more feminine than we like to admit, because the unifying, regenerative principle is a passion with us.*
— Dorothy Livesay

From *The Dictionary of Canadian Quotations and Phrases*

Her presence rested in the solace given me by the creek not yet iced into silence, the land rolling down to the coulee, the coyote day beds on the cutbanks, and the white-tail deer's egg-shaped resting places under windbreak trees. A ribbon of certainty fluttered below thought after I stood awhile in the stillness at Chimney Coulee. I was sure Mary would remember everyone who had been born or lived or died in the coulee that looks empty now, where even the crumbled fieldstone chapel in which she was Sainte Marie a little while for the Metis has worn away on the wind.

The Mary I found as the Virgin Mary and as a link to the oldest human ideas of female divinity fills other empty places, as well as city streets, homes, churches, prisons, and stories across the country. Mary the Mother of God knows Canada by heart. She has the recipe for a certain life-giving tea made from the bark of *Thuya occidentalis*, the eastern white cedar. Atop the pillar supporting Our Lady of the World in Marystown, Newfoundland, the Burin Peninsula's unemployment rate is on her mind, and in St. Norbert, Manitoba, she is Notre-Dame-de-Bon-Secours, Our Lady of Good Help, keeping an eye on the Red River levels near the Metis wayside shrine. She works cross-country days, and night

58  MARY OF CANADA

shift. She is Mother of Consolation in Winnipeg's north end and other Canadian cities' tough downtown neighbourhoods, while she steadies the wheel for tired drivers at Our Lady of the Highway on the road east of Vegreville, Alberta.

Mary of Canada knows how to make ice miracles, to soften winter, and to settle white water, whether these conditions are of the soul, or the Canadian landscape, or both. Only in Canada does Notre Dame du Portage join the Virgin Mary's consoling titles as the lady who hovered in the mist above the rapids to guide the voyageurs, and who now watches over a St. Lawrence River municipality named for her, as well as a Diocese of Thunder Bay parish serving anglophone, francophone, and native people. The 1905 Virgin who obligingly appeared in the harbour at St. John's, Newfoundland, on the 408th anniversary of John Cabot's landfall is the world's only Iceberg Madonna. And only in Canada can the much-travelled hero of Yann Martel's *Life of Pi* see the Virgin Mary smiling lovingly at him within the snow shaken from a tree branch and falling through sunlight.

Probably some form of Mary, whose name may be rooted in the Hebrew words for fragrant myhrr and light-bearer, has always blessed a hard-edged northern land in need of light and a measure of consolation. Her name cradles the country. Saint Mary, a.k.a. Sainte Marie, St. Mary, Ste. Marie, Our Lady, Notre Dame, La Sainte Vierge, and Mani (Algonquin Mary), inhabits Canadian geography and culture in hundreds of capes, bays, islands, rivers, streams, mountains, cities, towns, villages, streets, schools, businesses, and parishes named for her from the Arctic to the Atlantic and the Pacific coasts.

Canadian rock, ice, earth, and water have always contained Mother Mary as she changes to suit the times. In Notre Dame Bay, Newfoundland, she keeps care of a Beothuk infant's bones, and the tiny bark food containers and stone amulets lying with the beloved child's body. Alberta's St. Mary's River Reservoir, hard-used for crop irrigation

*An hour had not passed before a rifle shot rang out ... During the struggle, in the noise of the shots, the canoes, caught up in the terrible currents, bounded through the bubbles and foam, plunged and rose on the crest of the waves that carried them into their course ... "I saw nothing in the Seven Falls," later said Cadieux's wife, who was a pious woman, "I saw nothing but a noble Lady in white who hovered over the canoes and showed us the way!"*

From *Forestiers et Voyageurs*, by Joseph-Charles Taché

in the 2001–02 drought, has held the huge, silted footprints of a woolly mammoth for about thirteen thousand years. The mammoth baby's prints and an ancient people's hunting artifacts are nearby.

With enough yearning and imagination, the entire landscape enclosed by Canada's territorial waters and the forty-ninth parallel may yet come to resemble the shape of a Mary image. The nation where Mary maintains a continuing interest in Canadian football — the 2001 Vanier Cup starred a perfect-win season for Halifax's St. Mary's University Huskies — and appeared Christmas 1996, halo and all, in frozen elm-tree sap at Halifax, Nova Scotia, might yet be photographed from satellite camera angles as a space-blued cloak of a country, leaning over the continent like a benediction flowing down from the north.

✱

JOURNEYS ACROSS THE CANADIAN LANDSCAPE trace lay lines leading to Mary in Canada. My perceptions of her are always in progress, are always being glazed with the translucent colours of another possibility in the Mary-name of a New Brunswick credit union, or a British Columbia mountain, or some folded line of land flowing like a cloak or a calm profile under the First Air plane crossing the tundra from Yellowknife to the Arctic, or ahead of the car on gravel roads around La Ronge in northern Saskatchewan.

I have made pilgrimages to rivers and ideas as well as to Marian shrines at Marymount, Marystown, Newfoundland; Notre-Dame-du-Cap, Cap-de-la-Madeleine, Quebec; the Huron Chapel of Notre-Dame-de-Lorette on the Wendake Huron Reserve, Loretteville, Quebec; Notre-Dame-de-Roc-Amadour, Quebec City; Notre-Dame-de-Bons-Secours, St. Norbert, Manitoba; and Our Lady of Lourdes, Mission, British Columbia. I stopped at waypoints on the Mary road like the national historic sites at Batoche, Saskatchewan; Fort St. James, British Columbia; and Parc Historique National Cartier-Brébeuf, Quebec

City; and I travelled by boat into Nunavut's Coppermine River up to Bloody Falls Territorial Park. In churches far apart from each other in distance and style, Mary of Canada was present, as both herself, and mercy that overlooks the awkwardness of an itinerant stranger who occasionally makes a note during the service.

I travelled in Canadian history and other research all the while I was looking for Mary in the country. On the road through texts, I found Marian treasure in Canadian poetry and fiction, and stimulation as well as consolation in the luminous, expansive ideas of creation-centred Christianity in *Le Christ est amérindien — Christ Is a Native American* — by Achiel Peelman, professor of theology at Saint Paul University in Ottawa, and in the presence and poetry of Father René Fumoleau, who has been with Dene people in the north for fifty years.

I looked up other Canadians who had made long journeys across the land: the Virgin Mary herself, voyageurs, settlers, the North West Mounted Police, and a wayfaring pilgrim named Madonna, miracle tabby cat of Windsor, Ontario, who walked into her old home 280 kilometres away in Kitchener in September 2001, four years after she disappeared.

If I had tried to make a postal journey to Mary in Canada, my letter addressed to the Virgin Mary and consigned to Canada Post would have been forwarded to UMO, the Undeliverable Mail Office in Scarborough, Ontario, or Sydney, Nova Scotia. At UMO, unopened, and in the company of other letters mailed to the air in the sad absence of a findable street address, envelopes addressed to Mary are contemplated by grave, gracious Canada Post people who still shred them.

I never caught up with the shopping cart said to be festooned, nay laden, with all kinds of small Mary figures being wheeled through Vancouver's Downtown Eastside streets. By some unspoken understanding I had come, by then, to know as Just Canadian, it didn't seem to occur to my informants, or to me, that such a cart was all that wildly, madly strange. Unusual, yes. Beautiful, yes. But, given the times, given the Mary-buggy and its owner's location in the land where Mary of

Canada presides, a multitude of Our Ladies on wheels looked more like a sensible, even practical, choice for hope and solace.

The Virgin Mary has been shining out of Canadian history and church doors, and into Canada's everyday culture for a long time.

✸

IN QUEBEC CITY, across town from the St. Lawrence River harbour and the Ursuline convent to which Marie de l'Incarnation's dream of a Virgin perched in a "frightening" place had taken her, there is a good-enough anchorage on another river and another Virgin.

Wild, hard country had not seemed almost unbearably dangerous to one of the earliest Old World Marys to arrive in Canada. She was already at sea, making way toward a new land and its needs in 1534, the year the Jesuits were formed in Rome. Near the St. Charles River in Quebec City, on the sidewalk in front of St-François d'Assise church on Rue St-Martial, I could imagine my way back to her second landfall, a year later.

The captain may have walked into the bush alone at first. Probably his too-thin boots squeaked on the deep, crusted snow. Perhaps his thoughts chanted only HereisNotHomeNothomeNothome, meaning, this place contains neither the foreseen sway of a ship deck nor the sweet, static comfort of known ground. He was forty-five years old, and not unfamiliar with storms and war, but he might have been startled more than once by the gunshot snap of tree branches weighted with ice and snow.

Some way into the woods, out of sight of the ships lying behind him in the river, the captain opened his cloak to withdraw a small statue. His hands and feet must have been numb with cold. Perhaps he stumbled as he set the figure of a woman into the branches of a tree in the snow-thickened forest that nearly enclosed him.

The woman in the tree was not surprised by the strange cold land. She regarded the forest and the man kneeling before her in the snow with calm. The captain's plea to her may have been an almost incoherent litany of need and fear: "Aidez-moi, aidez-moi, je vous en prie." Help me. Help my men. So far from home. Help.

The man on his knees was Captain Jacques Cartier. The imperturbable lady who already seemed to know the New World showed one shape of Mary, Mother of God, the same Mary who still lives at Notre Dame Junction, Newfoundland; on St. Mary Avenue and at St. Mary's Self-Serve & Carwash in Winnipeg; along the Virgin River in Saskatchewan; and in St. Mary's Alpine Park in British Columbia.

In mid-November 1535, Cartier and the crews of the small sailing ships *Emerillon* and the two *Hermines* — *La Grande* and *La Petite* — began their first Canadian winter in a log fort near present-day Quebec City. The ships lay fast in two fathoms of ice on the St. Charles River, smothered in snow higher than the hulls. By February 1536, twenty-five men had died of scurvy, and most of the others in the 110-man company were desperately ill.

The crewman who kept the journal of Cartier's expedition recorded that "Our captain, seeing the misery and sickness so active had everybody put to prayers and supplications, and had an image of the Virgin Mary placed against a tree about a bow-shot distant from our fort across the snow and ice, and ordered that ... all those who could walk ... should go in procession, ... while praying the said Virgin that it might please her to pray her dear Child that he would have pity on us ... the captain bound himself a pilgrim to Our Lady who causes herself to be prayed to at Roquemado [that is, Notre Dame de Rocamadour, Cahors, France], promising to go thither if God should give him the grace to return into France."

Grace appeared in the form of the Iroquois from Stadacona, who told Cartier he needed "the juice and refuse of the leaves of a tree" and sent "two women with the captain to fetch some of it ... and showed us how one could strip the bark and the leaves from the said tree and put the whole to boil in water, then to drink of it every other day and put the refuse on the diseased and swollen legs ... They call the said tree in their tongue *amedda*."[1]

*er of God ✻ Mary, Queen of Hearts ✻ Miriam of Nazareth ✻ Mirror of Justice ✻ Mother of Christ ✻ Mother of the Church ✻ Mother of Consolation ✻ Mother of Divine Grace ✻ M*

Jacques Cartier most likely drank first to show his men the infusion held no harm. (Always, the captain has to do these things.) The amedda infusions and poultices, probably made from the vitamin-C-rich eastern white cedar tree, cured the sick men almost immediately. Jacques Cartier called the event "a real and evident miracle."[2] The sailors were so grateful for their recovery some of them insisted the grace of God, conveyed through Our Lady, had also eliminated their tertiary syphilis.

Not the grace of God inherent in the generosity of the Iroquois, or the marvellous tree, or the Isis of Egypt origin of France's ancient Notre Dame de Rocamadour were given any part in the miracle. Notre Dame de Rocamadour as the image Cartier placed in the tree is a sailors' Madonna whose first home is the Cahors district shrine, founded, in Christian legend, by Saint Amadour, the Virgin Mary's servant who took ship for Gaul to work as a missionary.

I walked across Cartier-Brébeuf Park to look at the river awhile, before I went into the church to find the Canadian shrine to Notre Dame de Rocamadour, and Jacques Cartier, wearing not-bad Canuck boots now, still striding through the snow. In St-François d'Assise church's huge painting hanging above a statue of Mary dressed in a peach-coloured robe, Cartier, followed by his limping, bandaged crewmen, stands before a picture of a fair-faced crowned Madonna and Child pinned to a leafless birch tree. Someone who might be an Iroquois crouches in the shadow of an evergreen on the left side of the painting.

On September 8, the Feast of the Birth of Mary, pilgrims' prayers in the sanctuary here still conclude, "Comme Jacques Cartier, je te remercie pour tes bontés," and the back wall of the church is lined with marble ex voto plaques thanking the Virgin of Rocamadour for favours and blessings.

The sun pouring through amber-coloured stained glass above the painting lights the snow, the birch tree, and Mary's face, but Mary has changed. Again. The fair-skinned, pink-cheeked Marys of the pilgrimage painting and the peach-robed statue do not resemble any image of Notre

*Vierge Marie,*
*notre peuple croyant*
*reconnaît dans son histoire*
*ta presence, ta protection, ta tendresse.*

*Nos pionniers t'ont fait connaître*
*Pour la premiere fois au pays sous le nom*
*de Notre-Dame-de Roc-Amadour.*

*Aide-moi a obtenir de ton Fils*
*la faveur que je te demande ...*

*Dès maintenant, comme Jacques-Cartier,*
*je te remercie pour tes bontés.*

*Amen!*

"Priére à Notre-Dame de Roc-Amadour, comme Jacques-Cartier" (Avec la permission de l'ordinaire, Québec, 8 septembre 1987) Fabrique St-François D'Assise, 1380 St-Martial, Québec, Québec, G1L 4Z4)

Dame de Rocamadour Jacques Cartier and his crew would have known. The original Notre Dame de Rocamadour is tall and dark, an ancient Black Madonna whose past incarnation as Isis, Oldest of the Old in Egypt, still lives in Canada. Poet Roy Kiyooka calls her "ISIS the Egyptian goddess and patron / saint of the movie house by that name / on 1st Street West between eleventh and twelfth / avenue in Calgary Alta."[3] And in Margaret Atwood's story "Isis in Darkness":

> The Egyptian Queen of Heaven and Earth was wandering in the Underworld, gathering up the pieces of the murdered and dismembered body of her lover Osiris. At the same time, it was her

own body she was putting back together; and it was also the physical universe. She was creating the universe by an act of love.

All of this was taking place, not in the ancient Middle Kingdom of the Egyptians, but in flat, dingy Toronto, on Spadina Avenue, at night, among the darkened garment factories and delicatessens and bars and pawnshops.[4]

Cartier brought the New World an enduring Virgin capable of adapting to any human circumstances, and connecting to human lives flawed even unto syphilis. More than one man sprung from prison in St. Malo to make up Cartier's crew trusted Mary to understand him, body and soul, in all his weakness and strengths. The faith Jacques Cartier and his crew gave to a Virgin intimately connected with their lives joins them to Christopher Columbus, who vowed a pilgrimage to Santa María de Guadalupe in Spain during an Atlantic storm, and to Champlain, who died at Quebec on Christmas Day 1635, certain the Notre Dame he had come to know understood the details of daily struggles in his tiny New France.

Explorers knew a Virgin responsive to days ordered only by no-turning-point risks and borderless dreams. That part-time daydreamer Sam Champlain, hunting with the Hurons in their country before Christmas 1615, lost himself for three days in the bush because he followed a bird whose beauty had enchanted him.

✸

EXPLORERS' EXPECTATIONS of a risk-taking Virgin Mary by their side are still alive in Canada and able to charge a more subdued form of Mary with their energy. Agnes Marie "Moony" Pottey, *New Waterford Girl* explorer in her own right, and all the other girls in the 2000 movie set in a Cape Breton, Nova Scotia coast small town, expect the Virgin Mary standing on a window sill as one more watchkeeping Mary Immaculate to dance

---

*The Black Madonna is sacredness in matter, the intersection of sexuality and spirituality.*

*The Black Madonna's energy has smoldered.*
*Rejected by the patriarchy,*
*now she is erupting*
*in the world and in us,*
*demanding conscious recognition.*

From *Coming Home to Myself, Daily Reflections for a Woman's Body and Soul,* by Marian Woodman with Jill Mellick

*They are spirits, sky people, coming with a message for us*
*They are coming to say, Rejoice (Be on top of life)*
*Marie, she has just given birth. Rejoice! Jesus, he is born.*

From a literal translation of St. Jean de Brébeuf's Huron words (Huron Carol), John Steckley, *Teondecheron*

lively in the real matters of their lives. Mary, as a small statue, will be used, briefly, as a microphone. (Another miniature, manufactured Mary works double shift in Alissa York's *Mercy* when a "foot-high porcelain madonna"[5] with a stopper holds coins and bills while other aspects of the Virgin name Mercy's Catholic Church and infuse blessings into the boggy wilderness at the edge of town.) The New Waterford Virgin will also sponsor a boxing match, supervise retribution dealt out to boys and men who use the girls carelessly, and see Moony off to her exploration of art and dreams in New York. All the while, in Mary's always true, always simultaneous way, New Waterford's beauty and the love it contains are rooting deeply within Moony, to be taken away with her in lasting, strengthening memory.

✳

FOR HUNDREDS OF YEARS after the first explorers' time in Canada, river waters were Mary's ways. The sailors' Virgin surging into *la rivière de Canada* with Cartier on the salt tide that narrows into fresh water at Anticosti Island became part of Notre-Dame-de-Foy who stayed here to be paddled and portaged from the St. Lawrence up to the Jesuits' mission on Lake Huron, of Notre-Dame-des-Anges at their seigneury west of St. Charles River, and of other river-borne, riverside New France Virgins. Our Lady of the fur-trade canoes eventually travelled a water road into the far northwest reaches of the new land. A riverine Mary running deep in Canadian history was an early and enduring aspect of the Virgin who remained in-country rather than returning to Europe on explorers' ships.

Sainte-Marie-aux-Hurons made the river journey, and thirty-six portages, up the Ottawa and Mattawa Rivers, across Lake Nipissing and down the French River to Georgian Bay on Lake Huron, then along the lakeshore to the Jesuit mission centre named for her on the River Wye near its Lake Huron entrance. Our Lady of the Snows also entered the *Huron Relation of 1635* as the Feast Day celebrated on Saint Jean de Brébeuf's

Good Counsel ✴ Our Lady of the Navigators ✴ Our Lady of the Sacred Heart ✴ Our Lady of Victory ✴ Our Mother of Consolation ✴ Panagia (All-Holy Queen Assumed into Heaven

Mary in Canada  69

arrival in Huron country. When Jean de Brébeuf and other priests were tortured to death by the Iroquois, the Jesuits burned Sainte-Marie-aux-Hurons's fortified buildings. On the riverbank in 1649, a chapel, lodgings for priests, Huron converts, visitors (and chickens), and a hospital, were put to the torch. At the Ottawa National Arts Centre 1977 performance of James W. Nichol's play *Sainte-Marie among the Hurons*, the stage directions — "(FATHER HENRI and FATHER DANIEL run down the audience aisles left and right, holding burning torches)"[6] — were followed.

The maize fields at Sainte-Marie-aux-Hurons went to seed, and a short-lived Ste-Marie II mission on St. Joseph's Island (now Christian Island, an Ojibwa reserve) was broken by starvation among the Hurons and the deaths of two more priests. In June 1650, three hundred Hurons and the last priests of Sainte Marie's mission in Huronia fled down the rivers to the mission near Quebec City they named Notre-Dame-de-Lorette.

Ville-Marie-de-Montréal's Virgin, as well as Notre Dame de Nouvelle France and Notre Dame de Québec accompanied thirty-five-year-old soldier Dollard des Ormeaux, sixteen volunteers from Montreal, and their newly baptized Huron and Algonquin allies through drift ice on the Grand Rivière des Algonquins — the Ottawa — to scout wild country that offered rich fur-trade opportunities as well as the Iroquois in April 1660. Some while later, upstream from the riverbank where Father Laforgue, played by Lothaire Bluteau in the 1991 film of Brian Moore's novel *Black Robe*, sang "Ave Maria," "the words of the hymn lost in the yells of the exultant Iroquois,"[7] at the place where the Ottawa River pours into the Long Sault rapids, Pierre (independent *esprit* — spirit — is my name) Esprit (independent fur-trading is my game) Radisson found the broken human remains of a week-long siege and tormented death.

Marie de l'Incarnation, the Ursuline sisters' Mother Superior in Quebec, learned the Long Sault news from a Huron who had escaped. She wrote to her son in France on June 25, 1660:

The Huron, who is named Louis (*Taondechoren*) and is an excellent Christian, was reserved to be burned in the enemy country, and for this reason he was guarded so carefully that he was bound to one of the Iroquois, so afraid were they of losing him, as well as another Huron that was destined for the same fate. They called upon God and the Blessed Virgin with such fervour and faith that they escaped as if miraculously, living on moss and grass along the way and running without drawing breath all the way to Montreal. Louis told me in our parlour of his great faith in the Blessed Virgin and how, while he was tied to the sleeping Iroquois, one of his bonds broke of itself and, being thus half-free, he quietly broke the others, and was completely at liberty. He passed through the entire army, though watch was being maintained, without any ill encounter and in that way escaped.[8]

✴

ALMOST THREE HUNDRED YEARS LATER, a young man who had grown up in an Outremont, Montreal, home where a marqueterie image of the Virgin Mary was inlaid in the stone over the main stairwell, and who sometimes wondered about adding Pierre Radisson's middle name to his own, asked some friends, "If Radisson and Desgroseilleurs were able to do it in the seventeenth century, why wouldn't it still be possible to do it today?"[9] Pierre Trudeau and three friends followed the Ottawa River canoe route, turning north at Mattawa to make Radisson and Desgroseilleurs' journey to James Bay.

✴

AT SAULT STE. MARIE, Mary's own rapids between Lake Huron and Lake Superior, on June 4, 1671, Ste. Marie's name added weight, if not permanence, to a formal New France declaration that all lands west of the

*Lend me your happy laughter,*
*Ste. Marie, as you leap;*
*Your peace that follows after*
*Where through the isles you creep.*
*Give to me your splendid dashing,*
*Give your sparkles and your splashing,*
*Your uphurling waves down crashing,*
*Then, your aftermath of sleep.*

From "Where Leaps the Ste. Marie," by Pauline Johnson, probably written on her recital circuit, 1894, at Sault Ste. Marie, where Pauline persuaded a Chippewa man to let her run the Ste. Marie (now St. Mary) River rapids with him.

Jesuit mission there belonged to the King of France. On that day, the Metis were the children of French Indian families living near New France missions and settlements, people named *boisbrule* — burnt wood — by the French. Western Metis, geographically and socially apart from European culture, knowing themselves as their own people, and their Sainte Marie as knowing them, were more than a century and many rivers ahead.

On the banks of the St. Lawrence in 1671, cherubs bore Mary, alone, aloft into a blue sky. The Virgin of the Assumption held sway in New France no matter the gap between European clerics arguing over whether or not her body as well as her soul had been taken up — assumed — into heaven, and the colonists: *filles du roi* — the king's daughters, girls without much family or money sent from France as marriage partners for the colonists — soldiers, independent fur-trading *coureurs des bois* — runners of the woods — and indentured labourers. Seventeen centuries of theological debate about the cherub-borne subject of *L'Assomption,* painted by Récollet artist Frère Luc (a.k.a. Claude François) to hang above the altar in Quebec's hospital chapel, would not end until 1950, when the dogma of the Assumption was proclaimed by Pope Pius XII.

Another Ursuline Virgin living near the St. Lawrence was lavishly embroidered during the eighteenth century. Marie Lemaire des Anges and her workshop of embroideresses stitched with gold and silver thread to create the Virgin adorning the silk altar cloth made for the convent chapel close to the Ursulines' flourishing girls' school.

Other rivers would bear these sometimes delicate Virgins of New France, as well as the sturdier mercy of Notre Dame de Montréal, dispensed through Jeanne Mance and later Sisters Hospitallers at Hôtel-Dieu since 1645, into distant, high country and transformations that would reach Indian and Metis people as far northwest of the St. Lawrence as Fort Chipewyan on Lake Athabaska in northern Alberta. The first passage toward a Virgin shaped by a new land was made in the late 1700s when North West Company fur-trade voyageurs paddled freight canoes forty-five to sixty strokes a minute through five thousand kilometres of river and lake waters opening the body of a huge, uncontrollably wild land.

✺

VOYAGEURS CELEBRATED their uproarious departure for *le pays d'en haut* above the Lachine Rapids on the St. Lawrence near Montreal while axes, guns, blankets, buttons, tiny brass bells, and other trade goods were crammed into the canoes until hardly a hand length's freeboard showed above the water lines.

From the canoe brigades' first push in the St. Lawrence, the voyageurs sang, lifting "La Plainte du coureurs des bois" into the water-washed rhythm of their long passages to the high country as bawdier, sometimes weepier, river-made versions of old French folk songs and ballads.

Lachine leave-takers soon halted pace for a brief pilgrimage to Sainte Marie's mother. Peter Pond, sometime North West Company partner and phonetic speller, recorded the voyageurs' "Saramony" for prayers to "St. Ann who Protects all Voigers,"[10] at Ste. Anne's (now Ste-Anne-de-Bellevue) chapel on the western edge of Montreal Island before every cross-country passage. Irish poet Thomas Moore created "Canadian Boat Song" from the ballad voyageurs sang while they rafted him and a friend from Kingston to Montreal in 1804: Saint of this green isle! Hear our prayers, Oh, grant us cool heavens and favouring airs. Blow, breezes, blow, the stream runs fast, The Rapids are near and the daylight's past.[11]

Along with Sainte Anne, Sainte Marie, and the earthly wild, wild women and /or lost, sweet maids of voyageur songs and jokes, a female presence with enduring mythic power crossed Lake Superior in the freight canoes. On Lake Superior's north shore, outbound west laden with trade goods, back east with beaver, lynx, marten, and fox pelts, voyageurs often sprinkled tea leaves or other treasure onto the water, "tributes to *La Vieille*, the old woman of the wind," Hugh Durnford and Peter Madely, editors of *Great Canadian Adventures*, write in "The Birchbark

*L'Assomption sash: a colourful sash 4 to 6 inches wide and 8 to 10 feet long, so called because the best such sashes were made in L'Assomption, Quebec, and widely distributed as trade goods by the fur companies, especially in the design known as the arrow sash.*

From *A Dictionary of Canadianisms*

*The Five Toasts of the North West Company's Beaver Club in Montreal: The Mother of All Saints; the King; the Fur Trade in all its Branches; Voyageurs, Wives and Children; and Absent Members.*

*My Lady Wind, my Lady Wind,*
*Went round about the house, to find*
*A chink to get her foot in*
*She tried the keyhole in the door,*
*She tried the crevice in the floor,*
*And drove the chimney soot in.*

*And then one night when it was dark,*
*She blew up such a tiny spark,*
*That all the house was pothered*
*from it she raised up such a flame*
*As streaked away to Weavers Frame,*
*And sleeping folks were bothered.*

Traditional

Brigade": "Some tobacco or trinket to invite her blessing. 'Souffle, souffle, la vieille,' they would chorus. (Blow, blow, old woman.) Then they would sit back, asleep or smoking, while makeshift sails of oilcloths or blankets did their work."[12]

✸

EVEN NOW, while Mary Star of the Sea minds the wind for sailors who can also get a marine radio weather forecast, a divine female in a starry palace belonging to Canada comes to life when the wind — "She's howling out there" — is a woman. Latin goddess Cardea, whose home castle glitters past the North Wind beside the polar hinge of the universe, made numbers, compass points, and winds "cardinal," from Latin *cardinalis*, or essential, born in a Greek word meaning to swing, as on a hinge.

When the weather bears down hard, the hinge between newly accumulated, learned modernity and ancient, instinctual human experience swings open. We claim, without pause or conscious thought, some inheritance of an older divinity who has wind and water and wilderness in her care. In an essay he called "West Talk," the late Victoria, British Columbia writer Charles Lillard noted neutral words becoming female when men worked outdoors: "The yesterday logger was an individual ... Perhaps it all starts with the separation between the pronouns 'her' and 'it' ... In the bush, you'll hear, 'I'll need my marlinspike for this job. She'll be stuck in behind the strawline drum where I hid her last night.' Once a man's imagination has made this important transition from it to her, anything is possible."[13]

✸

THE POSSIBILITIES CREATED in the intuitive, continuously shifting responses Quebec voyageurs taught themselves on waters wind-chopped across snow melt and torrent debris were a medium for Mary of Canada's making. River prayers — for a wind shift, for a turn of strength through one more (surely to *le Dieu* the last today) water riff — urgent supplications undiluted by ritual, made by human beings whose bodies and souls were becoming part of a wild land, may have been some of the first currents of invocation to shape the kind of responsive, in-country Virgin Kathleen Mary Flannigan, "Mrs. Mike," would see at Lesser Slave Lake one day in the twentieth century. She described a Mother of Sorrows whose warmth and sweetness carved in wood with a hunting knife might as well have been formed from *le pays d'en haut* itself, a figure very different from the delicate, young, and somewhat isolated Virgin of the Ursulines' altar cloth or the Jesuit missions.

The Metis French Indian families in the west, and their Sainte Marie, who would always know rivers, are in part the inheritance left by voyageurs tough enough to paddle and portage fourteen hours a day and merry-hearted enough to sing while they did it. They carried Sainte Marie to and from the fur-trade forts on the North and South Saskatchewan, up into the Athabaska River out of the Churchill system, along the Red and Assiniboine draining into Lake Winnipeg, up and down the rivers and lakes between Lake Winnipeg and Lake Superior.

Sainte Marie–Mary of Canada journeyed farther north and west, riding horses and railways with Metis people and mission priests through the long, slow nineteenth-century decline of the fur trade. Years after she had recognized Gabriel Dumont's need for a fast horse and the American border after the Metis were defeated at Batoche, she was making way with Metis freighters on river and lake systems in northern British Columbia, travelling by barge as well as canoe and, eventually, overland by pack horse train into the early twentieth century.

✸

THE MOST ADAPTABLE, river-wise Quebec voyageur could not have imagined the changes of heart, mind, and social climate needed before

Sainte Marie would be shown as a succession of possibilities in Denys Arcand's 1989 *Jesus of Montreal*. In the film centred on a contemporary Passion Play staged on Montreal's St. Joseph's hill, Sainte Marie may be one of the unwed mothers mentioned in the play's quiet opening narration referring to historical context. The Virgin's continuing mercy can be seen in the character named Constance, the single mother and sometime actress whose steady, balanced capacity for love, as well as her common sense and beauty, enfolds everyone in her life. It might be as Sainte Marie herself that Constance, wearing a robe, speaks words of love and courage to the Passion Play's audience after the Crucifixion scene while Montreal glitters and hums in the backdrop. Aspects of Sainte Marie, the Blessed Virgin who listens carefully, who is a loving mother, are also present in the crowd watching the play on the hill. And the entertainment lawyer with big plans for the Passion Play actors knows what he's about when he orders a round of Virgin Marys — seasoned tomato juice, no vodka — and Magdalen lobsters for their lunch.

✹

THE VOYAGEURS' VIRGIN, the noble Lady in white who showed the way through the Seven Falls rapids in their *La Complainte de Cadieux* ballad and legend, and who had a soft heart for any voyageur willing to paddle sixty-plus strokes a minute for hours to win Lake Winnipeg canoe brigade races (that is, every voyageur) still lives as Notre Dame du Portage. A St. Lawrence River municipality and a Kenora, Ontario's Diocese of Thunder Bay parish with an anglophone, francophone, and First Nations constituency all carry her name.

Imagine Kenora's Notre Dame du Portage smiling. She knows the in-joke. She remembers very well that this version of herself as the world's only Portage Madonna started out at Rat Portage, on the Winnipeg River north end of Lake of the Woods, where *Wauzhusk Onigum*, Algonkin "portage to muskrat country," was the first settlement. Later, the voyageurs knew the fur-trade post on Old Fort Island in the river as Rat Portage. The village of the same name moved to the lake shore and belonged in Manitoba in 1882. Only a provincial boundary change, and the first two letters of surrounding districts Keewatin, Norman, and Rat Portage, made the Ontario city of Kenora. Notre Dame du Portage in Kenora, who has, one way or another, known as many muskrats as people involved with portages, canoes, and rivers in Canada, would not be troubled by a reminder of the fur trade as a local place name in her title.

✸

I LIKE TO THINK that Mary of Canadian Rivers might also know a certain ocean-bound voyageur who slid out of a barely breaking-up snowmelt stream in Northern Ontario's Lake Nipigon watershed. His liturgy begins "Please Put Me Back in Water. I Am Paddle to the Sea."[14]

✸

THE YEAR the Hudson's Bay Company's fur-trade grant — "all lands watered by rivers flowing into Hudson Bay"[15] — was sold to a brand new country already looking for immigrants to fill its empty spaces, Mary of Canada had in mind the mélange of desperation, eagerness, hope, and fear that had always accompanied newcomers to Canada. She knew of their need to cling to whatever faith or denomination seemed most familiar to them, or safest, whether they had followed French soldiers or fishermen to fortified Louisburg on Île Royale, a.k.a. Cape Breton Island, in the 1700s, or had arrived in Ontario that year, just in time for the 1871 census.

The 1871 Ontario census records some evidence for common, if stereotypical, assumptions about connections between first homeland, family, and denomination:

Male: Born Ontario. Age 26. Head of House. Wesleyan Methodist. Ethnic Origin: English. Farmer.

Male: Born Quebec. Age 60. Has surname other than head of house. Roman Catholic. Ethnic Origin: French. Lumberman.

Male: Born Scotland. Head of House. Church of Scotland/Kirk/Scotch Presbyterian. Ethnic Origin: Scottish. Minister.

Male: Born England. Head of House. Church of England, Anglican. Ethnic Origin: English. Cabman.[16]

But many contradictions to automatically perceived linkages, and painful, desperate efforts to alter them, are also present in the nineteenth-century Ontario census lists. A woman with a last name known in New France is listed as "Born Quebec. Age 64. Has surname other than head of house. Episcopal Methodist. Ethnic Origin: French. Occupation: unknown code." Some Ontarians are recorded as "Anglican. Ethnic Origin: Jew."[17]

✱

SOME OF THE CENSUS CITIZENS believed in witches. One of the oldest Old World beliefs was alive in Canada before and after 1871, however blurred and faint its back trail. In 1557, Martin Frobisher's crew captured Inuit people in the Arctic, stripped one elderly woman to see if she were cloven-footed, then let her go on the grounds she was likely a witch anyway. Hundreds of years later, a Nova Scotia farmer's wife turned witch when she became a cat who muttered a German, possibly Dutch, word or two just before she tried to kill her twenty-sixth hired man. She was caught with the old cut-off-her-paw then see who's missing-a-hand-in-the-morning trick.

Nova Scotia was troubled by witches, even if 1831 poet Andrew Shiels thought one of them resembled the "Muse of the West … To human view she lived alone — Child or domestic she had none" in "The Witch of the

Westcot: A Tale of Nova Scotia."[18] Another Nova Scotia woman probably earned the title by refusing to remarry after her husband died in a nineteenth-century Baptist farming community. She proved herself a witch by creating a wind that flattened her old house on the very night her descendants were planning to collect her spinning wheel and other valuables after her death.

The witch of Port La Joye, opaque, still, within her folds of historical time and legend, belongs to Mi'kmaq, Acadian, and other Prince Edward Island stories. La Belle Marie was the daughter of a Basque woman living near the French fort at Port La Joye on Isle St. Jean in the early 1700s. The mostly Breton settlers' jealous talk about Marie's beauty, and about both women's ease with Mi'kmaq people, increased, perhaps, when the Basque fishermen were away at sea. In continuing Mi'kmaq oral tradition, La Belle Marie married the man she loved, the son of a Mi'kmaq chief. They may have lived happily ever after, or maybe only until La Belle Marie, still young and beautiful, took an arrow shot meant for her husband. Or she was declared a witch by church and civil authorities, and died in flames at the stake, November 17, 1723, at Port La Joye.

Nova Scotia Acadians exiled in the mid-1700s carried witch caution as well as the Virgin with them to Cajun life in Louisiana bayous. Cajun mothers knew that witches had been at the breasts of fretful, colicky babies in the night. A broom across the doorstep disposed of her. No witch will step over a broom.

Mary of Canada (whose cross-border mandate these days extends to Sanctuaire de Notre Dame du Sourire, the Quebecois church on Johnson Street in Hollywood Beach, Florida) sometimes had to go down to Louisiana to lend a hand. As La Vierge, she was already busy enough calming Cajun children trembling along paths they had been cautioned never to leave, not even to pick swamp lilies, or lavender, the money bush, for fear of a *loup-garou* or some other devil-spelled form. Sometimes, she was busy with grown-ups who stepped off bayou roads. One Cajun wife, childless and desperate to please her husband, was seduced off the trail by the sight of a baby boy lying sweet and healthy under a tree, gurgling with laughter and kicking his feet. La Vierge had answered her constant prayers, the Cajun wife believed as she knelt beside the infant to give thanks, but she would have to finish her devotions at home, she told La Vierge because the first words of her prayers caused the child to scream. Only a step or two had she taken with the baby in her arms when he began to grow, and blacken, becoming something either devilish or witchcrafted, or both. All the barren wife could do was call La Vierge's name, and make the sign of the cross. This gestured plea was enough to cause the creature from some dark, enchanted level of the world to disappear. No Cajun lady has left the bayou path since.

Other witches were killing oxen and pigs, stopping horse teams in their tracks, spellcasting illness, and spoiling maple syrup around Cashel, Ontario, not far from the Free Methodist Church. You could tell a witch by the scared look on her face, or her scars, or the way she smiled, according to David Trumble, 111 years old when his reminiscences were published as *The Road to St. Ola and Other Stories* in 1978. To break a witch's spell on a sick person, put a Bible under the bed, then "take the patient's urine, and boil it — hot. Pour that in a bottle. Take nine new needles, heat them red hot, drop them in the bottle of hot urine. Put the plug onto it. Nothing can get out ... And that bottle — glass, needles, urine, and everything — will fly into the witch. Then she gets all crippled up."[19]

Witchcraft rumours lasted into the twentieth century. Along New Brunswick's Northumberland Strait shore in Linda McNutt's 1997 novel *Summer Point*, Nana Whittaker, mother and grandmother of local ne'er-do-wells, is known to make moonshine from blood. And Mary Anne the Duck, adorned with necklaces and rings, treated with deference if not fear, told fortunes and maybe more on the South Side of St. John's, Newfoundland, in Helen Fogwill Porter's 1979 childhood memoir, *Below the Bridge*: "My grandmother and the others were, it always seemed to me, a little afraid of her ... She was rumoured to be a witch — Dot said she had even more cats than Minnie Warren — and we were always warned not to offend her."[20]

✴

ONCE UPON A TIME when there was Atlantic cod, I saw Helen's beloved South Side Hills across the harbour in St. John's, Newfoundland, from the height of a chain-link fence around the fuel dock over there. It was only a moon-washed glimpse because my hands needed to unclench while my feet scrabbled up the fence so I could jump down the other side, and decide never again to hitch a ride across St. John's or any other Atlantic harbour on a Russian trawling ship for old time's sake. I knew trouble would follow giving in to the almost irresistible temptation of forty days of hard labour at sea, then maybe Halifax, maybe Murmansk, even if the bent tin forks and spoons in the crew's mess room were familiar to my hands. Even if Mary were allowed to live on the main deck of Russian ships by then, in the messroom's icon corner beside a twig from the tree Russia calls the wonderful birch.

Helen had made me a gift of her company on the flight back across the country while I read her beautiful South Side of St. John's memoir, but a few years later when I called from Gabriola Island to tell her I was looking for Mary in Canada, I had forgotten this part of *Below the Bridge*: "Our family belonged to the United Church ... we didn't learn very much about Catholics and Protestants. We learnt a certain amount about God and Jesus, not very much about the Virgin Mary who was somewhat suspect to most of our congregation, and we were wary of crosses and any kind of statuary."[21]

On the phone from Gabriola to St. John's, Helen hardly paused, "Mary," she pronounced with great calm while I imagined all the land between us hanging in a silver net strung between seas. Then, "She's stood up well, hasn't she, Joan?"

Yes, Helen, I think she has.

**Let Me Fish off
Cape St. Mary's**

*Take me back to my western boat,
Let me fish off Cape St. Mary's*

*Let me sail up Golden Bay
With my oilskins all a' streamin'...
From the thunder squall — when I
   hauled me trawl
And my old Cape Ann a' gleamin'
With my oil skins all a' streamin'*

*Take me back to my western boat,
Let me fish off Cape St. Mary's*

From "Let Me Fish off Cape St. Mary's," a Newfoundland song in *Historic Newfoundland and Labrador*

✳

SHRINES, TOO, and other kinds of sacred grounds, have stood up well in Canada and are still being made. Needing and finding and making shrines as containers of the sacred from Latin *scrinium* — box or container — continues here, crossing time, language, age, and cultural boundaries.

A Canadian riverbank that Rome recognized as a pilgrimage place in 1644 is still sacred ground after three hundred and fifty years of political, cultural, and population change. Sainte-Marie-aux-Hurons has been rebuilt as a replica of Ontario's first European settlement, near the site now called the Martyrs' shrine on the Wye River at Midland, Ontario. In 1930, Jean de Brébeuf, Isaac Jogues, Gabriel Lalemont, Charles Garnier, Antoine Daniel, Noël Chabanel, René Goupil, and Jean de la Lande were named North America's saints and martyrs by Pope Pius XI.

The saints' bone and skull fragments are at the shrine, encased in a silver reliquary. Healings and other blessings are known here. Our Lady of Huronia abides in her grotto on the grounds, knowing that war founded in faith changing and fur trading is no longer the only choice for citizens of a homeland made strange to them by strangers, and that villages between the Great Lakes and the Gulf of St. Lawrence will not be ravaged by Europe's smallpox.

Canadian shrines the Catholic Church has dedicated to the Blessed Virgin Mary or Saint Anne or other saints differ from private shrines in their content, yet connect with them in the demonstration of our need for material designated as soul treasure. By means of this shared human need, the 1803 Quebec City Jesuit Martyrs chapel built by a Marian prayer group the Jesuits started in 1657 after the loss of Sainte-Marie-aux-Hurons is linked not only with the Midland, Ontario shrine, and the beautiful Huron chapel of Notre-Dame-de-Lorette near Quebec City, but also with the 2002 shrine in Doctor Josef Penninger's Toronto laboratory. The secular science shrine is made from champagne bottles and good luck charms marking the lab's every genetic-disease research victory. The Internet shrines for television's *Due South* (with RCMP officer Benton Fraser and his deaf wolf, Diefenbaker), and singer Shania Twain mark publicly worshipped entertainment divinities.

✶

WHENEVER A PIECE OF THE MATERIAL world is set apart from its usual context — the candle a young girl set at the door of the U.S. Embassy in Ottawa after September 11, 2001; some King City earth that was farmland north of Toronto before it was owned by a financier who named the lake there after his wife, Marie, later bought by the Catholic Archdiocese of Toronto to be enshrined as Marylake, a pilgrimage place for Our Lady of Grace; and the small stone in my pocket, provenance known only to me — sacred meaning is made.

An intimately personal shrine or an altar, an amulet, or an icon is created over and again every ordinary day in Canada. In these contemporary acts of assigning spiritual meaning to matter comes word from a far country. The small white crosses, sometimes snow broken, on the edge of Canada's northern roads, and the flowers left on city streets, never touched even after they fade, mark, not the physical graves of car accident victims, but the exact, ordinary places where great loss was incurred. Like the Assiniboine people who cut the wheel of life into La Roche Percée, and who covered beloved bodies with hyacinths forty thousand years ago in Neolithic caves, we need to make a sign that our awareness of consciousness has been carried beyond the physical.

The flowers and small crosses or other symbols marking sudden-death places are *descansos*, a Spanish word meaning resting places. In 1792, crewmen from Dionisio Galiano's schooner *Sutil* and Cayetano Valdes's *Mexicana* left a descanso, perhaps more than one, on Gabriola Island during Spain's west coast exploration out of the Spanish naval base at San Blas, Mexico. The Gabriola–Nanaimo ferry ties up in Descanso Bay, named in memory of those who died there. The Spanish sailors' descansos, likely accompanied by prayers to the conquistadores' Virgin de los Remedios, and contemporary Mexican Canadian artist Carmen Bizet-Irigoyen's expansive presentation of an altar for Our Lady of Guadalupe find a cross-country connection in Cape Breton, Nova Scotia.

Mary of Canada and the Unexpected is not surprised to find the only official Canadian shrine for Our Lady of Guadalupe in Johnstown on the south side of Cape Breton Island, near the Mi'kmaq people. As Madonna of the Americas, Our Lady of Guadalupe, the mestizo Mary, is treasured in many Canadian First Nations communities. The *Novalis Guide to Canadian Shrines* says, "In the sacristy of the church is a tiny art gallery consisting of 12 paintings of Our Lady of Guadaloupe in an aboriginal style by Brazilian artist Claudio Pastro."[22]

✸

MARY OF CANADA as Our Lady of Guadalupe knows that gray whales *Eschrichtius robustus* share a Mexican Canadian connection with her. The whales make a long, leisurely passage off the west coast of Haida Gwaii, Queen Charlotte Islands and Vancouver Island twice a year, to and from the Bering and western Beaufort Seas, and Mexican waters. A few small bands of grays stay year round in western Canadian waters, despite whale-watching boats.

Our Lady of Guadalupe may have been on board a small skiff in a Baja California lagoon with fisherman Francisco (Pachio) Mayoral in 1972. When a gray whale surfaced beside his little boat to look at him, Francisco Mayoral understood. He put out his hand and stroked the whale. His touch was the first friendly human contact eastern Pacific gray whales had known.

✸

NEITHER IS MARY OF CANADA startled by Bizet-Irigoyen's beautiful altar piece, a box in which the cherub holding the crescent moon at

*Our Lady of Grace* ✶ *Our Lady of the Assumption* ✶ *Our Lady of Good Counsel* ✶ *Our Lady of the Navigators* ✶ *Our Lady of the Sacred Heart* ✶ *Our Lady of Victory* ✶ *Our*

*Mary in Canada* 85

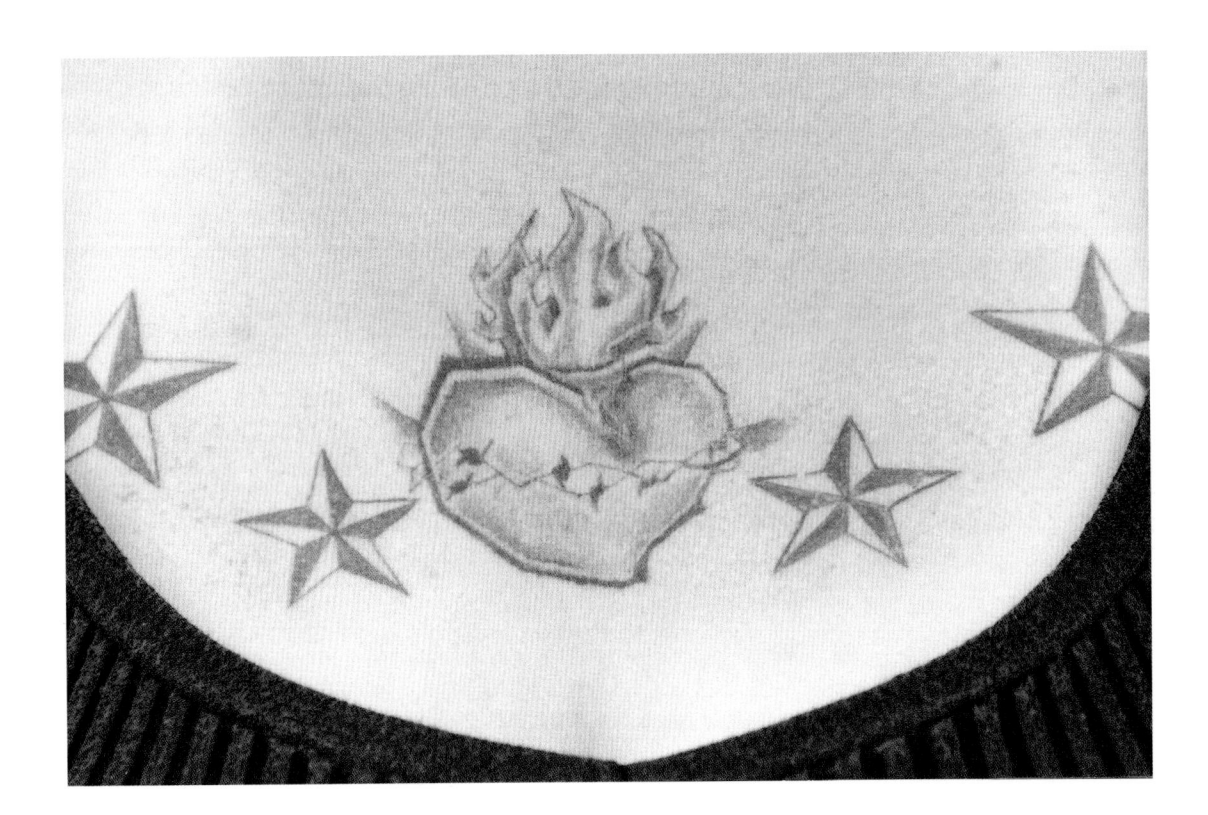

Guadalupe's feet is replaced by a small Aztec figure, and the image of a starry-robed Virgin with sunrays behind her (intended to mean that the pregnant Virgin is larger than the Aztec sun god) is crowned with a tiny bronze head of Tonatiuh, the sun god. The piece she titled *Guadalupe-Tonantzim* combines the Aztec divine mother with the new Madonna who appropriated her hill at Tepeyac, and includes Japanese origami paper cranes, made by Bizet-Irigoyen's daughter as peace prayers, and prayer symbols from Singapore. "*Guadalupe-Tonantzim* is a votive," she says, "a prayer for protection."[23] No, she would not sell it.

Our Lady of Guadalupe appears at the tattoo parlour in Canada these days, along with other Mary tattoo images. Around the corner from my place in Vancouver's West End, Sacred Heart Tattoos creates Marian skin art from pictures provided by customers. Although *Skin and Ink: The Tattoo Magazine* cites Canada for wondrous Guadalupe images, tattoo artist Mikel at Sacred Heart (named for the frequently requested design; no church affiliation) told me Mary's immaculate heart — "roses around it, with fire coming out the top" — is still requested.

An Irish Mary carrying a Gaelic harp adorns the right shoulder of west coast writer Terry Glavin (*The Last Great Sea: A Voyage through the Human and Natural History of the North Pacific*; *A Death Feast in Dimlahamid*; *Dead Reckoning: Confronting the Crisis in Pacific Fisheries*). At the other end of the phone on Mayne Island, while he was kindly searching his files for a Chinook-language Mary prayer for me, he said, "I just like Mary." And me, I like the last paragraph of Terry Glavin's July 2002 *Georgia Straight* review of some Mary books, "To her believers, Miryam stands as a protection against the unspeakable cruelties of the real world. She is a rebuke to the claims of scholars and clerics. For countless millions, she is the last line of defence against God himself."[24]

✸

VIRGINS OTHER THAN OUR LADY OF GUADALUPE, and not tattooed either, bracket Cape Breton Island in Lynn Coady's novel, *Strange Heaven*. John Donne's "faire blessed Mother-maid … whose womb was a strange heav'n" opens the book. The Virgin who closes it intimately knows Margaret P. She had "always been old, had always had spells, 'bad turns,' she called them, had lived in this room … saying the rosary, spitting into Kleenex."[25]

✸

ANOTHER MARITIME SHRINE holds traditions casting far back in Canada's history, and outward across distance and borders. The history of Prince Edward Island's Lennox Island Shrine of St. Ann on the

*Klahawiyam Mali,
maika pati kopa lagrace,
Sahalé-Tayé kanamokst maika,
maika ilep tlous kopa kanawé
 kloutchémin
ilep tlous maika tanas Jesu.*

*O tlous Mali,
iaka mania kopa Sahalé-Tayé,
mamouk stiwilh kopa Sahalé-Tayé
 pous nsaika,
massachi télikom, alta pi alka pous
 nsaika chako memelous.
Tlous pous kakwa.*

From *Ava Maria in 404 lingue*, "Ave Maria," Chinook language, contributed by David G. Landsnes, MD

reserve goes back to 1610, when Membertou, the Mi'kmaq high chief, was baptized. In the *Novalis Guide to Canadian Shrines*, Leonard St. John writes, "Around 1620, a concordat was drawn up between the Micmac (sic) and the papacy, giving the district chiefs almost the same powers as the priests, including the right to teach the faith. After the British conquest of Canada and the expulsion of the Acadians, the Micmac (sic) were responsible for the survival of Catholicism in the Maritime region ... From the earliest times the Micmac (sic) adopted St. Ann, the grandmother of Christ, as their patroness partly because of their great respect for grandmothers."[26]

Saint Ann/Anne's Sunday July feast day pilgrimage and celebration on the Atlantic coast at Lennox Island is joined to huge ceremonies far inland at Lac Ste. Anne in Alberta. They won't be blessing the fishing fleet out in Alberta, but as many as forty thousand native people will make the pilgrimage to the Virgin Mary's mother.

Acadian memory on Prince Edward Island has sustained in Canada a fragment from one of Europe's oldest pilgrimages. The nursery song "La Nourrice du Roi," recorded by l'Abbe Galland at Mount Carmel, P.E.I., in the 1920s, probably travelled to France from Montserrat, where the small Black Virgin seated with Christ on her lap and holding a pine cone would have been the miracle worker whose arms carried the missing baby, "Dans les bras de la Vierge tu le retrouveras."

Pilgrimages to Acadian history, as well as to a Calvary shrine, are made at Miscouche, P.E.I. Here, in 1884, the first *Convention nationale acadienne* affirmed Acadian culture, and remembered the Acadian families Britain expelled from their homes in southeast Quebec, eastern Maine, New Brunswick, Nova Scotia, and Prince Edward Island, from 1755 to 1763. The Acadian Genealogy Homepage reports, "The Acadian National Flag was adopted. The tri-colour flag of France (blue, white, and red) was chosen as the base flag. A yellow/gold star was placed in the upper part of the blue field ... the star, Our Lady of Assumption, represents Stella Maris, Star of the Sea, seeks the protection of the Blessed Virgin Mary and indicates hope and the guiding light of the future ... The flag is conserved at the *Museé acadien de l'Université de Moncton* ... in New Brunswick."[27]

Acadian people were pushed, in great travail, to other British North American colonies. Some Acadians went to France, others to Louisiana, where Evangeline and her beloved, lost, Gabriel (but not Longfellow's poetic licence in deleting New England's self-interest and the Massachusetts troops who herded Acadians into boats from *Evangeline*) are remembered at a tree named for them.

Antonine Maillet created a contemporary Acadian heroine in *La Sagouine*, "a scrubwoman, a woman of the sea, who was born with the century, with her feet in the water." *La Sagouine* suggests, "Jus' suppose that on a Christmas Day, the pr'cession made a wrong turn n' landed right here in our shacks — the shepherds, the Wise Men, the camels, Joseph n' Mary n' the baby ... we'd send for *Sarah Bidoche*, the midwife, to help jus' in case. But he wouldn' need *Sarah*'s help, that little one, cause it would all happen accordin to the Bible, like a miracle ... I can jus' imagine *La Cruche* whisperin' to the Holy Virgin, so she could tell her everythin', tell her everythin' she never would of told the priest, that's fer sure. Or, maybe she'd say not'n at all, but would jus' stay close to her, n' they'd laugh together, the two of them watchin' the baby."[28]

Every prayer at St. Joseph's shrine in Tracadie, New Brunswick, a village settled by returned Acadians, rises from a nation where Saint Joseph and Saint Anne are the patron saints. Joseph is also patron of the Metis, and of all workers and fathers. The newest version of *Saturday Night* magazine is published by St. Joseph Media.

Saint Joseph was the nickname striking miners gave the twenty-nine-year-old lawyer with the blondish beard who stirred them with his talk of justice and democracy in Asbestos, Quebec, 1949. Everyone at the labour meetings listened up to Pierre Trudeau, though.

(Besides, Saint Joseph, as a saint who protects families, helps with tough real-estate sales. Plant him in the ground in front of your house, near the for sale sign. Ask him to help. Believe.)

---

*Look at this vigorous plant, that lifts its head from*
    *the meadow,*

*See how its leaves are turned to the north, as true as*
    *the magnet;*

*This is the compassflower, that the finger of God has*
    *planted*

*Here in the houseless wild, to direct the travellers'*
    *Journey...*

From "Evangeline,"
by Henry Wadsworth Longfellow

Virgin Most Prudent ✷ Virgin Most Venerable ✷ Virgin Most Renowned ✷ Virgin Most Powerful ✷ Virgin Most Merciful ✷ Aeiparthenos (Ever-Virgin) ✷ Ark of the Covenant ✷ A M

✷

IN THE URGENT COMMONALITY of our need to make a physical sign of spiritual presence, holy places are joined. In our recognition of their intense meaning, the shrine where "An image of the Virgin occupied a niche in the chapel wall, and before it burned the silver lamp of Repentigny"[29] in *The Golden Dog*, Kingston, Ontario writer William Kirby's nineteenth-century Quebec historical romance is not so distant from the Toronto hotel bar table where Ilona, legendary lady of mysteriously enchanting comfort for the soul as well as the body, reigns in Morley Callaghan's *Our Lady of the Snows*.

In Katherine Govier's *The Truth Teller*, the "Manor School for Classical Studies in an unsuspecting Toronto" is a shrine to its founding couple, and to high art, if not truth, as the means of redemption for rich girls gone astray. One of the girls, Cassandra McVey, will strip coats of hypocrisy and illusion from the legendary school, and everyone in it. The Madonna will be part of the book's one true act of redemption: "On the front were a couple of Madonnas drawn by Ashley, a linocut transfer of a bee by Maureen / Delphine, the illuminated letter F contributed by Sara, and a pressed rose from the garden. In elegant cursive script, a specialty of Roxanne's, was written: 'Dear Ferdinand, The Ladies of the Manor have missed you and your truck. We are certain that the bad people who beat you and drove your truck into the lake have been punished for their wrongdoing, and that they are very sorry. They would probably never do anything like that again.'" [30]

Canadian fiction causes even holy miracle places to resonate with human contradictions. Don Hannah's *The Wise and Foolish Virgins* contains no shrine honouring Mary's visit to the spruce grove at the back of the nuns' pasture in Membartouche, New Brunswick, because no one is willing to believe the two Grade Seven girls who really saw her. In Alberta writer Mary Woodbury's short story "Not in Front of the Virgin," the Pietà Madonna who has appeared on Wally and Vera's bedroom wall creates media attention as an endurance test: "'Mr. Jarman was reluctant to talk. Hopefully, tomorrow, CFRN can bring you more details. After the case of the tree stump with the virgin on it in Sudbury, and the false claims from Kelowna of blood dripping from the wall, the latest phenomenon will be of interest to both the media and the religious authorities. In other news ...'"[31] The Alberta bedroom wall Madonna restores Wally's virility, though, while the small, glass-encased bones of poor little *tante* Jeanette, set up at a sudden roadside shrine in the township of Cobalt, Ontario, never actually, permanently, really truly cure anyone, no matter how often Farmer Lanthier refers to their former owner as the Blessed Jeanette. In Melissa Hardy's "Lightning" in *The Uncharted Heart*: "Old Farmer Lanthier sold the glass-encased skeleton of his little sister to the man who owned the sideshow — he was making a shopping trip through the district looking for such marvels as the two-headed calves, dancing chickens, and boys without limbs."[32]

Individual perceptions of sacred meaning are assigned daily. The forty-seven-year-old labourer who found two metal beams fused into a six-metre-tall cross in the rubble of New York's World Trade Center knew it was an act of God. The metal cross was blessed and became a pilgrimage site for other workers. In Jean-Claude Lauzon's 1992 film *Léolo*, the Montreal basement shrine where a small boy in a family wrenched by inherited mental illness attends his beloved sister, Queen Rita of the bugs, is part of his world of sacred matter. Leolo's earliest hiding place is deep in the swimming pool, "because the bottom is sky blue," and only the rose someone has chucked into the water is "scarlet plastic."[33]

At the edge of a pig farm in Port Coquitlam, British Columbia, the sacred intention within the flowers and photographs of more than sixty women missing from Vancouver streets, and the vigil their families maintain as police excavation of the murder site continues, may not be so far from Shelagh and John Greensides' farm in Marmora, Ontario, 190 kilometres northeast of Toronto.

In 1990, the Greensides visited Medjugorje in the Croatian area of the Republic of Bosnia-Herzegovina, where hundreds of thousands of people from many countries have been drawn to the hill on which Our Lady is said to have appeared to six Croatian children of the Franciscan Medjugorje parish on June 24, 1981, and on other occasions since then.

The Greensides prepared the Stations of the Cross in the woods on their land as a way to celebrate and give thanks for the Medjugorje apparitions with other local pilgrims on June 24, 1991. Thousands of people, and images of Our Lady, often in the sun and sometimes accompanied by the scent of roses, appeared at the farm within a year. Our

Lady is said to have directed that the natural spring on the property be a means for healing. Personal transformations and healings are known there.

✸

HIDING HEAT SICKNESS AND EXHAUSTION, I passed through Medjugorje in July 1995. No pilgrims, only convoys running slow in fierce summer sun. Looking back at Mary's hill from the side window of a jeep, I saw clouds gathering. The air cooled and rain fell most of the way up the Neretva River Valley to the Mostar checkpoint.

✸

MADONNA HOUSE IN COMBERMERE, Ontario, may have seemed as much a blessing as cooling rain to a troubled man in 1965. Artist William Kurelek, haunted by childhood grievances and doubts, found some peace in the Lay Apostolate community there. Madonna House was founded by Catherine de Hueck Doherty (1896–1985), who had integrated her Russian homeland and early Orthodox faith with Catholicism, a social work career, and a friendship with Thomas Merton before she decided on voluntary poverty and a life devoted to others in a simple house named for the Mother of God at Combermere Ontario. Our Lady of Combermere, a full-size, bronze Questing Madonna with open arms, approved by the Sacred Congregation of Rites in Rome, and blessed by the Bishop of Pembroke in 1960 as "the newest shrine in Christendom," watches over lay volunteers working the earth and dedicated to "apostolic farming,"[34] at Madonna House.

Earth, both Canadian and Russian, may be the sacred matter by which to remember Grand Duchess Olga Alexandrovna of Russia. A Campbellville, Ontario farm provided the peace Tsar Nicholas II's sister had last known at a summer home on a hill overlooking the golden dome of St. Tihon's

*Individuals and groups saw manifestations in the sun, including images of Jesus, Our Lady, the symbol of the dove, the sacred Host and the Cross. Hundreds of people focused their cameras on the sun, and later discovered on their film silhouettes of the Blessed Virgin ...Visitors take away with them a bottle of water from the natural spring which was blessed by Our Lady for healing ... Another phenomenon observed by many visitors is that of huge golden energy fields in the sky encircling the hill of the Way of the Cross, as well as the lower level of the farm. These sights have been witnessed by adults and children alike. Within these energy fields, Steven Ley said he saw the magnificent features of angels, some of whom were six feet high.*

From Marmora's Miracle Website at http://205.206.169.2/amorcanada/miracle.htm

The murmur of prayers are to me like
   stepping stones, the mysteries like
   wings.
All things spoken on the beads are now
   accomplished and today
I walk on their slender, incredible
   strength.

"Prayer," by Catherine de Hueck
Doherty, founder of Madonna House,
Combermere, Ontario, from The
Flowering of the Soul: A Book of Prayers by
Women, by Lucinda Vardey

Russian Orthodox monastery in Voronez province in 1902. The jewel-edged icons she still owned were taken by her sons before her death in 1960. The small, velvet-lined box containing a silver chain and a scent bottle that Anastasia, the real Anastasia, had given her Aunt Olga is in a landfill somewhere in Ontario. When Olga Alexandrovna died in November 1960, a handful of Russian earth was placed on her coffin in York cemetery.

A Romanov who had survived the Russian Revolution and two world wars would not have shown unseemly surprise had she ever learned that her cousin, Queen Marie of Romania, had kept southern Ontario in her heart alongside her devotion to the Orthodox Virgin. Queen Marie visited Canada in 1926 to see for herself the homeland of Lieutenant Colonel Joseph Whiteside Boyle, a.k.a. Klondike Joe Boyle, decorated by England, France, and Russia, and possessor of Romania's highest honours for his gallantry, and superb train- and ship-commandeering skills put to use during World War I and the Russian Revolution to save Romania's parliamentary hostages and national treasure.

When Joe Boyle died suddenly in London in 1923, Queen Marie said private prayers in the room where he died, and marked his grave with the Order of Maria Regina and an ancient Orthodox double-barred stone cross. In 1983, Joe Boyle's remains, and Queen Marie's monuments, infused with her love and the prayers she centred in the tender Virgin of Vladimir, were repatriated to the Presbyterian cemetery in his hometown, Woodstock, Ontario. Queen Marie died in 1938, holding an icon of the Virgin. (Hollywood bought the rights to Joe's story in the 1930s. Spencer Tracy had the lead until 1941 when the U.S. entered World War II, and the movie was cancelled.)

Other holy ground in Ontario and a trace of the Russian Orthodox Madonna as Theotokas — the God bearer — appear in Robertson Davies's *The Lyre of Orpheus*. A passel of Mary possibilities are tucked into Maria Magdalena Theotoky, "half Pole and the other half is Hungarian Gypsy," who is impregnated by a man disguised as her husband, a matter which,

*Puerto Rico: Our Lady of Divine Providence* ✳ *Uruguay: Our Lady of the Thirty Three* ✳ *Venezuela: Our Lady of Coromoto* ✳ *Mary, Mother of God* ✳ *Mary, Queen of Hearts* ✳ *Mi*

for the good of all concerned, must not be mentioned. Eastern Ontario seen from a train window in November briefly resembles the Garden of Eden after Darcourt discovers that the extraordinary, ostensibly sixteenth-century painting, *The Marriage at Cana*, is peopled by the "turn-of-the-century Ontario town" citizens of Blairlogie. Except for "the only figure in the picture graced with a halo. The Mother of God? Yes, for the convention in which the picture was cast demanded that. But more probably the Mighty Mother of All. As mother of everybody and everything, it was not necessary for her to look like anyone in particular."[35]

96  MARY OF CANADA

*eth  ✽  Mirror of Justice  ✽  Mother of Christ  ✽  Mother of the Church  ✽  Mother of Consolation  ✽  Mother of Divine Grace  ✽  Mother Inviolate  ✽  Mother Mary  ✽  Mother Most Aimial*

Bearing a resemblance to gentle, possibly saintly, Mary Dempster back in Deptford, Ontario, the small Madonna standing in a niche left intact in a shattered building during the Third Battle of Ypres in Robertson Davies's *Fifth Business* may owe a fraction of her fictional creation to World War I Canadian soldiers. Some of their writing only became more widely known when Barry Callaghan and Bruce Meyer collected work for *We Wasn't Pals: Canadian Poetry and Prose of the First World War*.

Fragments left by a burning shell
    Show where the altar stood
  A pile of bricks where the steeple fell,
     A Virgin carved in wood …

From "Laventie Church," H. Smalley Sarson (dates unknown; wounded Ypres)[36]

I tried to believe H. Smalley Sarson might have seen my grandfather in Regina Trench, or Alfred Gott from Lillooet, sniper in the same North Coast 102 Battalion, both men accompanied by memory streams of British Columbia rivers with attendant grizzly and black bears. When I could imagine all three men, along with Arthur and Simeon and Moise and two dozen other Canadian soldiers who bore the surname Sainte / Ste. Marie to the Great War, and thousands more tired, muddy faces, they were all looking up at Notre-Dame de Brebières, the golden statue of the Virgin holding the infant Christ atop the church at Albert on the Somme, bombarded from 1914 onward to an increasingly dangerous angle of lean over the troops until a stray British shell brought her down in 1918.

I found only the absence of the Mother of God in any idea of a Virgin of Victory in World War I or any other war. Notre Dame de Lorette, the height before Vimy Ridge that holds nineteen thousand French soldiers' graves, and a hill of bones estimated to mean thirty thousand more men, was a Virgin created by way of a war long before her name was given to the

*The wind buffeted the frozen Saint-François River; the stars, paralyzed by the cold, hovered on the horizon an extra measure longer ... And with his pocket knife, Nazaire began whittling the little branches that pushed through the walls of his hiding place. First, a little baby Jesus, as big as a finger, with a little round head, lying on some wisps of straw. A holy Virgin carved into a curved branch, better to bend over the infant. A St. Joseph with a bark beard ...*

From "The Draft Dodger,"
by Louis Caron

Huron Mission near Quebec City, the Manitoba parish, and the Paris metro as Our Lady of Loreto, patron saint of pilots because of the legendary angel-borne passage of her home from Nazareth to Loreto, Italy. Mary was made to move house by air after the Holy Land war when the Saracens took Jerusalem in 1291. (Our Lady of Loreto, the pilots' patron, was surely present in the cockpit July 23, 1983, when Captain Robert Pearson glided his powerless Air Canada Boeing 767, and sixty passengers on board the plane known thereafter as the Gimli Glider, to safe landing in Gimli, Manitoba, and in August 2001, when Quebec's Captain Robert Piché managed the same superb pilotage by gliding his Air Transat jet and 293 passengers onto a Terceiras Island runway almost fifteen hundred kilometres off Portugal.)

✵

THE GLOSSARY in *We Wasn't Pals: Canadian Poetry and Prose of the First World War* provides a definition new to me: "Lazaret: A small locker or storeroom for personal belongings not taken to the front."[37]

The lazaret I know is the between-decks space either at the stern or in the forepeak of the vessel, intended for gear stowage on long voyages. The lazaret latched tight against downflooding from water on deck in heavy seas once held lepers on pilgrimage to the Holy Land. The Gospel of Luke's "certain beggar named Lazarus ... full of sores"[38] and carried by angels to Abraham's bosom after his death made *lazar* the archaic form for leper.

Spare web, lines, and corks lived in the lazaret on wooden-hulled salmon seiners up the coast. Offshore, the lazaret on one Polish ship contained a net of copper tubing the electrician had woven into a still to produce alcohol that tasted the way nail-polish remover smells.

Because lazarets were assigned to World War I soldiers, this word is stored in my thoughts now alongside the other Lazarus, the friend Jesus raised from the dead in John 11:44.

Lazarus can also find its roots in the Greek form of Hebrew *Eleazar*, helped by God.

Lazaret may have come into use as a corruption of *nazaret*, from the fifteenth-century St. Maria di Nazaret church hospital for seamen in Venice.

✷

ALL CANADIAN GROUND became a shrine for the Holy Family in William Kurelek's children's book *A Northern Nativity: Christmas Dreams of a Prairie Boy*. Mary places a radiant child on packing straw in a box car in the 1930s CNR freight yards in Winnipeg. On another page, the Mother of God waits with her baby in the passenger seat of a broken-down car on the road beside the slag heaps at an iron mine. The car is green, maybe a '62 Chev. A worried-looking Joseph peers under the hood. But all is well on Christmas Eve in Flin Flon, Manitoba. The ore truck has stopped up ahead, and the driver is on his way back to the Holy Family with a tool kit.

Mary, Joseph, and the holy child find shelter in a country church in Prince Edward Island, and at the Star Service gas station in a small Alberta town where the New Bethlehem Motel shows a no vacancy sign. At a Regina construction site, Joseph stands over a fuel-drum fire outside the night watchman's trailer, surrounded by cranes and concrete forms, talking with the watchman. Mary, wearing a Ukrainian embroidered blouse, is safe and warm in the trailer with her baby on her knees.

This Mary, the Holy Mother made knowable, even familiar, by her clothing or by being in a place Canadians recognize, is a frequent figure in Canada. She wears denim and glasses as a middle-aged woman in Chris Woods's stunning Stations of the Cross for St. David's Anglican church in Vancouver. In front of a pile of tanks and shattered buildings labelled Bethlehem, she appears with Joseph in the *Globe and Mail*'s editorial cartoon, April 2002.

---

*The Blessed Virgin had given her mother's heart to understand that her son was in heaven. All of his sins, his oaths, his blasphemies, the caresses he had given the girls of the village, and especially the girls in the old country where he had gone to war ... all these sins of Corriveau had been pardoned; the Blessed Virgin had breathed it to his mother ... The old lady felt it in her heart that God was obliged to pardon soldiers who had died in the war.*

From *La Guerre, Yes Sir!*, by Roch Carrier

Canadian artists see Mary, the shape-shifting Madonna, contained in forms as far apart as Elvis Presley (Shari Hatt's photograph of Elvis altered to resemble the Virgin) and a pine tree (Thoreau MacDonald's 1926 *Pine Tree Madonna*). Mary of Canada also appears at the bank. That's Mary, resting in the almost cave-painting lines of the Mother and Child window that Toronto artist Sarah Hall made for the *All That Glitters* mural in Toronto's Scotia Plaza. The same, but different, Mary with strong bones, full lips, and wide, direct-gazing eyes lives in the stained-glass windows Hall made for Immaculate Conception Church in Woodbridge, Ontario. But that's her, too, in Toronto artist Barbara Klunder's mischievous Madonna holding Saint Pinnochio on her knee.

*Our Lady of the Assumption* ✴ *Our Lady of Good Counsel* ✴ *Our Lady of Grace* ✴ *Our Lady of Mercy* ✴ *Our Lady of the Navigators* ✴ *Our Lady of Sorrows* ✴ *Our Lady of the*

Winnipeg-born artist Marianna Gartner's work mixes childhood memories, images both beautiful and fearsome, and some traditional Mary references into portraits of a Virgin who is only partly, provocatively familiar. In *Reading Pictures: A History of Love and Hate*, Alberto Manguel's richly informed reading of the world's works of art includes her paintings: "Old photos are the inspirational basis for many of Marianna Gartner's canvases ... They are plucked and transformed on the canvas to something else. And it is in this sense that Gartner subverts the traditional art of portraiture."[39]

Now living in Budapest, Marianna Gartner has been told that one of her Mary paintings is in Rideau Hall:

Mary in Canada 101

To the best of my knowledge, it's being rented by the Governor General from the Canada Council Art Bank. I think it's a 1990 painting called *This Dark Edge of Monkeys*. It features a little girl in her confirmation (or Holy Communion) outfit, and beside her in the background is a statue of the Virgin Mary. Beneath her, looming up from a dark background, is a screaming baboon. This piece's initial inspiration came to me when a friend of mine showed me an old snapshot of her mother, which became the basis for the top part of the painting. The bottom part comes mainly from my own thoughts on religion and being raised in the Catholic faith, but is also a representation of the horrors and nightmares that some young children fear when they are sleeping, things that go bump in the night, and so on.

*ueen of All Saints* ✳ *Queen of Confessors* ✳ *Queen Conceived Without Original Sin* ✳ *Queen of Families* ✳ *Queen of Heaven* ✳ *Queen of Martyrs* ✳ *Queen of Patriarchs* ✳ *Queen o*

✻ Queen of Prophets ✻ Queen of the Most Holy Rosary ✻ Queen of Virgins ✻ Refuge of Sinners ✻ Saint Mary the Virgin ✻ Saint Mary of the Angels ✻ Settena Maryam, Our Lady

104   MARY OF CANADA

Another Virgin Mary type painting I've done more recently is in a collector's home in Victoria, I believe. It's a fairly large piece that is called *Mary – aged 7 years*. It shows a young girl with long blond hair, dressed all in white, holding a baby also dressed in a white gown, with a rather worried expression on its face. The piece is loosely based on typical portraits of the Virgin and Child, but in my painting, the girl, who seems older than seven, but *Mary – aged 7 years* is what was written on the back of the original old photo that I painted the young girl from, has a skull formation where the top half of her face would normally be. There are also some strawberry plants on the ground around the girl's feet, again inspired by an old painting of *The Virgin with Strawberries*.[40]

Poet Robert Service made Mary so familiar that she is "a woman from the street, Shameless, but, oh, so fair!" even if only the artist in "My Madonna" knows a prostitute is the model for his portrait of Mary who, "hangs in the church of Saint Hillaire, Where you and all may see."[41]

Another Mary is so ordinarily Canadian that she uses the bank machine at the mall (with a card labelled Mary Theotokos) when she visits Diane Schoemperlen in *Our Lady of the Lost and Found*: "I should not have been surprised. After all, she was not some primitive *naif* who had been popped into a time machine and then dropped down unceremoniously into this day and age. She did not exist in a vacuum and she had not spent the last two thousand years in a cave. She had been here all along."[42]

These companionable, chartered bank–attending, jeans-wearing versions of Mary written and visually formed as a familiar figure bear a connection to the Holy Mother who finds warmth and safety in trappers' camps, fishermen's sheds, and other places of refuge among ordinary Canadians in William Kurelek's *Northern Nativity* children's book. In the nativity dream, "Across the River from the Capital," even the Parliament

---

*I hailed me a woman from the street,*
*Shameless, but, oh, so fair!*
*I bade her sit in the model's seat*
*And I painted her sitting there.*

*I hid all trace of her heart unclean;*
*I painted a babe at her breast;*
*I painted her as she might have been*
*If the Worst had been the Best.*

*She laughed at my picture and went away.*
*Then came with a knowing nod,*
*A connoisseur, and I heard him say;*
*"'Tis Mary, the Mother of God."*

*So I painted a halo around her hair,*
*And I sold her and took my fee,*
*And she hangs in the church of Saint Hillaire,*
*Where you and all may see.*

From "My Madonna," by Robert Service

Buildings are made radiant by the presence of Mary and the child on the bank of the St. Lawrence River.

※

MARY, THE MOTHER OF GOD whose glorious light takes in Canada's Parliament Buildings at Christmas, is also a sometime lawn ornament. *This Other Eden: Canadian Folk Art Outdoors* shows her standing in a blue, upended bathtub dug into an Ontario garden, and consorting with pink flamingos in Alberta. The Virgin Mary attends chartered banks with Canadians all the while she is lending her name, coast to coast to coast, to hundreds of street signs and businesses, including the Notre Dame Auto Body Shop, 10 Notre Dame Avenue in Notre Dame de Lourde, Manitoba. Mary of Canada appears regularly in all Canadian auto body shops anyway, monitoring rust removal and paint jobs from her place on dashboard altars. She's come a long way down a well-lit, carefully maintained Canadian cultural highway since she stepped ashore with the Vikings more than a millennium ago.

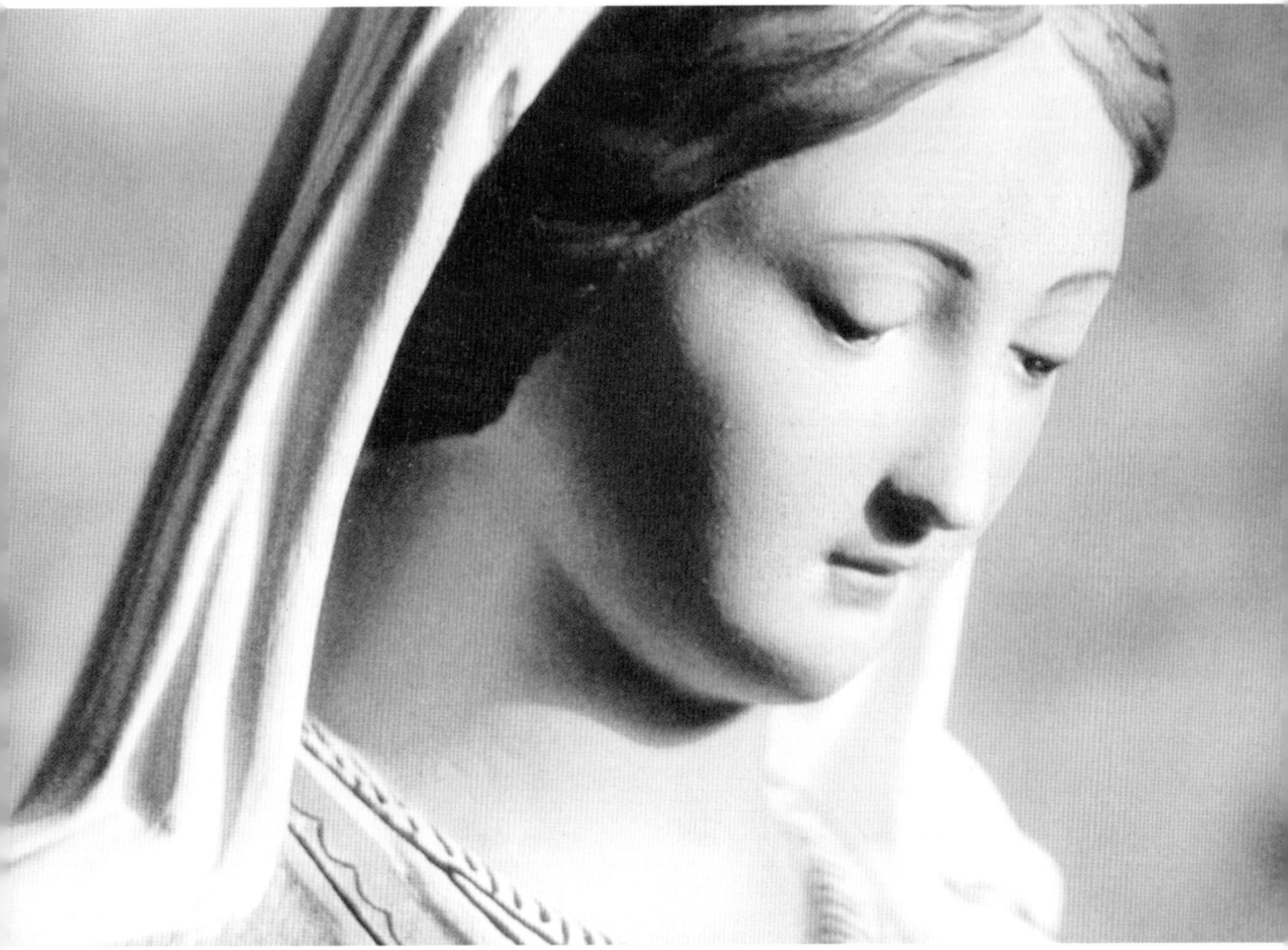

※ CHAPTER 4 ※

# *Eastern Settings*

EVEN GUDRIDUR THORBJARNARDOTTIR, VOYAGING VIKING GRANDDAUGHTER OF AN IRISH FREED MAN, BROUGHT MATERIAL FROM HOME TO NEWFOUNDLAND SO SHE COULD SET HERSELF NEAR THE BEGINNING OF EASE IN HER NEW WORLD. I IMAGINE HER HOLDING THOUGHTS OF MARY THE MOTHER OF GOD AROUND THE PALM-SIZED PERFECTION OF A SOAPSTONE NORSE SPINNING WHORL FROM ICELAND WHILE SHE LABOURED, GIVING BIRTH TO THE FIRST EUROPEAN CHILD IN NORTH AMERICA AT L'ANSE AUX MEADOWS MORE THAN A THOUSAND YEARS AGO.

In this way, I keep something of rivers and the bush in mind in the city, and I carry a portion of the Pacific Ocean to the Atlantic coast.

Too much so, sometimes. At Mary and Bill Kelly's kitchen table in the house behind Kelly's general store in Lawn on the Burin Peninsula in Newfoundland, I opened a Rite-in-the-Rain notebook left over from offshore fisheries work ("Use it up, wear it out. Make it do, or do without" — a 1930s fishermen's saying still needed in Alert Bay and Prince Rupert, British Columbia) to see that I had unaccountably brought to Newfoundland my list of all the wind words in the *English–Polish Handy Seaman's Dictionary*: wind rose, leading wind, land wind, windbound, high wind, head wind, hauling wind, freshening wind, free wind, foul wind, fall wind, dead wind, cross wind, beam wind, baffling wind.

Apart from my notebook, there was no wind, or any need to write in the rain, in the Kellys' kitchen, just tea with Mary and Bill while the Virgin Mary regarded us kindly from her garden on the wall calendar, and the Kellys' promise to see me along to the Virgin with open arms who stands on a pillar at the top of the hill overlooking Marystown tomorrow.

I was still back on the west coast, though, when the Powerhouse Brook in Lawn, Newfoundland, ran through my dreams. We were anchored for the night near the mouth of the Kakweiken River in Thompson Sound, listening to the river pouring into salt water. The mainland inlet was sharp-cold in late fall, but the old salmon seiner in my dream stayed warm, leaking familiar smells of coffee — a grain or two charring on the dull black surface of the oil stove — diesel, and damp wood. In the evening, when the engine was shut down, the boat became a nursery of night sounds, her own and those common to all old wood-hulled work boats: soft static under the words of the marine weather report on the turned-down radio in the wheelhouse; the rattle from the anchor chain falling down the last fathom, then tapping along the hull when the tide changed; the strained, high whine of the sink pump; the clatter of Yahtzee dice on the ridge-edged galley table before supper.

*Sick ✶ Help of Christians ✶ Holy Mother of God ✶ Holy Virgin of Virgins ✶ House of Gold ✶ Madonna of the Americas: The Virgin of Guadalupe ✶ Argentina: Our Lady of Lujan ✶*

Compliments of
**KELLY'S STORE**
GENERAL DEALER
**Phone 873-2493**

LAWN,                    NEWFOUNDLAND

| JANUARY | | | 1992 | | JANUARY | |
|---|---|---|---|---|---|---|
| SUN | MON | TUE | WED | THU | FRI | SAT |
| ● 4 | ☽ 13 | ○ 19 | 1 NEW YEAR'S DAY | 2 | 3 | 4 |
| 5 | 6 TWELFTH NIGHT | 7 | 8 | 9 | 10 | 11 |
| 12 | 13 | 14 | 15 | 16 | 17 | 18 |
| 19 | 20 | 21 | 22 | 23 | 24 | 25 |
| 26 | 27 | 28 | 29 | 30 | 31 | ☾ 26 |

*Eastern Settings* III

Lady of Copacabana ✳ Brazil: Our Lady of Aparacida ✳ Chile: Our Lady of Carmel of the Maipu ✳ Columbia: Our Lady of Chiquinquira ✳ Costa Rica: Our Lady of the Angels ✳ Cu

## The Devil and the Blessed Virgin Mary

*A girl roved out one evening to view her father's land.*
*She met with a deep sea captain; he took her by the hand.*
*He said unto his comrades, "If it was not against the law,*
*I'd have this fair one with me to lie beneath the cold stone wall."*

MARY:
*"Hands off, young man, hands off, young man, hands off, young man," said she.*
*"I'm to view my father's dwelling, where the green grass grows so tall,*
*So I won't comply with you to lie beneath the cold stone wall."*

DEVIL:
*"I will put to you six questions and you'll fulfill them all:*
*'What is deeper than the sea, what's higher than the wall?*
*What's a young man's sense in a fair maid's heart, I you on duty call?*
*And you'll comply with me to lie 'neath the stone cold wall.'"*

MARY:
*"Now hell is deeper than the sea; the sun is higher than the wall.*
*The Devil's sense in a fair maid's heart on you on duty call.*
*I won't comply with you to lie 'neath the stone cold wall."*

DEVIL:
*"Now what is deeper than the sea; what's higher than the wall?*
*What bird sings best when the lark is at rest in the spring when the dew first fall,*
*Nor you'll comply with me to lie 'neath the old stone wall."*

MARY:
*"Now hell is deeper than the sea; the sun is higher than the wall;*
*The thrush sings best when the lark is at rest, in the spring when the dew first fall.*
*I won't comply with you to lie 'neath the old stone wall."*

By morning, walking up the shore road to the hill above Lawn harbour in the clear, yellow Atlantic light, I remembered that I only knew the way to the hill path before I ever got to Lawn, and how to find the Kellys and Mary in Newfoundland, and the recipe for boiled dinner (Soak salt beef in cold water overnight. Lash the pot down, or leave it in the sink. Put the meat in fresh water in the morning and boil a while. Turn down to simmer and add turnips first, then carrots, cabbage, and potatoes until done.) because trawl fishermen from the Burin Peninsula and other Newfoundland places had carried some of the east coast with them when they fished British Columbia waters on the draggers working joint-venture hake offshore with the foreign ships.

Lawn harbour on the southwestern shore of Placentia Bay's wider, wilder waters was waiting for me, that day in Newfoundland, as a reminder to expect the unexpected on journeys toward Mary. The Basque cod fishermen's port of refuge has been Lawn since the 1760s, when a young Englishman was so taken with the hill's meadows and mosses glowing incandescent green against the grey Atlantic that he gave the place a garden name from a home he seldom saw. Years before Captain James Cook ever dropped anchor in Nootka Sound on the west coast of Vancouver Island, or anywhere else in the Pacific Ocean, Cook had been sounding and charting the waters wind-kicked white beyond the harbour entrance below me.

Cook sharpened his chart-making skills in the preparation of provisional river charts that resulted in his log entry of September 13, 1759: "at midnight all the Row Boats in the fleet made a faint to Land at Beauport ... to favor the landing of the Troops above the town on the north Shoar ... the English Army Commanded by Gen Wolfe attacked the French under the Command of Gen Montcalm in the field of Aberham behind Quebec."[1]

Only once, when a powder horn blew up in his right hand, did James Cook pause a day or two during the ice-free seasons 1763–7 while he was making the carefully depth-sounded Newfoundland and Labrador coast

*DEVIL:*
"For breakfast you must get for me a fish without a bone,
And for dinner you must get me a cherry without a stone,
And for my supper you must get me a bird without a gall.
Now you'll comply with me to lie 'neath the old stone wall."

*MARY:*
"Now when the fish is first born, I'm sure it has no bone,
And when the cherry is in full bloom, I'm certain it has no stone.
The dove she is a gentle bird; she flies without a gall.
So I won't comply with you to lie beneath the old stone wall."

*DEVIL:*
"You must get for me some of that fruit that in September grew;
My mother has a silk worm cloak that a shuttle never went to;
You must get me a sparrow's horn or yet on duty call
Nor you'll comply with me to lie beneath the old stone wall."

*MARY:*
"My father keeps some of the fruit that in September grew;
My mother has a silk worm cloak that a shuttle never went through;
A sparrow's horn is not hard to find; he has one on every claw,
So I won't comply with you to lie beneath the old stone wall."

"There's a man outside my father's gate; he is waiting to come in;
I am sure that man was never born, nor yet committed any sin;
His mother's side was cruelly pierced, if you on duty call.
"You fly from me, Devil," said she, "right through that old stone wall."

From Folk Ballads and Songs of the Lower Labrador Coast

charts for which his name was blessed by fishermen well into the twentieth century.

The St. Lawrence River and Newfoundland-Labrador lay half the world around from Kealakekua Bay on the island of Hawaii where Cook was killed on the beach in 1779. The Hawaiian people burned the body of the man they still considered a god and distributed his bones as sacred relics. The small portion of human remains returned to Cook's crew were identified as his because the hands, the right bearing his Newfoundland powder-burn scar, had been preserved in salt. The Anglican service for Burial at Sea was held on board the *Resolution*.

Bridegrooms of the Sea, Newfoundlanders sometimes call men lost at sea. On the hill overlooking Lawn harbour, Bridegrooms of the Sea known to me on both coasts kept company with James Cook and Mary of the ocean. Like seafarers and fishermen before and long after his time, Captain James Cook's last earth-bound presence was consigned to an ocean the Church of England's *Book of Common Prayer* knew to be female: "We therefore commit his body to the deep, to be turned into corruption, looking for the resurrection of the body (when the sea shall give up her dead), and the life of the world to come, through our Lord Jesus Christ ..."[2]

※

I WENT ALONG THE BURIN PENINSULA to Marystown, then back to St. John's on Slayney's taxi-bus, always knowing I was entirely on the Atlantic coast. Another time, I made a St. Lawrence River journey to be surprised by the unexpected again, and to find other forms of Mary in eastern Canada, even though I was still packing some of the west coast with me there, too.

✷

WAFIK, the taxi driver at Quebec City airport, knew of a park that might be named Jacques Cartier, but he didn't know the man himself, he said, and he didn't recognize Notre-Dame-de-Rocamadour. But Mary, yes, he knew her. And speaking about Mary, Wafik said, he himself needed, urgently, to rest, rest in someone's arms. All the same, I got out of his taxi at St. François d'Assise church not far from the St. Charles River.

Afterward, when I came out of the 1919 church where I had been daydreaming my way back to Jacques Cartier's faith in Notre Dame de Rocamadour's ability to cure scurvy in the winter of 1535–6, a backhoe was beginning sidewalk repair on the streets between the church and Cartier-Brébeuf Park on the river. The Lincoln-Mercury dealer was open. The body shop was busy. And Wafik and his taxi were waiting.

Not much busy, he said, waving away my surprise. On the way downtown, Wafik, who had been raised in Egypt as a Coptic Christian, wanted to talk about the Mary his memory had carried to Canada, and about the street in Cairo where you still cannot make bread. His right hand rose from the steering wheel to form a bowl and bread dough in the air beside me in the front seat. But the dough will never rise on that Cairo street. To this day. Because on that street, Mary was refused a piece of bread after she and Joseph had obeyed the instructions from the angel of the Lord to take their young child and "flee into Egypt"[3] (Matthew 2:13).

Parked in front of the Cathedral of Notre Dame des Victoires on Place-Royale (American and English attacks defeated, thanks to Our Lady, Frontenac's guns, and fog in the Gulf of St. Lawrence), Wafik said, "No charge for this airport, and the Mary, and now this church." And, "Sorry about the resting in arms."

We sat together, silent, in the taxi for a minute or two. I wondered if I would have given Mary a piece of bread when I didn't know who she was. I hope so, but I never let myself count on good behaviour in the imaginary past. I have always known I would have been the scrawny Jerusalem dancing girl on the edge of the crowd around Jesus, figuring he was bad for business. Before I got out of his taxi, Wafik and I agreed that Mary has tolerated much from most of us, in Egypt and Canada and everywhere.

Because of Wafik's bread story, another kind of Mary, smaller, sometimes so tired the blue cloak dragged in the dust, and hungry, travelled with me on the bus from Quebec City to the Notre-Dame-du-Cap shrine at Cap-de-la-Madeleine farther up the St. Lawrence.

✹

YEARLY NOW, Our Lady of the Cape receives a million or more visitors on the riverbank where the ice never formed in the mild winter of 1878–9 until she made an ice bridge in response to rosary prayers. The stone for her new church could then be freighted from the south shore in horsedrawn sleighs, and a shrine was dedicated to her, as promised.

The Virgin Mary's (and Mary Magdalene's, Mary Poppins's, Marie Antoinette's, and Bloody Mary's or Mary I of England) attachment to the south shore of the St. Lawrence is sustained in Ann Lambert and Laura Mitchell's 2000 play, *The Mary Project*, set in "the South Shore town of Marieville, in a greasy spoon called *Chez Ma Mère*."[4]

Along the St. Lawrence from Cap-de-la-Madeleine, on L'Isle Verte, children played *La Demande de Graces à la Sainte-Vierge* — Asking Favours from the Holy Virgin — well into the twentieth century: a girl with a makeshift veil over her hair sits on a chair while the players bring forward the child who wants to ask a favour. The pretend Virgin asks the applicant to come closer, closer to her, so she can sprinkle her or him with water from the mouthful she has been holding since before the game started. Across the country, in *My Name Is Seepeetza*, British Columbia Salish Nation writer Shirley Sterling's novel based on her own experiences, the girls at Catholic-run Kalamak Residential School gather around Adelia, "queen of the junior girls,"[5] whose shoulders are draped with their kerchiefs as she receives gifts of candy, gum, and comics.

For two and a half centuries before the 1878–9 ice miracle at Cap-de-la-Madeleine, Mary of Canada as Sainte Marie and Notre Dame had been busy along the St. Lawrence River. As Notre Dame de Recouvrance for Samuel Champlain, she had retrieved Quebec from the Kirke brothers' illegal English-flag possession in 1632. As Notre Dame des Victoires, she had assisted Governor Frontenac's disposal of an English invasion in 1690, and had organized fog, wind, and Admiral Hovenden Walker's ineptitude to push British ships out of the St. Lawrence in 1711.

In the countryside, she sometimes turned her hand to helping parishes too poor to spare a horse to haul church building-stone. Mary, dressed in white, would appear leading a black stallion, a devilish strong horse, whose bridle was Never To Be Removed. A similar coal-black steed bore the tall stranger who dropped by the seventeenth-century dance "in a remote village on the banks of a great river"[6] in Cyrus Macmillan's oral source tale called "The Shrove Tuesday Visitor." Splendidly, the stranger danced with the young girl of the house and fine were his clothes, but the girl's old aunt noticed his wrath whenever the Virgin Mary's name was uttered. Only the sudden appearance of the village priest caused the stranger and his black horse to disappear with a sound like thunder.

The Virgin Mary entered stories from many traditions made Canadian in the mouths of their tellers. In this country, a long quest story known as "The Prince and the Arm Bands" in India, the Middle East, and Europe became "The Green Flag and the Devil's Head." The princess with the golden apple now crosses a forest as well as the Red Sea, and the blinded hero is healed at the Holy Virgin's miraculous spring. The Canadian layer of the story included maple trees and a moose quarter as well as Mary in the version New Brunswick fisherman Johnny Larocque used to tell.

Marius Barbeau's collections of early Canadian folk tales and legends include stories combining Huron and habitant traditions, like the tale of a "young woman … beautiful as a dream" who appeared "out of the air" to "Hurukay, the … Huron," carrying "the Child of all the people in this

---

*Oh, Pat was an awful drunkard. The priest was always getting after him. One day he saw him drunk and he said to himself, "The rascal, he hasn't been to church for six months, an' he's always soused up." So he went up to Pat and says to him, "Say, Pat, when are you goin' to stop gettin' drunk, an' come back to church?"*

*Pat pulled out his watch an' said, "I'm goin' to pawn this, Father, an' pay off an IOU. Then after I do that, I will change an' become a good man."*

*The priest says, "Why don't you go in church and pray to the Blessed Virgin, maybe she'll send you the money."*

*Pat says, "That ain't bad. All right, I'll do it, Father." So he went in the church an' he prayed to the Blessed Virgin for ten dollars.*

*He prayed so hard the priest thought he really meant it. So he got up on a balcony and dropped down a five-dollar gold piece. "There now," he said, "maybe that'll cure Pat."*

*But a few hours later a boy came up to the priest an' said, "Father, Father, shure an' Pat is comin' up the road beastly drunk."*

*The priest said, "The rascal, gone an' took my five dollars an' got drunk off 'n it. I'll fix him." So he got a big sheet an' wrapped it around him. Then he hid behind a thorn hedge. Just as Pat come up, he jumped out an' said, "Hello!"*

*Pat looked at him an' said, "An' who are you, begorra?"*

*The priest said, "I'm God."*

*Pat said, "Begorra, I've been lookin' for you all day. Your mother owes me five dollars."*

From Folklore from Nova Scotia,
by Arthur Huff Fauset

Eastern Settings  117

land, with straight black hair, dark eyes and a brown complexion. Its dress, instead of being linen embroidered in rainbow hues, seemed to be of tanned deerskin trimmed with rabbit." In the story, Hurukay tells of how he saw the Child "under the Tree of Dreams." [7]

That tree is rooted deep in transformative maternal earth that Mary of Canada may remember from the earliest versions of a tale that would also be transformed in Canada and woven into other stories. The Acadian girl named Souillon whose stepsister is Cat'line, and who must go down into the Nova Scotia creek leading to fairy land to search for her prince-husband who went to war after their magical wedding, then disappeared for seven years, started out as another girl, ash-stained to show her grief, weeping over her mother's grave. From the earth, the mother answers her daughter's sorrow by sending forth a tree for Cinderella to water with her tears until it bears the fruits of life, including the apples and pears that accompany some early Madonnas, and attracts the white doves who will help her daughter.

"The Algonquin Cinderella," "a noble lady" who "understood far more about things than simply the mere outside which all the rest of the world knows," appears as sister and guardian to the Invisible One whose sled-string is the Rainbow, and bowstring is the Milky Way: "'So you have seen him,' said his sister. She took the girl home with her and bathed her. As she did so, all the scars disappeared from her body. Her hair grew again, as it was combed, long, like a blackbird's wing. Her eyes were now like stars ... Then, from her treasures, the lady gave her a wedding garment, and adorned her." [8]

✴

THE MAGICAL TRANSFIGURATION made possible by a Mother Earth–born blessing still lives in Canadian culture as the name given to Canola, Cinderella Crop of the Prairies. The poor-sister rapeseed oil that lit the lamps of Mesopotamia before it ever lubricated World War II

*Our Lady of the Iceberg* ✸ *Our Lady of Peace* ✸ *Our Lady of the Prairies* ✸ *Our Lady of the Presentation* ✸ *Our Lady of Providence* ✸ *Our Lady of Perpetual Help* ✸ *Our Lady of the*

ship engines was made over as a nutritious, low-cholesterol cooking oil pressed from a prairie cash crop by the nonmagical efforts of Canadian farmers, seed scientists, and commercial processors.

✸

AT FIRST, Cap-de-la-Madeleine seemed to be a mall containing a parking lot, a huge concrete basilica, a cafeteria, a souvenir shop, and an information centre where the attendant and Oblate Missionaries of Mary Immaculate priests who bless rosaries were kind to the English-speaking non-Catholic.

In the garden outside the basilica, I found the old shrine, the small, stones-over-ice church where the statue of the Blessed Virgin once opened her eyes, which "appeared to be black, well formed and in perfect harmony with the rest of her face. Her look was that of a living person; it was partly severe mixed with sadness,"[9] said Father Frederic, the Franciscan priest who was there on the miraculous evening in 1888, in the absence of concrete.

I was comforted more by the bright width of the St. Lawrence River than by the Virgin and her church at Cap-de-la-Madeleine, and the familiarity of freighters in ballast, hulls high in the water, easing down-river past the shrine, and the spring. Pilgrims filled plastic bottles, though the Notre-Dame-du-Cap information centre's site map clearly states the spring is "from a natural source; has no miraculous origin."

Still, when I drank from the spring at Cap-de-la-Madeleine, then lay on the grass to rest, I remembered other, older places where water is holy: the head of the creeks in the Queen Charlottes where Creek Women, one to each stream, call home the salmon; the spring below the oracle cave at Delphi where I held my son's small hand to keep him from touching a coin and two icing-sugared crescent-shaped cookies left on the rock beside the bubble of clear water coming from the ground.

I was grateful, then, for those other water memories, and for other Madeleines whose histories I began to discover at Cap-de-la-Madeleine, the St. Lawrence riverbank the Jesuits called Blessed Mary's fief in 1659. Monsieur de Magdelaine, the seventeenth-century landowner whose name gave reason for the presence of Saint Mary Magdalene, a.k.a. Sainte Marie Madeleine at the Cape, is recorded in *Le Journal des Jesuites*, September 11, 1646, as having "the concession" of the river frontage. By 1653, the Cape had been granted to the Jesuits, and had become Cap de la Magdalene, listed also under Cap-de-la-Madeleine in the Jesuit Journal index. The parish of Sainte-Marie-Madeleine was recognized here by the first bishop of New France in 1678.

Saint Mary Magdalene was a relief when I was far from the Pacific, and farther yet from the Virgin Mary as the remote-eyed woman born without sin who stood inside the new basilica and the old shrine church. Mary Magdalene seemed familiar, a woman from Magdala, a place the

*Catholic Encyclopedia* describes as "a prosperous and somewhat infamous fishing village on the western shore of the Sea of Galilee."[10] Magdala is a town I know under other names, on another coast, and in this century.

   This Mary is easy to know. She was the unnamed woman who bathed Christ's feet with her tears, and with ointment from an alabaster box because she was "a sinner,"[11] in Luke's gospel, as well as the woman from whom seven devils were driven. And a whore, the early Christian church decided. Her legendary repentance reached as far as the Magdalen Laundries in Montreal where Joni Mitchell's "Peg O'Connell died today."[12] The Magdalens were associated with the Sisters of the Good Shepherd, who recruited them from "the penitents," former prisoners who stayed on with the sisters to further their rehabilitation. The 1888 Magdalen steam laundry, where reform and industrial school girls like Peg O'Connell worked, became the Congregation of the Good Shepherd's principal income source.

※

I HAVE DECIDED TO BELIEVE that Mary Magdalene was a hopeful woman whose faith surged wide and deep as her sins, whatever they were. The story goes that after she saw the risen Christ in the garden near his sepulchre, she drifted to the coast of France in a rudderless boat with no sails, then talked to people about Christ and Mary before becoming a holy hermit. I left Cap-de-la-Madeleine hoping Our Lady of the Cape was sharing her earth with Marie-Mary-Magdalene-Madeleine, sinner and patron saint of penitents and contemplatives.

   Easier, always, to assume a need for penitence even if I am not certain for which act. Acts. Easier to attach myself to that Magdala girl with the shadowed past, even if she is now a saint, rather than to the one who has always, forever, been good.

   Saint Mary Magdalene's emblem is the ointment jar. Undoubtedly not intended to mean the twenty-first-century moisturizer that tempts me because it is advertised as miraculously luminous. On the bus along the St. Lawrence to a secular shrine consecrated only in my mind by its connection to an endlessly resourceful New France vagabond, I considered turning in my pilgrim licence on grounds of grotesque personal unsuitability. Unease settled around the memory of fairy godmothers and princesses met in childhood, and always set aside in favour of Robin Hood, Mowgli, Huck Finn, and, later, the explorers.

In Trois-Rivières, Pierre Esprit Radisson's hometown, I convinced myself that he, too, would have been a haywire pilgrim at a concrete Cap-de-la-Madeleine, and that he would have gone north as soon as possible to mend his spiritual and other fortunes.

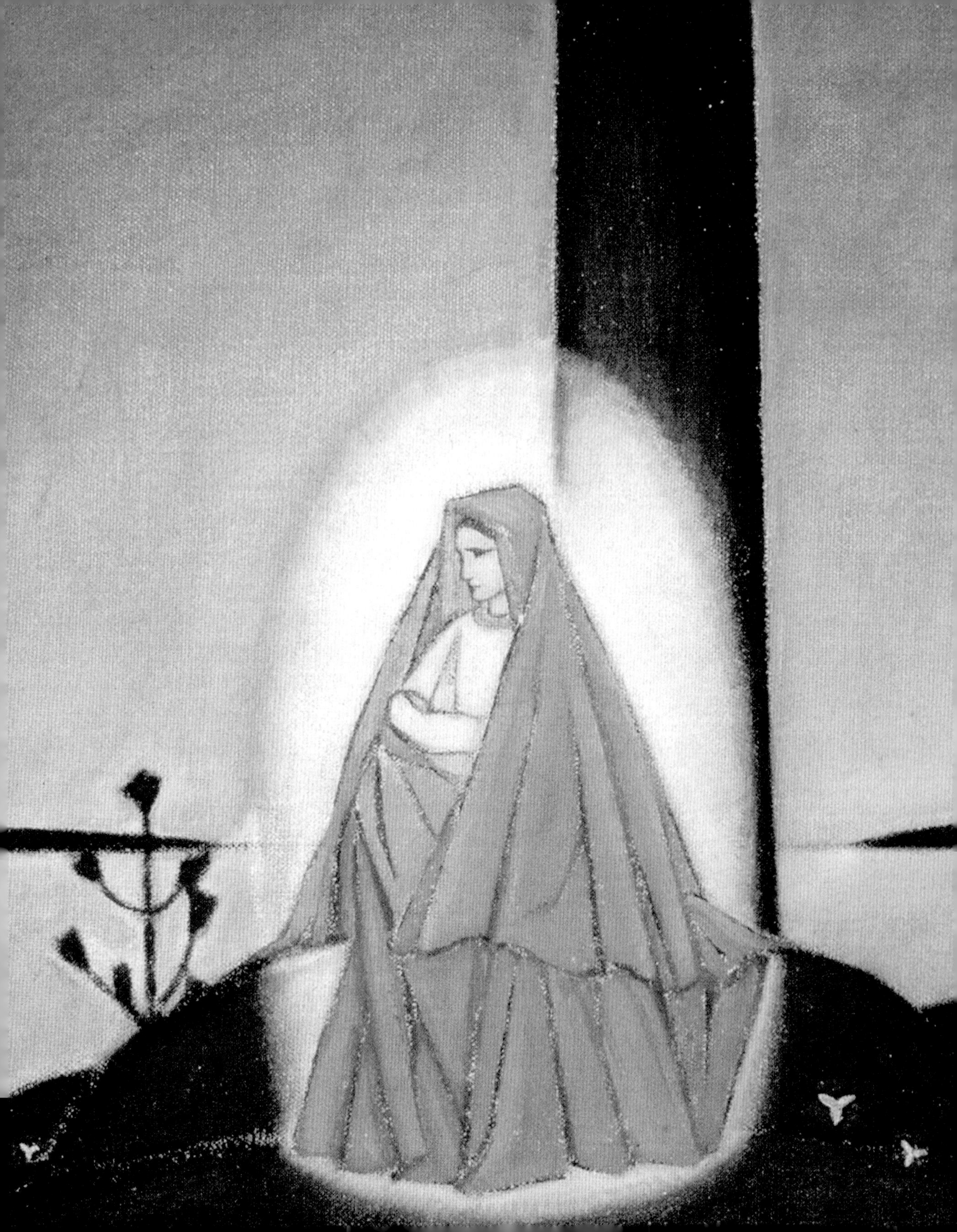

\* CHAPTER 5 \*

# Northern Blessings

NORTH MEANT THE BLURRED MASS OF TREES FLOWING TO THE END OF THE WORLD FROM THE MOUNTAINS ACROSS VANCOUVER HARBOUR WHEN I WAS A CHILD. THE DISTANT, CROWDED DARKNESS OF THE FOREST TOOK SHAPE IN THE FAR REACHES OF MY MIND AS A REFUGE. I, OR ANYONE ELSE WHO WANTED HARDER, MORE HONOURABLE WAYS, COULD GO INTO THE WOODS, I THOUGHT, WHEN WE CAME TO THE END OF OUR STRENGTH. THE FOREST WOULD WAIT FOR US FOREVER, I BELIEVED.

All the way through southern Canadian grade-school definitions for an icebound Arctic, almost empty tundra, and slightly treed taiga, I continued to believe north would be a place where a person could make way in good faith. But then, I also believed Dick Prince, hunter hero of the fur trade at Fort Chimo in R. M. Ballantyne's 1858 novel *Ungava*, was a figure from history sadly neglected at school.

Going along hopeful in the north is true, though. The CN train still slows down so you can jump off at Kitwanga bridge up the Skeena River in British Columbia. From there, the way to Meziadin Junction will be paved with gold, if only in the Eskay Creek high-grade gold-silver ore dust left in the truck returning from the mine load-out yard near the rail line at Kitwanga.

No matter how bad the winter road condition looks when you're standing beside a frozen suitcase at Meziadin Junction, or how many times you need to blunder through the snow to warm up at the Last Store until Dease Lake a couple of hundred kilometres north, some driver grinding up to Whitehorse or Anchorage will stop. On the old logging and mine haul gravel road now partly paved and graded into Highway 37 North, the going will be slow. When night comes and snow is still falling into the narrowing white tunnel that is the road, pairs of pit-lamped eyes gleam out of the dark. If you stop to step into the muffled, white world, the snow shows tracks: slurred marks from snowshoe hares; light prints that might belong to a fox; deeper, longer moose strides, and other four-footed signs, all made by creatures who seem to have been strolling, even sauntering, around their front yard before you arrived. The prints fill with snow while you look at them, becoming only small, slightly rolling hills on a smooth, white plain.

Somewhere between Good Hope Lake on 37 North and Teslin on the Alaska Highway this side of Whitehorse, the landscape given over to calm, white silence appears to be true North at last, a country in care of Our Lady of the Snows in the Yukon.

✳

Our Lady of the Snows' first flakes drifted out of a summer sky long ago in a land some distance from the Yukon Territory. When the Virgin Mary appeared in the dreams of a fourth-century Roman patrician and his wife who wanted to leave her their fortune, she asked them to build her a church. The August snow Our Lady caused to fall in the gardens on Rome's Esquiline Hill outlined the site for Santa Maria Maggiore, Rome's principal church dedicated to Mary.

✳

In Our Lady of the Snows' country west of Whitehorse, near the crossroad of the Alaska Highway and Haines Road at Haines Junction, another Yukon Mary of Canada lives now as Our Lady of the Way, offering travellers rest at her church on the old Coastal Tlingit and Chilkat trade trail. On clear days, she can look over her shoulder west-southwest across Kluane National Park's icefield ranges to glimpse a tough, old mountain man she knows to be as good a traveller as she herself is, and eternally faithful to God. The Prophet Elijah of the Bible, Ilyas / Elias of the Koran, in Canadian form as the country's 5,889-metre, second-highest peak, has travelled farther than the distance between his home mountain in Palestine — *Jebel Mar Elias* (Arabic), Mount Carmel (from the Hebrew *karmel*, garden) — and the high coastal ranges of the Yukon. The eight-hundred-year-old Catholic Carmelite mendicant religious order believes Elijah trekked out of Old Testament time in the twelfth century to encourage the hermits who had a chapel dedicated to Mary alongside his everlasting spring on Mount Carmel. The Carmelites claim both the great Jewish prophet and Our Lady of Mount Carmel as spiritual inspirations.

Northern Blessings 127

Father O'Leary *established a mission in an isolated settlement in the Northwest Territories. After some years, the Bishop paid him a visit.*

*The Bishop asked him, "How do you like it up here in the wild?"*

*"Just fine," replied the priest.*

*"And what about the weather?"*

*"As long as I have my rosary and my brandy, I don't care how cold it gets."*

*"I'm glad to hear it. Say, I could go for a shot of brandy myself right now."*

*"Sure thing," said the priest. "Rosary! Would you bring us two brandies?"*

From *The Penguin Book of Canadian Jokes*, by John Robert Columbo

From inland, Our Lady of the Way might be able to see, even now, on the North Pacific past Kluane's ice mountains, some sea-worn icon of herself as a shadow-faced, enigmatic Virgin with infinitely patient eyes on board Vitus Bering's ship. In 1741, Bering and his Russian crew, sailing under orders drafted by Tsar Peter the Great, named the mountain on Canada's most westerly ground after an Orthodox saint whose full title was Saint Elias the Prophet, a.k.a. the Prophet Elijah, home address: the Hebrew Bible and /or the Old Testament, and the Koran.

The Russian sailors will have known that the height of a grand mountain visible from the coast under a sky full of ravens was the right place for a prophet fed by ravens in the wilderness of the Book of Kings not long before he crouched by a spring now called Elijah's fountain on Mount Carmel, looking out to sea again and again for a sign of God.

✹

BACK AT HAINES JUNCTION, Our Lady of the Way in Yukon Territory knows she is also, sometimes, called Our Lady of the Quonset Hut, thanks to the enterprising priest who found a home for the new Catholic church in one of the handy, half-circle aluminum huts left behind by the World War II U.S. Army building the Alaska Highway.

✹

THE HIGHEST, DEEPEST NORTH inside the 66.5° N Arctic Circle is rightly made from bear stars, *arktos*, the Greek term for Ursa Major. I know this now, even though my own northern entrance is anywhere the other side of 54° N. I know the word *tundra* rests inside Saami people's close-up look into a profusion of mosses, lichens, poppies, caribou, and lemmings, flick-eyed into seemingly endless distance, and taiga is a swampy, subarctic, sometimes muskeg-quilted Russian word for the land where smallish coniferous trees slow march south to easier boreal forest ground.

The idea of north as refuge I still keep underneath facts and experience may not have changed much since childhood. I have come to think that the meaning of north, and its boundaries, are individual choices no easier to enclose within words than is Mary, the mother of God and all.

North meant the backdrop for heroic adventure fiction to Robert Michael Ballantyne, who did fur-trade clerk time at Norway House on Lake Winnipeg and York Factory, Hudson Bay, before he returned to Scotland to write for younger, mostly British readers (including a dreamy lad named Robert Louis Stevenson). Ballantyne used a factual setting to create an entrance for belief in the romance of *Ungava: A Tale of the Esquimaux Land*. The fur traders' journey to Fort Chimo's building site on Ungava Bay begins at Moosonee and Moose Factory where "the headquarters and depot of the fur-traders, who prosecute their traffic in almost all parts of the wild and uninhabited regions ... stands on an island near the mouth of Moose River ... a broad river, which ... flows into James Bay. As everyone knows, this bay lies to the south of Hudson's Bay in North America."[1] As everyone knows ...

✹

THE IDEA OF NORTH as a blessing source is older than the hills in the Bible. The wind blowing out of northern regions human culture would make luminous with benevolent possibilities was part of the cooling, drying catalyst that slowly shifted Canada's 140 million BCE geology toward present time. As soup-warm seas on the prairies leaked from a rainy, tropical land, the ambiguity between solid earth and liquid sea sharpened into edges on Pacific, then Atlantic and Arctic coastlines.

On north wind currents, eons of itinerant possibilities for food to sustain human bodies and souls drifted through cool air, along with seeds for the early birch, maple, and pine species that gradually covered the ground. New warm-blooded creatures belonging to the earth slowly overtook the fish, reptiles, amphibians, and ancestral bird forms that

*duras: Our Lady of Suyapa* ✼ *Mexico: Our Lady of Guadalupe* ✼ *Nicaragua: Our Lady of the Immaculate Conception of El Viejo* ✼ *Panama: The Immaculate Conception* ✼ *Paraguay:*

thrived in an amorphous, watery world. North American mammals began the long evolutionary passage to their present shapes, and their spiritual roles in Canada's first people's creation myths and legends.

Here, a cooling northern benediction nourished spiritual seeds that sprouted a thick-branched Tree of Life. The fruit of its future blessings would one day include a Kwakiutl man's prayer while gathering fronds from young yellow cedar as medicine for his wife:

Please have mercy on her
and, please, help each other with your powers,
with our friend, acrid roots of the spruce,
that my wife may really get well.

130 MARY OF CANADA

the Miracles of Caacupe ✳ Peru: Our Lady of Mercy ✳ Puerto Rico: Our Lady of Divine Providence ✳ Uruguay: Our Lady of the Thirty Three ✳ Venezuela: Our Lady of Coromoto ✳

>   Please, Supernatural One,
>   you, Healing Woman
>   you, Long Life Maker[2]

A version of the Tree of Life bearing Mary's roses embroidered with special rose-on-white beads on First Nations' gloves and medicine bags, and Smoking Lily, a Victoria, British Columbia fashion designer who silkscreens Mary's image onto hot pink silk cushions and T-shirts would also be among the blessings.

Bodily and spiritually contained within a naturally perfect world that included the Land of the North Wind, one far day to be called the district of Keewatin, the Cree name for the north wind, Canada's First Nations were the only human presence here when Homer was writing the *Odyssey* on the other side of the world, recording his certainty that the north wind was "born in the bright air." Old World tales of Boreas the North Wind first carried him as a goddess's protector, then swept the Virgin Mary into the story flow.

Boreas, the uncontrollably wild north-wind god, attracted wind cult devotees in parts of Greece, as well as across the Adriatic in Thrace (now part of modern Bulgaria), where Orpheus, the poet-musician, was king. Wind deities, the three-realm gods who created good or ill fortune on land, on water, and in the air or breath, were already old when Boreas was blowing his living power. Egypt's 1290–23 BCE psalm writers saw "the Lord of the Gods coming as the north wind, with pleasant breezes before him."[3] A desert people's wind cult stirs the sandy texts of the Old Testament and the Book of Prophets following the Hebrew Torah when Jehovah's mountain, and the gusts of glory blowing from it, appear to the north in Isaiah, Ezekiel, Job, and the Psalms. The Hebrew words *Ruach YHWH* for the wind or breath of God carried God's spirit.

Hyperboreans — north-wind priests and their congregations — believed that behind Boreas's farthest northern realm, sheltered and safe, stood the glittering castle where the divine queen whom poetic myth historian Robert Graves called the White Goddess once lived. Her business was poetry, memory, fate, and wind. Whistling three times to honour the White Goddess and raise a wind for sale to desperate sailors and fishermen is witchcraft tradition that lasted long enough to live in the minds of Orkney Islanders boarding Hudson's Bay Company ships sailing for Canada from the last Scottish provisioning port at Stromness. Whistling on deck is still not welcome on Canadian Navy ships and on fishboats, east or west coast, even though some of the vessels may well have been built with their keels traditionally laid north-south, for good luck at sea.

North as a container of female power, and a possible sanctuary, thrived in mythologies geographically distant from each other. The Finns knew the Virgin of the Air, who lived in a palace roofed by a rainbow, behind the northern lights and within a wall of mist. In stories from the Black Sea ports, the Queen of the World once lived beyond the icebergs on the other side of seven Caucasus mountain ranges. On the far banks of three rivers — one flowing with milk, one with honey, and one with oil — sweet, ripe fruit hung heavy on the branches of the Queen of the World's orchard trees flourishing in the snow. If you ever made it to the Queen's shining northern chamber, you would see the moon, whose influence over fertility and the ocean Mary would inherit, hanging on her forehead.

The Northern Goodness inheritance was given to the Good Witch of the North in Frank Baum's 1900 *The Wonderful Wizard of Oz* and in Hollywood's 1939 musical *The Wizard of Oz*. The King of the Winged Monkeys explains: "'There lived here then, away at the North, a beautiful princess who was also a powerful sorceress. All her magic was used to help the people, and she was never known to hurt anyone who was good … She lived in a handsome palace built from blocks of great ruby.'"[4]

Boreas, the wind who protected the goddess in the north, appeared in mythological versions as complex and shifting in emphasis as any long-lived, well-travelled tale, the more so, maybe, because sailors were spreading some of the Hyperborean beliefs around the Mediterranean,

Black, and Adriatic Seas. Long before Boreas appeared in Britain as the protective Sir Bors in the King Arthur saga, or moved to northern Canada as the aurora borealis, Homer's *Iliad* described him as a lusty wind impregnating beautiful mares on the plains of Troy. Late in the third century after Christ, Lactanius, a Christian scholar, felt able to explain the Virgin Mary's pregnancy by likening the ways of the Holy Spirit to those of Boreas, the north wind.

A wind with the same unstoppable, impregnating power as Homer's Boreas would one day blow through the landscape of Ojibwa creation legends half a world away from the New Testament. A wind from the north breathed its spirit into the early twentieth-century summer that Dakelh Dene Simeon Prince died at Fort St. James in British Columbia, "A sudden gust of north wind blew the door open at the moment of death," his granddaughter Lizette Hall writes in her memoir, *The Carrier My People*. "Apparently he was a dreamer of the north wind."[5]

Wind, earth, water, and sky ways of older, wilder worship have flowed into Christian devotion to the Virgin Mary since the day men and women began to tell each other about the Marys who appear in the Gospels: Mary Magdalene, and Mary, the mother of James the Less and Joses, who is possibly also "Mary the wife of Cleopas,"[6] half-sister to Mary, the mother of Christ in John's account.

In the early evening after Christ's Crucifixion, "there came a rich man of Arimathaea, named Joseph, who also himself was Jesus' disciple: He went to Pilate and begged the body of Jesus. Then Pilate commanded the body to be delivered. And when Joseph had taken the body, he wrapped it in a clean linen cloth. And laid it in his own new tomb, which he had hewn out in the rock: and he rolled a great stone to the door of the sepulchre, and departed"[7] (Matthew 27:57–60).

Three hundred years later, Joseph of Arimathaea, by then a saint, was starring in a word-of-mouth story that had expanded Matthew's Gospel verses to include a voyage to Britain, and a miracle that rooted Mary in sacred ground. Joseph's thorny walking staff burst into bloom when he

*orning Star* ✽ *Mystical Rose* ✽ *Mater Dolorosa* ✽ *Notre Dame du Portage* ✽ *Notre Dame de Bon Secours* ✽ *Our Lady of Good Help* ✽ *Our Lady of Good Hope* ✽ *Our Lady of the H*

thrust it into Glastonbury earth to mark the building site for a Marian chapel long before King Arthur and the Holy Grail enshrined the same site at the heart of early English Christianity. The saint's flowering staff was likely the hawthorn branch that had earlier been sacred to Cardea, a Roman form of the White Goddess.

✸

SALT AND SWEET WATERS cherished as sacred in pre-Christian times were rededicated to Mary. More than one hundred ancient holy wells in Britain were made over to Christian saints, most often the Virgin. St. Mary's Spring in Haida Gwaii, Queen Charlotte Islands, was called after one of England's renamed wells. Only in Canada, though, would a logger have fired up his chainsaw to hack out a figure of the Virgin to go with the local spring.

In Canada, waters the first peoples knew as enspirited were sometimes claimed by Christianity. Lac Ste. Anne, Alberta, an Oblates of Mary Immaculate nineteenth-century mission site, is now a shrine dedicated to Sainte Anne as the Virgin Mary's mother. Every summer, on Sainte Anne's feast day, thousands of native people make a pilgrimage to the healing waters the Cree called *Manitou-Sakahigan* — Lake of the Spirit — before a European presence in Canada could be imagined.

✸

LIKE HEALING WATERS, virgin births were known in Canada before missionaries arrived. Mythology scholar Joseph Campbell thought the miraculous virgin births in many cultures might symbolize an unbroken, perfect union of physical and spiritual natures giving birth to consciousness and compassion. Before the rose that had symbolized Aphrodite and Venus was cut and soldered in lead-lined stained glass for the Virgin

Mary's beautiful Rose of France window on Notre Dame Cathedral's west wall, other virgins were giving birth in a far, northern land.

✸

Somewhere along the Nimpkish River on the northwest coast of a huge unnamed continent, a young Kwakiutl woman sat, perhaps knelt, on her bed, weaving wool. Maybe mountain goat wool. The bed might have been cedar boughs covered with finely woven cedar bark. Or deer hide. Anyway, the sun was shining. On her back. As this young weaver woman had no husband and had known no man, her child was named Born-to-Be-the-Sun, sometimes called Mink, because he was also that tricky one. Of Born-to-Be-the-Sun's ascent to the sun on an arrow ladder, and his return to us, of all his marriages and foolishness and power, there will be much to tell other nights this winter.

✸

Far across the northern land, seasons of walking and paddling days east and north from the Pacific coast, the daughter of Ojibwa grandmother Nokomis heard someone commanding her to turn her back to the north wind, and bend over. She was alone on the land, then, and could only obey. From this time, the daughter of Nokomis was pregnant. Maybe four children grew strong in her belly, maybe so strong they quarrelled with each other, pushing and pulling until their mother's body burst open and the four directions were born into the world. Or only one child was born to the daughter of Nokomis and the north wind, and he was Nanabush, now the trickster, now the hero, bringing creatures into being, then imitating them, so he was enough for the Ojibwa, and his mother.

ood Counsel ✱ Our Lady of the Navigators ✱ Our Lady of the Sacred Heart ✱ Our Lady of Victory ✱ Our Mother of Consolation ✱ Panagia (All-Holy Queen Assumed into Heaven)

✱

From skies that had glittered as pre-Christian heavens, Canada would receive residual gleams from the Ladies of Light who shone as Queens of Heaven, Mothers of Stars, and Stars of the Sea to guide and comfort sailors long before the Virgin Mary, haloed with stars, was elevated to stand on the moon. The earlier titles had belonged to aspects of female divinities who had been lifted from earth to sky, such as Astarte, a Syro-Palestinian goddess; Venus, the morning star; Aphrodite; Diana; and Isis. In *The Great Code: The Bible and Literature*, Northrop Frye writes, "Similarly, Isis in Egypt moved her center of gravity from the lower to the upper cycle, although there had always been sky goddesses in Egypt. In Christianity the Virgin Mary took on some attributes of a Queen of Heaven with her blue robe and her star (stella maris) emblem, which had also been attached to Isis. Some developments in Judaism assigned something parallel to a female Schekinah or divine presence."[8]

The Egyptian Mother Goddess who created life, fertility, and order along the Nile with Osiris, her brother-husband, wanders far from Egypt when Osiris dies, searching a dark world for her husband's body to complete the myth that means death as departure from the realm of physical needs and desires, and rebirth into spiritual consciousness. Isis's resurrection of Osiris, and the virgin birth of their son, Horus — the mythological, eternal Pharaoh Egyptian artists often sculpted or painted as a child sitting or suckling on his mother's knee — were absorbed into early Christianity. In the Roman Empire's fourth-century Gaul, Our Lady of Light was Isis. By the time Gaul had become France, and an adventurer named Jacques Cartier was setting out for a New World, Isis's French temples had been closed, and her worship forbidden for a thousand years. The dark, sombre-faced Isis, Our Lady of Light who had come to Canada as Notre Dame de Rocamadour with Jacques Cartier, was given another make-over to become the blank-faced, white-skinned

*The earth-mother also tends to take on the characteristics of a sky goddess: we can see something of this development even in the Bible. In the period of the judges a fertility goddess was worshipped in Israel, usually called* Asherah, *because she was a tree-goddess, and asherah or wooden poles were her emblem (Judges 6:25 and elsewhere). By Jeremiah's time (Jeremiah 44:15ff.) she was a Queen of Heaven. When Jeremiah reproached the women of Israel for returning to her cult, they told him calmly that they had had no luck since they deserted her, and they had nothing to lose by renewing their fidelity …*

From *The Great Code: The Bible & Literature,* by Northrop Frye

Northern Blessings 137

*Dear Mother Earth! I think I have always specially belonged to you. I have loved from babyhood to roll upon you, to lie with my face pressed right down onto you in my sorrows. I love the look of you and the smell of you and the feel of you. When I die, I should like to be in you, uncoffined, unshrouded, the petals of flowers against my flesh and you covering me up.*

From Emily Carr's journals and inscribed on her gravestone at Ross Bay Cemetery, Victoria, British Columbia.

Virgin wearing the robe and crown of a French queen on the wall of a Quebec City church.

Our Lady of Light, firmly wrapped in the Virgin Mary's cloak, re-emerged in Arctic Catholic churches, and in a parish north of Ottawa where she was Notre Dame des Lumières, while the luminous north wind traditions of Mediterranean and Middle Eastern myth were sometimes breezing along in folklore. Sweet, magical love bears north in the old Cajun Acadian charm recorded in *Gumbo Ya-Ya, Folk Tales of Louisiana*. *Poudre de Perlainpainpain* binds a young girl's lover to her forever if she can pluck from the wind seventeen thistle seeds floating in their down, then rub the seeds over the honey sac of a bee caught on a clover blossom leaning north. The seeds mixed with salt measured from a black thimble are rubbed into a man's clothes to guarantee love everlasting.

The divine queen who lives in a polar castle blew across Victorian England's Canadian Arctic obsession. She appeared as the wind herself in George MacDonald's 1870 fairy tale *At the Back of the North Wind*, explaining how she works:

"Oh, never mind your clothes. You will not be cold. I shall take care of that. Nobody is cold with the North Wind."

"I thought everybody was," said Diamond.

"That is a great mistake. Most people make it, however. They are cold not because they are with the North Wind, but without it."[9]

*At the Back of the North Wind* includes a travellers' description of the country at the back of the north wind where the ground smells sweet, the rivers are pure, and the month is always May.

✸

THE IDEA OF A FEMALE NORTH — a pure sanctuary, a safe refuge for the besieged, and a redemptive possibility — has lasted in Canada. Early in 1939, when war looked likely, and the governor general was dying, the Canadian north was the only place he could imagine for soul-making. John Buchan's — Lord Tweedsmuir's — last book was *Sick Heart River*, a novel formed from an invented Arctic quest undertaken by an unmistakably autobiographical Sir Edward Leithen who is weak with tuberculosis, "although he would not sink to self-pity. He had been brought up in a Calvinist household and the atmosphere still clung to him, though in the ordinary way he was not a religious man. For example, he had always had an acute sense of sin, which had made him something of a Puritan in his way of life. He had believed firmly in God, a Being of ineffable purity and power, and consequently had no undue reverence for man."[10]

Far along on a cold, hard fictional journey that has frequently included Leithen's increasing inability to continue without the tender care given him by other northern pilgrims — men escaping the city — as well as Metis guides and starving Indians, "a change had come over his world of thought." Under stars hung like lamps in a clear night sky, Leithen remembers:

> He had welcomed the North because it matched his dull stoicism ... Now there suddenly broke in on him like a sunrise a sense of God's mercy ... Out of the cruel North most of the birds had flown south from ancient instinct, and would return to keep the wheel of life moving. Merciful! But some remained, snatching safety by cunning ways from the winter of death. Merciful! Under the fetters of ice and snow there were little animals lying snug in holes, and fish under the frozen streams, and bears asleep in their lie-ups, and moose stamping out their yards, and caribou rooting for their grey moss. Merciful! And human beings, men, women, and children, fending off winter and sustaining life by an instinct old as that of the migrating birds. Lew nursing like a child one whom he had known less than a week ... Surely, surely, behind the reign of law and the coercion of power there was a deep purpose of mercy.[11]

*Sick Heart River* gives most of its last words to Father Jean-Marie Duplessis, O.M.I., the Arctic missionary priest who had looked after Leithen while he burned the last of his strength working alongside native people exhausted by starvation.

Father Duplessis says, "I witnessed the rebirth of a soul, but that is not quite the truth. The soul, a fine soul, was always there ... But he had been frozen by hard stoicism which sprang partly from his upbringing and partly from temperament ... He had always bowed himself before the awful majesty of God. Now his experience was that of the Church in the thirteenth century, when they found in the blessed Virgin a gentle mediatrix between mortal and divine. Or perhaps I should put it thus: that he discovered that tenderness and compassion which Our Lord came into the world to preach, and, in sympathy with others, he lost all care for himself."[12]

"Down North," from the north country insiders' name for the homeland where all rivers run down to the Arctic Ocean, is John Buchan's 1937 London *Sunday Times* essay describing the seven-thousand-mile bush-plane and canoe Canadian northwest tour that convinced him the north nourished hope and mercy. In southern Ontario sixty years later, *Up North* was the title art curator Andrew Hunter chose for the Tom Thomson Memorial Art Gallery exhibition that joined Thomson — machinist, fishing guide, and artist — with Bashing Bill Barilko, No.5, Toronto Maple Leafs defenceman, 1946–51. The link between them, shared by Andrew Hunter, was their need for northern sanctuary. The north had blessed all three men with pleasure and refuge, as well as with the gifts of distance, silence, and beauty.

*Up North* combined Tom Thomson's blazing northern paintings and Bill Barilko's brief, glorious hockey career (including his 1951 Stanley Cup–winning overtime goal for the Leafs) within the exhibition's subtitle, *A Northern Ontario Tragedy*. The *Up North* collection included a suspended canoe to note Thomson's drowning death on a northern lake in 1917, and images of the shattered Fairchild 24 float plane in which Bill

Barilko died between James Bay and Cochrane in Northern Ontario the summer after his triumphant '51 season.

✱

I NEVER SAW *Up North*, but when I heard how Andrew Hunter's exhibition text had merged Tom Thomson and Bill Barilko's work with their imagined inner lives as they dreamed each other into an abundant, irresistible north, I remembered the Ontario Northland train rocking gently up an old rail bed to Moosonee on James Bay, lulling along a narrow line cut through black spruce so thick along the track after Cochrane, the snow and sky seemed to darken. Bill Barilko, twenty-four years old, mine-camp kid out of Timmins, had been in the clear light up north of the black spruce country, fishing his first Arctic char in the wide, shallow mouth of the Seal River where the last of the northern boreal forest begins to trail into tundra on James Bay. On the flight back to Timmins, the little plane was swallowed by the bush about 150 kilometres north of Cochrane.

You could never have seen the crash site from the train. No one saw it for ten Toronto Maple Leafs hockey seasons minus the Stanley Cup, while Bill Barilko was alive in a northern legend.

Like Henry Hudson, not the overconfident Timmins dentist flying the Fairchild, but Captain Henry Hudson who didn't freeze or starve in 1611 when he was cast adrift in Hudson Bay, Billy was out there somewhere in the north, smiling. Henry Hudson had landed on the eastern shore of his own bay to be received so kindly by the Inuit that he married into a prominent hunting family to live happily ever after, and Bill Barilko was smuggling high-grade gold ore out of the country, or he had defected to the Soviet Union because of his Russian family background, and was teaching their hockey players more than they needed to know about playing defence.

Billy's coffin was so light, his pallbearers said. The Fairchild and its cargo of bones had been spotted by a provincial government helicopter on a routine flight on May 28, 1962. The saving grace from Bill Barilko's northern tragedy survives in Gord Downie's "Fifty Mission Cap," the Tragically Hip song included in the *Up North* exhibition: "Bill Barilko disappeared that summer ... The last goal he ever scored won the Leafs the Cup. They didn't win another until 1962, the year he was discovered. I stole this from a hockey card, I keep tucked up under my fifty mission cap, I worked it in to look like that."[13]

In the north that persists as the promise of hope, something is always saved from a northern tragedy, or still waits to be found. From the dead men's gold in unnamed northern creeks running on forty-year-old scraps of paper for which the identifying river-system maps have disappeared, to Samuel Hearne's *A Journey from Prince of Wales' Fort in Hudson's Bay, to the Northern Ocean ... in the years 1769, 1770, 1771 and 1772,* first published in 1795, and still able to cool a New York heat wave for Elizabeth Hay in *Captivity Tales: Canadians in New York*, something from the north that has been shaped around hope always survives. Even the vessel name *Hopewell* lives. The *Hopewell* tried the Labrador coast for the Northwest Passage as an East India Company barque in 1606, carried Henry Hudson aboard a sturdy little sloop on his 1607 passage-seeking voyage, then took to working twentieth-century west coast salmon as a wood-hulled seiner.

The bowhead whales who saw Sir John Franklin's 1845 Northwest Passage expedition ships *Erebus* and *Terror*, and doubtless know where their much-sought-after ice-wrecks rest, are still alive, too. Ivory harpoon heads found in whales taken by modern Inuit hunters, along with examination of the whales' eyes, show that bowhead whales live up to two hundred years. By another kind of northern knowing, sad-faced, capable Lieutenant Francis Crozier, captain of the *Terror*, is supposed to have survived the long, desperate trek from the ships abandoned in the ice to the barren grounds, then lived peaceful years with the Chipewyans.

✸

FOUR OR FIVE Ontario Northland hours this side of Moosonee, two people wearing snowshoes stood between the tracks and the black spruce, waiting for the train to pass. Bundled, they were, and calm, trappers, maybe, or others at home in the northern muskeg country before the tundra. I think of them surprisingly often, those two, and how they were standing at ease with winter in the bush, and the way I wanted to fall to my knees when I got off the train at Moosonee, wanted to give thanks for the James Bay light pouring onto the frozen salt and river water there. As everyone knows ...

✸

TOM AND BILL were young men with paintings and goals yet to make. If they had lived through northern miracles to survive their accidents, they would most likely have been drawn back to the north they needed as much as art and hockey.

"Mrs. Mike" went back. Benedict and Nancy Freedman's biography of "the Boston girl who married a rugged Canadian Mountie,"[14] records Katherine Mary Flannigan quitting the Northwest Territories after the winter when the 1918 flu took her babies, along with thousands of other northern mammals, human and animal, except, mysteriously, for bears. Sergeant Mike said nothing bothered bears.

After a lonely, discomforting season in now-alien Boston, Mrs. Mike went home with a wider, deeper acceptance of the north as the same combination of ferocious pain and sweet joy she had once recognized in the Lesser Slave Lake mission church: "I opened my eyes and looked into the face of the Mother of Sorrows. She was carved in wood. The work was crude. It looked as though it had been done with a hunting knife. But the face was not cold, like expensive marble faces. A great beauty was there, a great love and sincerity that made you forget its awkwardness and the strangeness of its proportions. The purity of the expression haunted me, the sorrow of the eyes, the sweetness of the mouth."[15]

Years later, Mrs. Mike told her biographers that once she was back north again, she saw the pattern. "Stretched on the loom was the huge white cloth of the North. We were the threads. Short and long, our ways stretched across it."[16]

✷ Costa Rica: *Our Lady of the Angels* ✷ Cuba: *Our Lady of Charity of El Cobre* ✷ Dominican Republic: *Our Lady of La Altagracia* ✷ Ecuador: *Our Lady of Quinche* ✷ El Salvador: (

Group of Seven artist Lawren Harris would have agreed with her about the north being fertile, giving ground for life lived with meaning and awakened spirit. While Thoreau MacDonald painted a version of a specifically female northern icon in *Pine Tree Madonna*, Harris's early Arctic pictures are visions of the shining northern purity he believed in as "A source of a flow of beneficent informing cosmic powers behind the bleakness and barrenness and austerity of much of the land."[17] The

*Northern Blessings* 145

presumption of purity in Canada's north is a marketing gift for Aurias, a.k.a. "True North. True Love. True Canadian Diamonds." Aurias's *Fashion Magazine* advertisement reads, "Your Canadian diamond is a lasting symbol of true purity in the very deepest sense ... as one would expect from diamonds found in the wilds of the Canadian north."[18]

North as a place in the mind where a safe home coexists with a needed wildness has staked a claim in the imagination of some southern Canadians. Already a brilliant pianist, a very small boy named Glenn Gould devoted his dream time to the paradisial island in northern Canada where he would make a home for stray and aging animals, and live there himself. Stephen Leacock would have understood: "I never have gone to the James Bay; I never go to it. I never shall. But somehow I'd feel lonely without it."[19]

✱

IN THE CANADIAN ARCTIC SUMMER, a remnant of the oldest, sweetest northern sanctuary mythology remains in the scent of wildflowers with a faint, dry undernote of reindeer moss, and in the mild air over a calm sea in Coronation Gulf. Saint Brendan the Voyager would have set sail on a day like this c. 550 CE. The saint, who was an Irish abbot, and seventeen of his monks, were looking for the Isles of the Blessed. They were certain that although north itself might well be a chaotic, barbaric place, behind the north wind would be a warm garden. Saint Brendan and his crew reportedly encountered a floating crystal castle, probably an iceberg.

✱

IN THE HIGH NORTH lives the most powerful, most fertile, most abundant, and probably most practical, conception of the Canadian north as an ancient metaphor for mythic female blessings. Sedna, Inuit Sea

Mother, now lives under the Arctic Ocean, after experiencing suffering and betrayal as a human form, still sending forth her blessings. Her fingers were chopped to the knuckle bones by her father as she clung to a kayak to try to save herself from drowning. Now, undersea, from these wounded, fingerless hands, flow all the fish and animals of the sea.

In summer 2000, I learned a little of her in Kugluktuk (formerly Coppermine), Nunavut, by walking the shore road along Coronation Gulf to Our Lady of Light church, boarded shut in the absence of a priest, and by reminding myself that Mary's consolation flows through boards and other barriers. Our Lady of Light, known as a gift for all nations, may have already been planning her silent, dove-accompanied 1968 appearance to Muslims, Jews, and Christians at Zeitun, Egypt's Coptic Church when she entered the Northwest Passage from the west, not far from here during World War II.

✷

ON THE ALREADY near-twilight morning of February 13, 1942, Mary, Our Lady of Light, passed by the beach ice in front of Coppermine-Kugluktuk's old Hudson's Bay Fort Hearne building, paying no mind to the marker which read "Here the first regular Masonic lodge was held north of the Arctic Circle, August 30, 1938. Lat 67°48′ Long W 115°15′." Among the Eldorado Mines and Hudson's Bay Company names on the monument are geologist J. B. Tyrrell, who retraced Samuel Hearne's Northwest Passage trek down the Coppermine River in 1893, and Henry Larsen, captain of the RCMP Arctic patrol vessel *St. Roch*.

Our Lady of Light had business farther along the Northwest Passage that morning. She was needed, suddenly, unexpectedly, in Pasley Bay on the Boothia Peninsula. *St. Roch* had left Vancouver harbour June 23, 1940 on a wartime mission to make the first Pacific–Atlantic Northwest Passage. The tiny ship and her crew were enduring their third winter in the ice.

Constable Albert ("Frenchy") Chartrand, one of eight men on board, had just died of a heart attack. Our Lady was needed, not only to ease the soul of Frenchy Chartrand, whose passage to heaven was entirely assured on the strength of his loving heart and his good right arm, which had just helped to bridle the bow of the *St. Roch* so she could escape being crushed by ice floes, and his ability to remain good-humoured at fifty below, but also to sustain Captain Larsen and his crew.

They had loved and depended on their large, immensely strong shipmate, and his utterly unanticipated death shattered them. A coffin was made and Chartrand's body was set into a snowbank. In Henry Larsen's understated autobiography, *The Big Ship*, he says, "He had been the only Roman Catholic of the crew and all the others shared my opinion that the last rites of the Church should be administered, knowing as we did how much this meant to members of his faith. The nearest priest was more than four hundred miles away, down at Pelly Bay in the Gulf of Boothia, where Father Henri of the Oblates had a little mission. We decided that I would go down and get the Father to come up and bury poor Chartrand."[20]

This quiet galley table plan for movement across frozen distance to honour Frenchy Chartrand's spiritual beliefs contained the first possibility of easing the shock of his death in a place where darkness, cold, and ice-trapped time weighed on them all. The difficulty of arranging for *Requiem aeternam dona defunctis, Domine. Et lux perpetua luceat eis* — Eternal rest give unto the dead, O God. And let perpetual light shine upon them — to be spoken on the deck of the *St. Roch* offered the men meaning and purpose for continuing their careful, calm police and civil work onshore, all the while trying to keep faith in a voyage that became imaginary every time ice stilled them.

Three months of slow, determined motion, and faith in itinerant light was necessary. In the Arctic, light is a presence that needs remembering in its absence, needs sheltered, luminous space made in mind and heart during winter. Saint Roch des Aulniers knew this. Light had filled his cell the night he died in a fourteenth-century French prison, allowing those around him to know he must have been telling the truth about being a homecoming pilgrim, not an imposter or a beggar, despite his rags. On pilgrimage to Rome, Roch des Aulniers started out as an ordinary-enough wealthy young man until he halted his journey, and used his money time and again to nurse, and sometimes, somehow, cure victims bearing the Black Death sign of the world's end — the bubonic plague. When he fell ill himself, and lay dying alone deep in some forest, a dog carried bread to him day after day, and slept beside him to warm his body until he recovered.

Frenchy Chartrand would have been happy about the dog in Saint Roch's story. He had loved the RCMP's sled dogs — a mix of black Mackenzie dogs and heavier-coated Huskies, who lived on board when they weren't working — and he did not even mind cooking their winter mash — rice, cornmeal, rolled oats, tallow, and seal blubber — in a ten-gallon drum over two primus stoves. He got as far as lighting the stoves the morning he died.

Saint Roch's name had been given to a village on the south shore of the St. Lawrence, and a Quebec parish in the constituency held first by Sir Wilfrid Laurier, then by Ernest LaPointe, the 1928 minister of justice. LaPointe named the 104-foot RCMP schooner, newly built from Douglas fir at Burrard Drydock in North Vancouver, and sent the healer saint to work in the Arctic, iced in or not, through Long Nights into light seasons.

The spring equinox had to tilt light back to the Arctic before seals appeared on the ice so Inuit hunters could bring Father Henri up the Boothia Peninsula from Pelly Bay. On May 19, 1942, Captain Larsen and his crew attended Requiem Mass for Albert "Frenchy" Chartrand on *St. Roch*'s deck. The snowbank grave was blessed and tons of rock were hauled to make a cairn. Larsen recalls, "Chartrand had always liked to have everything neat and orderly, and I think it would have pleased him to know of this lasting monument erected in his memory, not too far from the Magnetic North Pole."[21]

Shortly after midnight on August 3, in noonlike light, the ice around the *St. Roch* moved. Sixteen hundred pounds of gunpowder were needed to blast the ship out of the ice not far from Pasley Bay, but she made Halifax harbour easily enough on October 3, 1942.

Henry Larsen and his crew received Polar Medals from King George VI. Our Lady of Light noted that one of her stars was named for Albert Chartrand in 2000.

※

IN THE FALL, when light lessens on the west coast and I am landsick and slow, the *St. Roch*, also on the beach, is some consolation. Sitting on blocks at the Vancouver Maritime Museum more than fifty years after her Arctic work, she still holds the sweet smell of damp wood and marine diesel. The healer saint himself still hangs over the gridded wooden galley table, looking plenty tough enough to take on the Northwest Passage and/or ferocious illness, though slightly startled as he glances over his right shoulder at the small angel behind him.

Up top, a Scandinavian tourist pokes his head into the wheelhouse to say he's just come through the Northwest Passage on the German cruise ship *Hanseatic* out of Greenland. "Easy trip. Interesting."

Henry Larsen, who is present once I am alone again in the wheelhouse, smiles. He reminds me that from the first time he took *St. Roch* through Dixon Entrance up the west coast, on course for the Bering Sea in a northwest gale, she pitched and rolled worse than any vessel he had known, and that he loved her like no other. I know. Like *Lana Janine*, the old black cod boat who let herself lean down into even the easiest swells, taking the men, and the Madonna Mexican fishermen had fastened to the storeroom bulkhood when they worked on board, and me, with her. *Lana*, like the *St. Roch*, was sea-keeping. Like this: when she, the offshore wind, is up, then she, the sea, is high and here on board, over the decks, into the galley, and rushing out on the rise. And back in again on the pitching, sliding fall. Breathe now, with the sea and the boat together. The Madonna up top is surely breathing with the ocean and *Lana*. She is within them, and the long, watery North Pacific light.

Henry Larsen allows as how he might go north again, maybe say hello to Aimé Anhegona in Kugluktuk, and others he remembers. Aimé, named 'beloved' "in my orphanage,"[22] he told me, was a boy when he knew Henry Larsen on the *St. Roch*, and an old man in a skiff in the summer of 2000 when he took me to the Coppermine River entrance. The ice was far away across celadon green open water that year, pushed up against Victoria Island the other side of Coronation Gulf, softened by distance and a pour of light so pure my eyes now see clear Pacific days washed faint blue, and Atlantic light glowing minutely, translucently yellow.

On the high banks of the Coppermine, other, more tremulous light can only be imagined now, flickering on broad black hearth stones that mean Pre-Dorset, Thule, and other Inuit people have fished Arctic char here for more than thirty-five hundred years. Inside the Copper Inuit's summer skin tents, oil rendered from seal flesh would have been transmuted to pools of soft light in stone lamps the size and curved shape of a woman's hand.

✺

Arctic char are sent into the Coppermine by Sedna, the undersea mother also called Nuliajuk or Takannnluk, Big Woman Down There, or forty more Inuktitut names. She is the same source of ocean abundance and fertility who is Samna, the One Who Lives Below in the Chukchi Siberian world, and goes by similar names in Greenland.

Once, the undersea mother who is sometimes half woman, half fish, knew us all. Once she was human, so in love with her girlhood she refused marriage until her father insisted she wed his lead dog. The dog children were born, but Sedna's weary father weighted the dog husband's pack with rocks to drown him because he couldn't hunt to feed his family.

Sedna sent some of her dog children south, meaning them to come home to the north when they had learned all they needed to know to take care of themselves in the world. The rest of her dog children became the first people of the north. They would need to learn how to hunt and fish.

A storm bird in human form lured Sedna into a second marriage, then carried her away to a lonely island to torment her.

Or the dog, part husky, part wolf, was Sedna's beloved companion who whined to warn her when he smelled a storm in the spirit world on

her handsome suitor. She can never heed this warning. Even if the legend's Arctic Ocean waves, not the storm bird, cry out for her to return to them, her story must finish with the same pain, and the same blessing every time.

When Sedna's father crosses the water in his *umiaq* to rescue his daughter, the supernatural bird husband awakes and beats all the northern seas into a storm, shrieking for his wife's return. Despairing, Sedna's father pushes her out of the skin boat into the sea. She flails in the waves, sinking, then churns to the surface again, reaching out for the edge of the umiaq to save herself. As her hands curl, clutching the side of the little boat, her father raises his knife. Sedna's severed fingers fall slowly through the still, dark salt water beneath the surface storm. Now, she, too, falls away from this side of the world, growing in power and blessing as she sinks into the sea. From Sedna's fingers, and her long hair, flow all fish and sea creatures.

*Nuliajuk: Mother of the Sea Beasts* stars in a 2001 Canadian film directed by John Houston, son of James Houston, the Arctic naturalist and writer who worked as Canadian Arctic civil administrator for development of the Inuit Art Co-op. Marina Jiminez's August 25, 2001, *National Post* article reports:

> The film captures, for the first time, Nuliajuk's story, as it was passed down from pre-Christian Inuit legend. Mr. Houston and his crew travelled by snowmobile in −59°C weather to far-flung communities, where they built tents in the snow and lit sealskin lamps, patiently interviewing in Inuktitut more than 30 Inuit elders, including a shaman who has since died, and one of the last Inuit women tattooed in the traditional way to gain the sea goddess's favour.
>
> Through these interviews, the film-makers made a remarkable discovery: the veneration of Nuliajuk, long suppressed by

Christian missionaries, has quietly continued in the North, in a kind of underground syncretism similar to that which exists in Brazil and Mexico, where local deities merge with Christian saints.

"Today there are Inuit who say they are Christian and they are not going in any way against Christianity, but when they are out on the sea, they do not break old observances," says Mr. Houston, who narrates the film.[23]

Mary of Canada supported spreading Nuliajuk's story beyond the north by sending the filmmakers some help from her university in Halifax. St. Mary's University ethnologists digitally recorded the Inuit elders' words for a permanent archive.

✷

NELVANA OF THE NORTHERN LIGHTS (alternate identity: Alana North, Secret Agent), the Triumph Adventure Comics superhero, owes her creation to Nuliajuk, a.k.a. Sedna. Comics artist and writer Adrian Dingle heard of the Inuit's mythically powerful woman from the Group of Seven's Franz Johnston, who had travelled to the Arctic in 1939. Nelvana's mother is mortal, but her father is the heavenly Koliak the Mighty, King of the Northern Lights.

✷

ON LONG SUMMER DAYS, the Mother of Sea sends *Salmonidae Salvelinus alpinus* up the Coppermine in the world's largest Arctic char run. On the cliff above the falls, Aimé and I lie on our bellies to see that light had moved the char into the side pools, charging the hormones urging the silver, sweet-fleshed fish into freshwater to spawn.

Near the pools, Aimé showed me where to climb down to the river. This was the place, we thought, where an old, blind Inuit woman once knelt by the river, spearing char so plentiful even she could take them. Samuel Hearne saw her in summer of 1771, intent on her work, so deafened by the roar of the water she didn't know the Chipewyans and Copper Indians guiding Hearne had slaughtered all of her people asleep in the tents above the river. They killed her, too. Samuel Hearne named this place Bloody Falls.

✴

WHEN THE RIVER WIDENED into Arctic Ocean salt water on July 18, 1781, Samuel Hearne would have been flooded with truth and light. The light bounced between sky and open water now, and the truth emerged from the copper legend he had been hearing the Chipewyans tell during the long expedition from Prince of Wales Fort on Hudson Bay across the tundra, and down the Coppermine. Hearne was searching for the Northwest Passage, and a copper mine on the river his Hudson's Bay Company orders described as "called by the Northern Indians *Neetha-fan-fan-dazey*, or the Far-off Metal River."[24]

A clear Northwest Passage did not look likely from the wide rocky river mouth that was ice-clogged in the summer of 1781. And the copper …

Truly, truly, Copper Woman willingly showed travelling hunters her home. But when the men used her cruelly after they pounded out all the richly gleaming rock they could carry, she vowed to sink back into her source and disappear. The first year the hunters returned, Copper Woman merged with the copper up to her waist, and some mineral could still be seen. Next year, she and her copper were gone.

Despite the beautiful tools made from native copper that eventually named Coronation Gulf's Copper Inuit, neither Samuel Hearne nor any mining company has found ore worth mining for copper extraction in the Coppermine region.

Samuel Hearne probably knew nothing about other great ladies of copper. But privately devout Pierre Trudeau, who paddled his beloved

Coppermine River from Yellowknife to Bloody Falls, likely knew that Fidel Castro's Mary, patron Virgin of Cuba, is *Nuestra Señora de la Caridad del Cobre*—the Virgin of Charity of Copper.

The mulatto Virgin of Cobre has belonged to all Cubans since 1606, when the fishermen who found her in the sea carried her to El Cobre, Spain's colonial copper-mining town. In Cuba and in Canada, she is also the syncretistic Afro-Caribbean Santeria religion's Oshun, the maternal presence of love, femininity, and water who appears as beauty shining in the bushes along a Nova Scotia river, and as the woman whose "true name is Oshun. Or Ocean,"[25] in George Elliot Clarke's *Whylah Falls*.

Cuba's Copper Virgin Mary also has an address in Madrid, Spain, and she may bear a long intricate link back to Venus, the Roman version of sea-born Aphrodite Marina, whose largest shrine lay in Cyprus, Isle of Copper, where the classical world's copper was mined.

✳

MORE THAN ONCE, searching for Mary of Canada, I have needed to remember seafoam-born Aphrodite known as Cypris, and the oldest prayer of the seafarer in trouble on land: Dear Cypris who savest those at sea, I perish, wrecked, ashore. Save also me.[26]

✳

ROBERT GRAVES'S *Hercules My Shipmate*, inscribed to Henry Larsen as a gift from James Houston, is one of the few novels in Larsen's tiny library on *St. Roch*. The book looks well read, but certainty, or knowledge of Henry Larsen's response to myth, is not possible.

It's only possible to light a Nuestra Señora de la Caridad del Cobre candle from Amy's Loonie-Toonie-Town in Vancouver, $3.75 plus PST and GST, *Hecho en México*, and wonder if Cyprian Aphrodite, mythic

*...de los Remedios* ✸ *Mystical Rose* ✸ *Mater Dolorosa* ✸ *Seat of Wisedom* ✸ *Spiritual Vessel* ✸ *Stella Maris, Star of the Sea* ✸ *Theotokos (God Giver)* ✸ *Vessel of Honour* ✸ *Virgin Mos...*

mother of Hercules the sailor; Copper Woman of the Chippewyan legend; and Our Lady of Light, who is also the Virgin of Charity and Copper, may all belong on the same huge, shimmering circle around human culture on which Mary of Canada moves, and changes.

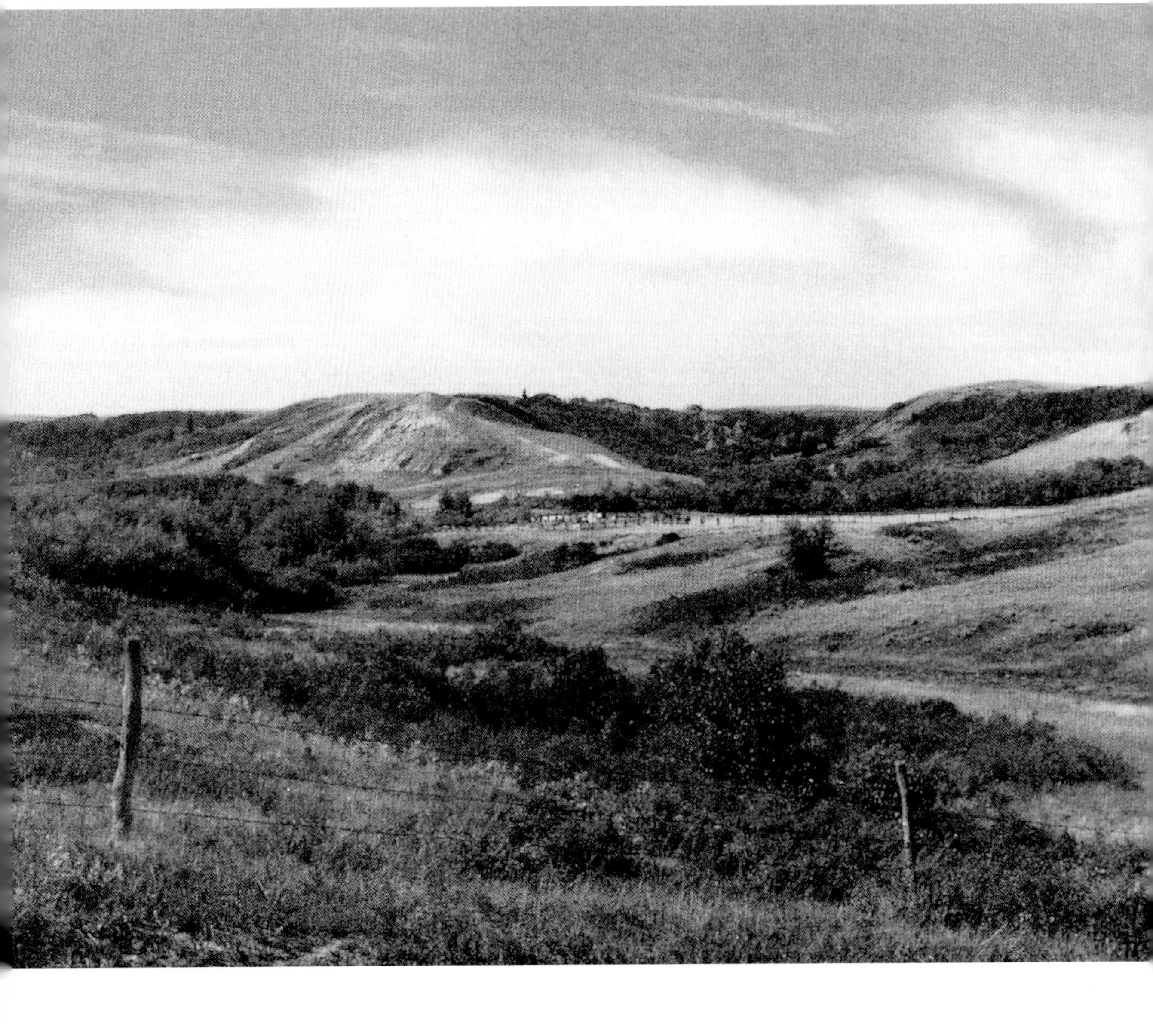

✳ CHAPTER 6 ✳

# *In the West*

CHIMNEY COULEE NEAR EASTEND IN SASKATCHEWAN'S CYPRESS HILLS IS THE ONLY COULEE I KNOW. CANADIAN METIS MADE COULEE A GENTLY SLOPED, STREAM-BEDDED GEOGRAPHICAL NOUN FROM THE FRENCH VERB COULER, TO FLOW, ROOTED IN THE LATIN COLARE, TO FILTER OR STRAIN. ACROSS WESTERN NORTH AMERICA, THE SHELTERED RAVINES THAT MOVING WATER EASED DOWN BETWEEN PRAIRIE HILL SWELLS ARE COULEES NOW.

*arthenos (Ever-Virgin)* ✷ *A Mercy for the Worlds* ✷ *Ark of the Covenant* ✷ *Cause of Our Joy* ✷ *Comforter of the Afflicted Consolatrix Afflictorum* ✷ *Domina* ✷ *Gate of Heaven* ✷

*The Englishman's Boy had to give the breeds their due. The cabin was as stout as his Pap's ... In a corner where a pitch lamp burned there was even a picture; he could see it from where he sat. One of them Cat-licker Jesus pictures ... He and Ed made easy at the table drinking boiled tea, black as coffee while granny clattered at the stove. A little twig of a girl of two, with gold rings in her ears, Rose Marie, stood clinging to the table leg, watching Grace wide-eyed. Every time he winked at her, she hugged the table leg all the harder.*

From *The Englishman's Boy*, by Guy Vanderhaeghe

In the Chimney Coulee earth under my boot prints in the snow, the meaning of home is being filtered along with the archaeological fragments sifted from the site earlier named Chapel Coulee for the tiny field stone church that housed Metis' devotions to Christ, born of "Marie, pleine de grace." For thousands of years before the Metis lived here, the coulee was likely be spoken with other words for the mercy of home as known, sweet ground. Grains of material left by the plains' earliest native people may rest in the soil under layers of fur-trade scraps, North West Mounted Police uniform buttons, square-headed nails, broken crockery, and spent, often misfired, Martini Henry .44 and Winchester .66 cartridges.

Home, home on the range / Where the deer and the antelope play / Where seldom is heard a discouraging word / And the skies are not cloudy all day ...[1] Even under cloudy November skies, Chimney Coulee is a wayside shrine to home in paradise west. When the buffalo roamed while the deer and pronghorn antelope played in the Cypress Hills, home was unconfined in imagination and physical reality. An entire, intimately learned geography, and the seasonal sanctuaries it contained, was home. The gentle slope where Chimney Coulee at last breaks the northeast wind off my back was one of many beloved home sites when the idea of home still held its hunting-gatherering dimension as the whole, divinely given, already perfect, promised land. For prehistoric bison hunters, Plains Indians, Metis, and cowboys who knew they were already dreaming about paradise lost when they sang "Home on the Range," the western plains had needed only knowing, not changing.

People don't live in Chimney Coulee anymore. At the coffee shop in Eastend, they say Gabriel Dumont's uncle used to stay here. On the run from Canadian troops, and lost Metis lands and hopes after the Battle of Batoche in 1885, Gabriel probably rested awhile in the coulee before he rode for the Montana border. But nobody lives here now. I knew that before I got out of the truck to belly under barbed wire in the snow. Plastic-covered archaeological excavations of Metis chimney foundations are the only human signs above ground. The fieldstone chimneys themselves are gone. Their flat, cut-edged stones were taken to line homestead paths or have winter-cracked and crumbled into the wind. The chimneys used to heat long, low buildings about four metres wide and fifteen metres long, divided for family groups.

Only miniature domestic spaces such as shepherd's field cottages, hermit's huts, and children's playhouses can "offer us at least a semblance of peace,"[2] says W. G. Sebald's Jacques Austerlitz early on in his relentless, uneasy study of Europe's monumental architecture. Long before the novel unfolds Austerlitz's memory of the bewildered four-year-old *Kindertransport* child he was in World War II Britain, where no one mentions his Jewish parents or his lost home in Prague, he knows he has been forever dispossessed of the means of homemade peace, however small.

I only know the snug Metis home measurements because old Jean Laframboise told someone, who told American writer Wallace Stegner, who told me in *Wolf Willow: A History, a Story, and a Memory of the Last Plains Frontier*. The broken, grass-grown stones in Chimney Coulee are also the matériel of Stegner's childhood in Eastend between 1913 and 1921, and of *Wolf Willow*.

Through the late-nineteenth-century winters when Sainte Marie wintered here with the Metis, the fires under the coulee's fieldstone chimneys warmed Jean Laframboise — Jean of the sweet, wild raspberry — and hunters, guides, freighters, and midwives whose skills plains newcomers needed, then.

"I wish I had known some of this," Stegner wrote, lamenting the lack of Cypress Hills stories in his Eastend elementary school history class. "Then, sunk solitary as a bear in a spider-webby, sweaty, fruit-smelling saskatoon patch in Chimney Coulee on a hot afternoon, I might have felt as companionship and reassurance the presence of the traders, metis, Indians and Mounties whose old cabins were rectangles of foundation stones under the grass."[3]

I know some of the stories Stegner yearned for as a child, and am not much comforted by them. The Metis-built post Hudson's Bay trader Isaac Cowie set up in the coulee had been abandoned by spring 1872. Cowie's pack horses and carts carried 750 grizzly bear skins and 1,500 "red deer" — elk — hides in their last load. Buffalo-hunting and fur-trade river freighting faded through the 1870s. Even the buffalo bones and skulls, piled in white cliffs alongside the new rail lines to be shipped back east and used for fertilizer, eventually disappeared.

Sitting Bull and the Teton River Sioux, winter-camped between Chimney Coulee and the Frenchman River after the Little Big Horn, were gone by the early 1880s, starved back across the border. The North West Mounted Police log cabin post in the coulee, and work for the tall, bearded Metis trackers and hunters (at ease on the summer grass beside the post in museum photographs back in town), lasted until the 1890s. No one in Eastend or on the new Cypress Hills ranches marked the early-twentieth-century year the stone-built winter homes were left empty in Chimney Coulee.

Others who move home by the seasons, knowing every landmark and source of food or joy in their geography, still live in Chimney Coulee. My footprints run alongside winter-pasture horse tracks and shallow, delicate marks left by a small four-footer holding his — her? — tail sideways in the snow. Hidden on the coulee's higher slopes, tail-circling, tired coyotes have likely scooped out their day beds. Other home signs rest in the clustered ovals of melted snow that mark mule and white deer sleeping places in wind-break retreats. Magpies shriek civil-defence warnings as sharp-edged as their black and white plumage when I pass the huge, ragged nests sagging in bare poplar and alder trees.

Only the pines look untouched by winter. No cypress trees grow here, or anywhere else in the Cypress Hills. The Metis were told the French word for cypress, rather than pine, so the country here became La Montagne de Cypre — the Cypress Hills — not the lodgepole pine *Pinus contorta*, centre-of-the-home-tent-pole hills.

I am embarrassed — ashamed is not too large a word for me, now — even in Chimney Coulee by myself, because I no longer recall the difference between lodgepole pine and jack pine trees. I still remember a story about a guy named Jack Pine, though. Once upon a west coast time, a new crewman in a logging camp signed "Jack Pine" on his credit advance for the caulk boots he needed before he could start work. No one came clean come payday.

Loggers' Quitting Poem: "Slack the main / Call the plane." And exit Jack Pine, De Havilland Beaver—borne out of the bush with new boots, bound for a better camp.

Back there, back then, upcoast fallers, fishermen, log salvagers, and boom men told Jack Pine's tale between beers, assuming their listeners — like the tellers themselves, like Jack, like me — contained seasons of shifting ideas about home: bunks in this camp, then another, and summer quarters in the fo'c'sle below the seiner's waterline, then in the wheelhouse of next year's gillnetter; winter-time weekly rooms; houses with friends or families on reserve, or somewhere near the dock up in Prince Rupert, down in Vancouver, or at any port in between; squatters' land up the inlets; cabins on not-yet-paid-off acreages and other green-drenched refuges built from two-by-four fir, cedar-sided dreams. All the fourteen-thousand-kilometre indented length of the west coast, like the bright, horizon-edged, disc of grassland starred by Chimney Coulee, used to be home when home was an entire landscape of seasonal grounds sanctified by their already known, already loved contours.

This morning in Chimney Coulee, I only need to know, or at least believe, that one or two sketchy twig platforms below my knee level in the berry bushes are mourning doves' homes. I want these nests to have been built by birds whose name and utterance mean sorrow, and who still keep house in a brushy coulee neighbourhood they will remember and return to next spring.

✱

ALL NORTH AMERICAN DOVES and pigeons descend from Old World wild rock doves. In Luke's Gospel, Miriam and Joseph of Nazareth, carrying the infant Christ, take two sacrificial doves up to Jerusalem's Temple of Israel for traditional Jewish ceremonies dedicating their first male child to God and purifying Miriam-Mary after childbirth.

Then they went home, Luke says. They returned to a safe shelter already known to them, a place the earliest English speakers called *ham*, the Anglo-Saxon word for a cluster of huts at the forest edge. If all the layers of time, the memories of ease and sustenance experienced when people lived in Chimney Coulee, are embedded in this winter-quiet earth, then pilgrimage to home as a movable feast can still be made here.

When the coulee was a sometime home place for journeying people, its riches included mule and white-tail deer, elk, antelope, and bear. The creek that watered the animals and their hunters is running fast today, not yet iced into static silence. Human safety in Chimney Coulee rested, once, in possibilities for hiddenness among the trembling aspens, willows, and pines tangled with chokecherry and saskatoon bushes down by the creek, combined with a long view from higher ground on the cut-banks.

Safety for body and spirit song-chained to words for house or home in the earliest English poetry. In Old English kennings, the body was *life-home* or *bone-house*, meaning the home that is most movable and easiest to forget is the body. By the twelfth century, a nameless Anglo-Saxon poet was calling the grave a house without windows.

Our first home was more moving water than still, solid earth. Before birth, we roll contentedly on our own sea. Faintly salted water within a membraneous sac in the womb moves as the mother's body moves, shifts its form to shelter the creature it contains. When the waters break around us and pour away, another passage begins. The first watery home seeps from memory, unless the elusive reassurance river systems offer me in their slide down the land into the sea summons a cloudy remembrance of another kind of home-seeking.

Chimney Coulee's creek has no choice about running home to the salt water its stream bed used to know. The Cypress Hills were islands when the Western Inland Sea joined the Arctic Ocean to the Gulf of Mexico in Late Cretaceous times. Now, the Hills are a continental divide, a height of land to tilt the creek south into the Frenchman and Milk Rivers flowing down to Missouri-Mississippi waters and into the Gulf again, or north on the farthest western tributaries on the Saskatchewan River system as it drains into Hudson Bay.

✳

On the western plains, the song of older spiritual meanings for ocean, and west, and the colour that meant life long before red-jacketed North West Mounted Police built an outpost cabin in Chimney Coulee, still sounds a long, reverberative note within the Virgin Mary overseas and eastern Canadian settlers brought to the prairies.

Ancient ceremonial reverences now sometimes associated with Mary still rest in Saskatchewan fields. In *Wild Stone Heart*, Sharon Butala writes of the Cypress Hill's Bracken Cairn Site, not far from a cairn in the beloved field on Butala land that is the physical and metaphysical ground of her book: "I was sure I was looking at a cairn made by Amerindians at some time in the last twelve thousand years, and now I wanted to know what this was, what it was for, if it was for anything. In one of my books I found an undated photograph of the Bracken Cairn Site ... In the photograph, the cairn looked just like a smaller version of the cairn I was looking at, and it was in a similar location, that is, on a high point with an unobstructed view for miles in three directions."[4]

The Bracken Cairn marked an almost three-thousand-year-old burial place for three adults and two small children, one newly born. Their skulls were turned west, and Gulf of Mexico seashell pendants had been set into the earth along with the bones. Other ancestral First Nations' burial sites in the Cypress Hills contained Atlantic Ocean shell beads.

The red ochre stains, meaning life was here and treasured, were present on the Bracken Cairn bones, as they were in the east coast Beothuk sites, and in the neandertaloid and archaic *Homo sapien*'s Skhül Cave burial places on Palestine's Mount Carmel where the Old Testament prophet Elijah had defeated the priests of Baal by calling on God for heaven's fire to consume a sacrificial bullock, and torrents of rain to end a two-year drought.

In I Kings 18, Elijah's one, true God sends fire and rain down to the mountain the Hebrew Bible calls Karmel, the garden, a place of oracle, prayer, and beauty known as sacred ground as far back as any Egyptian or Greek or Roman scholar of Biblical times could discover, perhaps as far back as the red-stained prehistoric hunters' bodies laid to rest inside the holy mountain fifty-five thousand years ago.

In Saskatchewan, Mount Carmel rises in a wheat field east of Saskatoon on Highway 5. The homestead hill Plains Indian and Metis buffalo hunters had called the "Big Brute" now supports as much religious and cultural change as connection with the biblical mountain where pine, prickly oak, myrtle, and olive trees flourished among herbs and wildflowers on sweet-smelling high ground that had been a spiritual retreat before Elijah's time, and before King Solomon's Song of Songs had likened the head of a beloved woman to the beautiful mountain garden called Carmel.

The high meadows of the Hebrew Bible were the earthly places where the meaning of a Canadian hill shrine for Our Lady of Mount Carmel was made when Christianity was new. In *The Great Code: The Bible and Literature*, Northrop Frye writes, "The two symbolic women in the life of Christ, the virgin mother and the bride who is the body of his people, are closely associated in imagery. The bride of the Song of Songs is also the Virgin who is impregnated by the Holy Spirit ... the enclosed garden ... is also the body of the Virgin."[5]

The white Carrera marble Lady on a smallish hill, where the air smelled of summer-heated, clean earth, and green wheat when I climbed up to her, contains a sea-born Marian metaphor formed on Mount Carmel. Twelfth-century hermits, who are claimed as founders of the Roman Catholic Carmelite order, wondered if the cloud God had caused to appear over the sea after Elijah's sacrificial prayers for rain to soak a parched land and its people could also be a form for Mary, bearer of the Messiah who would end spiritual drought.

In Muenster, Saskatchewan, at the St. Peter's Abbey–administered shrine on land donated in 1921 by homestead farmer John Bunko, pilgrimage day for Our Lady of Mount Carmel is the Sunday following July 16, near or on July 20, the Orthodox Church saint's day for Elias, who is also the Jewish prophet Elijah and Elias or Ilyas of the Koran. The light diffused by the white marble Madonna gleaming in Saskatchewan sunlight is refracted from high mountain air illuminated by prayers and meditations made for thousands of years in one of the world's oldest holy places, as well as by her Catholic title. Into the eighteenth century, Jews, Muslims, and Christians journeyed together to celebrate the feast of the holy prophet on Palestine's Mount Carmel, called Jebel Mar Elias by Arabs.

On spring mornings in Saskatchewan, when the earth smells green and new, the Lady whose Flos Carmel prayer begins *O Beautiful Flower of Carmel, most fruitful vine, splendor of heaven*[6] remembers the scented garden mountain in Palestine.

East of morning at the Saskatchewan shrine, the Prophet Elijah has been up for hours already, having checked in at St. Elias Church (Ukranian-Greek-Catholic Eparchy of Toronto and Eastern Canada) in Brampton, Ontario; at St. Elias the Prophet Roumanian Orthodox Church in Lennard, Manitoba; and in the dining-room-corner triptych at icon-maker Gary Robertson's farm near Elma, Manitoba. In Robertson's triptych, a replacement for a similar icon bought by the Canadian Museum of Civilization, Elijah tops the left-hand scene, then appears again, swinging up to heaven in his fiery chariot, below the Virgin and Child.

✳

Like the mountain in Palestine, the Virgin's western Canadian hill now called Mount Carmel is a height where older sacred ways were known. The nineteenth-century Cree and Metis buffalo hunters who wintered at the foot of the hill knew that fur-traded red banners entered the brush-walled lanes and corrals of Plains Indians' buffalo pounds as spirit matter. The poundmaker, a man or woman whose prayers included placing sacred objects near the pound entrance and central tree or pole, tied two-or three-metre-long strips of red flannel onto the buffalo medicine pole.

Western fur traders with red flannel, Hudson's Bay Company blankets, rifles, and sugar were followed soon enough by whisky traders. Blaze-belly, a.k.a. rotgut whisky, enflamed fears felt by native people and newcomers, all of whom were either grieving or creating ferocious changes across a landscape where change had come over people and animals slowly, or not at all, for thousands of years. By 1874, another kind of red cloth, and any number of forms of Mary of Canada were on their way west.

✳

Red coats resembling British Army uniform jackets were chosen for the North West Mounted Police in part to mark the new force and their mandate — one law for all in the west — as sharply distinct from the U.S. Cavalry "blue coats." All native people supposedly knew red to be a friendly colour since Chief Tecumseh and the Shawnee, as well as Mohawk Chief (and British army captain) Joseph Brant and four of the

Iroquois Six Nations had fought alongside British soldiers in the War of 1812.

A new police force similar to a cavalry regiment — 275 red-jacketed officers and men, 73 wagons, 114 Red River carts crammed with gear and ammunition, 93 cattle for slaughter, mowing machines to cut fodder, two field guns and a pair of mortars, field kitchens, and a forge — set out west from Dufferin, Manitoba, on July 8, 1874. Red River Metis men of both French-Native and English or Scottish or Orkney-Native families were with the wagon train as carters, wagon drivers, and guides.

Four days along the trail, the NWMP men, like almost every largish collection of Canadians before and after them, noticed their personal gear included interior baggage labelled "religion" or "denomination." Early in the morning of July 12, 1874, Sub. Inspector Sévère Gagnon wrote in his journal, "Orangemen Day. They are easily noticed for they are all displaying flowers on their hats or on the heads of their horses."[7]

Innocent wildflowers probably scattered unnoticed seeds of irony among the men and animals making way toward good water at the foot of Manitoba's Pembina Hills. The commemoration of a 1690 Protestant victory at Ireland's River Boyne battle — Holland's Prince of Orange, crowned King William III of England in 1689, defeated England's deposed King James II — may have been marked for the first time on the western plains with Mary's wild roses, blooming as *Rosa woodsi lindl*, the prairie rose.

Ultra-Protestant Orange Order ballads may have been sung while spurs jingled. Perhaps some of the recruits knew "The Battle of York Point, 1849, St. John, New Brunswick": "It was on the twelfth day of July, in the year of '49, / Six hundred of us Orange boys together all did join / to celebrate the glorious Twelfth, in memory of our King. / Who from popish chains and idol gods he did us all redeem. (Chorus) Then we will sing, our Orange boys, of courage bold and free, / Resolved to die before you fly from the popish enemy."[8]

In *Riots in New Brunswick: Orange Nativism and Social Violence in the 1840s*, professor Scott W. See says the first known British North American meetings of the militant, devoutly British fraternal order took place in Halifax in 1799, then in Montreal a year later. Brockville, Ontario, claims the continent's first formally established Loyal Orange Lodge in 1839. All major Protestant denominations were represented in the Orange Lodge, though most members were Anglicans, Presbyterians, Methodists, or Baptists.

Seventeenth- and eighteenth-century European state power struggles, ill-understood and labelled as Christian denominational conflict, then shaped as ferocious, paramilitary British Protestant political power in Ontario, parts of Quebec, and the Atlantic provinces, were headed west with the NWMP. The Orange Order's mix of borrowed Masonic ritual, loyalty to the British Crown, and membership that "admits no man within its pale whose principles are not loyal and whose creed is not Protestant"[9] was now part of western as well as eastern Canada.

✸

WATCHING THE MEN SADDLE UP at five in the morning, Mary of Canada may be imagined here wearing a cloak clouded with prairie dust and a thoughtful expression. She might have been saddened, but on the whole, unsurprised, to be considered a popish, un-British idol even though she was riding with the Anglican members as the Church of England's Mary the Blessed Virgin whose liturgical references Calvinist Prince William of Orange ("King Billy") had accepted, along with the title Defender of the Faith, when he received the crown of England as King William III in 1689.

She was, as ever, aware of all Canadian contradiction, confusion, and collective memory loss, past and present. She may have been praying that someone, anyone, in Canada would sooner rather than later remember the Irish River Boyne's deepest, oldest meaning. The Boyne's pools are

od Counsel ✳ Our Lady of the Navigators ✳ Our Lady of the Sacred Heart ✳ Our Lady of Victory ✳ Our Mother of Consolation ✳ Panagia (All-Holy Queen Assumed into Heaven

home to the Druids' salmon of knowledge and inspiration, the fish that feeds on the hazelnuts fallen from the nine riverbank trees of poetic arts.

Mary of the long memory may also have been thinking of the time twenty years before the Battle of the Boyne when the choices of another English king had fired up an operation that had affected every soul living in the land the NWMP were crossing, and most of the families and friends they had left back east. Despite the "Hudson Bay Hymn Book" (the factor's accounts of trappers' debts), used by the outfit known in the bush as "Here Before Christ," fur-trade profits, not forms of religion, had been the reason for Charles II's 1670 grant of all lands watered by rivers flowing into Hudson Bay to the "gentlemen adventurers." The Hudson's Bay Company had sold much of Canada to the new Ottawa government just three years before the NWMP was formed. The farthest western tributaries to the Saskatchewan River systems draining into Hudson Bay still lay two months, march ahead of them.

Concerning devotion to dead royalty, Mary of Canada might well have glanced east, and wondered if anyone in the NWMP recalled Princess Sheila, who had, by all accounts in Carbonear, Conception Bay, Newfoundland, set up housekeeping at a homestead there sometime between 1600 and 1610. Sheila Na Geira, of legendary beauty and ancient, perhaps Celtic, Irish royal family, was captured in the English Channel by Dutch pirates, then rescued by pirate and/or privateer Peter Easton, voyaging to Newfoundland to enforce British law in the colony at the behest of Queen Elizabeth I. Sheila of Ireland and navigator Gilbert Pike fell in love on the Atlantic crossing, were married at sea by Captain Easton, and lived happily ever after in Newfoundland, where everyone, especially the Pikes, knows their story.

✳

STILL LOOKING EAST, and back in time from the western plains on Orangeman's Day, July 12, 1874, Mary may have smiled with a mother's fond bemusement at the 1847 petition for a new Orange Lodge in her very own parish of St. Mary's, New Brunswick. Her smile would have stayed in place when she turned west to see Vancouver's twenty-first-century real-estate listings ahead. The rooming house at 341 Gore and Hastings, built in 1904 as a four-storey fraternal hall for the Grand Orange Lodge of British Columbia, is for sale as a Chinatown heritage building. Asking price: $2.2 million.

❋

ONCE IN A WHILE, we can see for ourselves how funny we are in our Marian confusions. Jane Urquhart's 2001 novel *The Stone Carvers* sets disconcerted but almost enthusiastic Orangemen, along with King Billy's white horse and the Virgin Mary, into a joyous Corpus Christi day procession through the nineteenth-century Ontario countryside some of the NWMP recruits had just left behind.

Mary knew how time and distance soften, or harden, or otherwise change history. She knew that while the NWMP wagon train and men were moving west on Orangeman's Day, some Quebec Catholic farmers working their fields through the summer afternoon were likely whistling and singing a few bars of a sixteenth-century song about an earlier, sweeter-natured, Prince of Orange. Their man — "Le Prince d'Orange, La! Grand matin s'est levé"[10] — was light-hearted enough to joke with the priest about his sinless life (except for a certain little maid) as he lay dying from an Englishman's sword thrust. "C'était Le Prince d'Orange," sung in the 1500s in France, survived long enough in Quebec to be recorded in the 1920s by anthropologist Marius Barbeau.

Mary of many names and changes was riding with the NWMP from the start of their trek west. Between slow-walking cattle, short rations, mosquitoes, a summer hailstorm, broken-down carts, and haywire boots, there didn't seem much to be thankful for, but the new police force halted for church services after eighteen days' march, anyway. The men attended ceremonies conducted by senior officers after they made camp at La Roche Percée on the Souris River in Saskatchewan.

La Roche Percée, the Assiniboine people's *Imyan-Oghnok*, was an eight-metre-high sandstone rock form in two parts, pierced, the Assiniboine said, by its arch-roofed opening. When the 1857 Palliser expedition geographers and the NWMP saw the rock, it was marked with many petroglyphs, and its crevices held offerings: tobacco, beads, and certain small stones.

Other invocations of the sacred were made at La Roche Percée on July 26, 1874. "Ave Maria Stellis, Show thyself a Mother, May the Lord divine, Born for us your infant, Hear our prayers through thine," the same ninth-century hymn to the Star of the Sea Jacques Cartier's crew had included in their prayers, was sung far inland more than three hundred years after Cartier's landing in Quebec during the Catholic North West Mounted Police service near La Roche Percée.

The Virgin Mary was also present at the Church of England's Anglican NWMP service that day. She was trailing wisps of early British Christianity flavoured with both Celtic tradition and Eastern Orthodox underpinnings that Winston Churchill (*The History of the English Speaking Peoples, Volume I*) understood through Saint Colomba's mission to Britain: "From the monastery which he established in the island of Iona his disciples went forth to the Briths kingdome of Strathclyde, to the Pictish tribes of the North, and to the Anglian kingdom of Northumbria. He is the founder of the Scottish Christian Church … The Celtic churches therefore received a form of ecclesiastical government which was supported by loosely knit communities of monks and preachers, and was not in those early decisive periods associated with the universal organization of the Papacy."[11]

Celtic versions of Mary — "Queen-maiden of sweetness … faithfulness … peacefulness / And of the peoples … well of compassion … root of consolations … living stream of the virgins / And of them who bear child" — survive in *Carmina Gaedelica, Charms of the Gaels: Hymns and Incantations*

*Orally Collected in the Highlands and Islands of Scotland in the Last Century* by Alexander Carmichael: "I will build the hearth, / As Mary would build it. / The encompassment of Bride and Mary, / Guarding the hearth, guarding the floor, / Guarding the household all."[12]

The Anglican Virgin Mary plodding across Canada's western plains with the NWMP already knew that the nightly chorus of "Home Sweet Home" — An exile from home splendour dazzles in vain / Oh, give me my lowly thatched cottage again![13] — sung by British Canadian recruits would not prevent change in their minds, hearts, and bodies, or in their ideas about home.

She herself had withstood Church of England changes more substantial than buffalo-chip campfires instead of ovens, and a round of unknown country rather than already squared and settled Ontario, Quebec, Nova Scotia, New Brunswick, Prince Edward Island, and Newfoundland.

In 1938, the Anglican Church restored to its original purpose the Lady Chapel and its seven-second echo for exquisite music in England's nine-hundred-year-old Ely Cathedral. But the statues of the Virgin beheaded during the Reformation, the medieval glass smashed out of the Lady Chapel, the glorious wall paintings that had been burnt, and the seventh-century Saint Ethelreda Saxon shrine destroyed near the cathedral were as absent and irreplaceable as they had been for four hundred years.

The Anglican service at La Roche Percée on July 26, 1874, was taken by a British Royal Artillery officer, acting North West Mounted Police Commissioner George Arthur French. Commissioner French would have read from the *Book of Common Prayer* prepared on Thomas Cranmer's watch as Archbishop of Canterbury for the new Church of England in 1549. This first complete English-language prayer book was meant to accord with the Protestant Reformation's refusal of priestly Latin in favour of commonly understood speech and text, though many of the English words formed familiar Catholic rites. Mass eventually became

*al Vessel ✽ Stella Maris, Star of the Sea ✽ Theotokos (God Giver) ✽ Vessel of Honour ✽ Virgin Most Faithful ✽ Virgin Most Prudent ✽ Virgin Most Venerable ✽ Virgin Most Renown*

Divine Service, and a certain troublesome matter — a Catholic pope who could supersede England's state power — was deleted from the structure of the new Church. By the time England's Virgin Queen — Elizabeth I — was crowned on earth in 1558, the Virgin Mary was standing on steady liturgical ground in the new Anglican Church, ready to take ship for Canada.

Archbishop Cranmer's calendar of holy days honouring the Blessed Virgin Mary's Conception, Nativity, Annunciation, Purification, and Visitation as well as saints, martyrs, and bishops from the first century of Christianity onward opened *The Book of Common Prayer and Administration of the Sacraments According to the Use of The Church of England in the Dominion of Canada* given to my mother as a 1929 birthday gift from my Yorkshire-born grandmother on Vancouver Island.

In Canada, the Anglican *Book of Common Prayer* that included Cranmer's sixteenth-century plea for patience with his efforts to please God, as well as to satisfy those who wished to change either everything or nothing from the Catholic Latin liturgy — "in our times, [when] the minds of men are so diverse"[14] — influenced Canadian military chaplains' services and the liturgies of other denominations.

At the Vancouver School of Theology, Anglican priest Reverend Doctor Richard G. Leggett says,

> The 1662 prayer book, used in Canada for three hundred years, came out of Cranmer's book. In both Canada and the United States, Lutherans in the early nineteenth century moving from German, Swedish, Norwegian, or Danish into English often looked at the *Book of Common Prayer* as a resource for English-language texts.
>
> Another group that would make use of texts based on the *Book of Common Prayer* would be the early Methodists. Prior to union in 1925 [with Congregational churches and about two-thirds of the Presbyterian congregations as United Church of Canada],

*Blessed be the great Mother of God, Mary most Holy.*
*Blessed be the name of Mary, Virgin and Mother.*

From the Divine Praises, St. James' Anglican Church, Vancouver, British Columbia.

Canadian Methodists would make use of liturgical rites which were highly influenced by the *Book of Common Prayer*, particularly on sacramental occasions.[15]

At the Anglican morning prayer service under an already fierce sun at La Roche Percée, the liturgy offered Commissioner French and his policemen congregation a choice of the Apostles' Creed or the Creed of Saint Athanasius.

Despite staunchly faithful fourth century CE Bishop Athanasius's exile from Alexandria in desert country not unlike the western plains, Commissioner French most likely chose the same Apostles' Creed taught to early Christian converts, who learned how each of the Apostles had pronounced an article of this creed after the descent of the Holy Spirit upon them at the first Pentecost.

The Apostles' Creed — beginning "I believe in God, the Father Almighty, maker of heaven and earth, and in Jesus Christ, his only Son our Lord, who was conceived by the Holy Ghost, born of the Virgin Mary" — became the outline of Christian faith still recited in Canada's Catholic, Anglican, Orthodox, and Lutheran churches, and sometimes used in Presbyterian and United churches.

The Presbyterian Church of Canada and the United Church of Canada do not require the Apostles' Creed as a fixed liturgical text. The United Church was formed in the understanding that "The historic creeds formulated by the ancient Christian church are recognized as valuable guides to the understanding of our relationship with God. Membership is not related to the specific acceptance of a catechism or creed, but to a general acceptance of the central truths presented in the gospel."[16]

Sometime during the hot Sunday morning of July 26, 1874, at La Roch Percée, Mary of Canada and of the Apostles' Creed recalled that amen began as the Arabic words *amn*, for safety and security, and *amana*, to believe, together meaning to become secure in belief.

✴

NORTH WEST MOUNTED POLICE records do not indicate if Commissioner French reminded his men that their Anglican prayer book calendar, as well as the Roman Catholic missal being used in the next shade patch along the Souris River, marked that date, July 26, as feast day for Saint Anne, mother of the Virgin Mary. Possibly, the officers and men felt no need of Saint Anne's particular concern for safe childbirth. They may not have wanted rain, another of Saint Anne's gifts, or yet planned any underground police assignments. Anne is patron saint of miners. But she is also saint of metal workers and blacksmiths. Many of the NWMP bloodstock horses were ill-shod for long days on rough ground. Some of the brilliantly designed, wood and leather, buoyant-across-rivers (notoriously squeaky-wheeled) Red River Metis carts full of gear had already been abandoned with broken axles. You would have thought ...

✴

THE PROTESTANT CHURCH of England's Blessed Virgin Mary and her mother, Saint Anne, had already been at work in Canada for more than three hundred years. In Arctic waters on Saint Anne's feast day in 1578, her ancient, probably pre-Christian Celtic, concern for sailors was working hard on behalf of a stout-hearted, sometime-slaver, oft-times pirate and his men "in this storme being the six and twentieth of July, there fell so much snow, with such bitter cold air that we could scarce see one another ... nor open our eyes to handle our ropes and sayles." After five storm days in ice, fog, and tides "nine hours flodde to three ebbe,"[17] Martin Frobisher, commissioned by Queen Elizabeth I to find the Northwest Passage, or gold, or both, made harbour near the tip of Baffin Island.

Far to the south about a century later, a lady of sacred legend who had probably started out as Celtic Ana before she was transformed to the legendary Breton duchess who became Sainte Anne (patron saint for Anne of Austria, Queen of France and New France), gentled a storm for Catholic fishermen from Brittany in search of New World cod. Her protection would result in the St. Lawrence River chapel at Beaupré that grew into Sainte-Anne-de-Beaupré, the world's largest Sainte Anne shrine. Not to mention "Haldimand Hills Spa Village, Home of Ste. Anne's," unaccountably moved to several Ontario locations.

Up on Countess of Warwick's Island, now called Kodlarnun (white man's island), on July 31, 1578, Reverend Wolfall, the Anglican priest on board Martin Frobisher's ship, led the crew in North America's first thanksgiving "for theyr strange and miraculous deliverance."[18] Holy Communion in the Arctic, celebrated from Thomas Cranmer's still brand new *Book of Common Prayer*, would have included the Virgin Mary of the Nicene Creed that is older than the New Testament.

The words recited by exhausted Arctic sailors were first set down amid the scent of Morrocan rose incense and beeswax candles afloat in the soft Maytime air of a Sea of Marmara city (now Iznik, Turkey) already old in 325 CE when the Council of Nicaea formed the creed: "We believe in one Lord, Jesus Christ, the only Son of God, eternally begotten of the Father, God from God, Light from Light, true God from true God, begotten, not made, of One Being with the Father. Through him all things were made. For us and for our salvation, he came down from heaven, was incarnate of the Holy Spirit and the Virgin Mary" [Ecumenical English Language Liturgical Commission translation from the Greek original].

The seventeen-hundred-year-old Nicene Creed that preceded the formal designation of the books of the New Testament, as well as any division between Orthodox, Catholic, or Protestant, is still recited in Canadian churches.

Liturgy professor Richard Leggett says, "The Nicene Creed is regularly used in Lutheran, Anglican, Presbyterian, and Roman Catholic parishes on Sundays, also in Orthodox and Eastern Rite Catholic churches. The Nicene Creed would be an option for use in other churches, such as the United Church of Canada, although more often than not they would use the so-called new creed."[19]

*Attention to the term hokmah, meaning "spirit" in Hebrew (translated to Sophia in Greek) led to the study of feminine wisedom linked with the Holy Spirit in later Christian teachings.*

From *The Flowering of the Soul: A Book of Prayers by Women*, by Lucinda Vardey

The United Church of Canada's 1968 New Creed avoids the Virgin Mary by way of "We believe in God / who has created and is creating, who has come in Jesus, the Word made flesh."[20]

But the Nicene Creed's long-eyed Byzantine Virgin Mary still looks down from the north wall of the fourth-century church built in Nicaea to celebrate the creed's making. Like *Hagia Sophia*, Holy Wisdom, the gloriously incandescent sixth-century cathedral in Constaninople/Istanbul, the Nicaean church was named for Sophia, the Greek and eastern tradition's spirit of female wisdom, God's female soul, sometimes symbolized by Aphrodite's dove.

Hagia Sophia's Canadian address is 270 Gladstone Avenue in Toronto. St. Anne's Anglican Church, a National Historic Site as well as a working church, was built in the soaring, vaulted arch Byzantine style of Constantinople-Istanbul's fourth-century Hagia Sophia cathedral. The walls were painted in the 1920s by artists, including the Group of Seven's J. E. H. MacDonald, F. H. Varley, and F. Carmichael, working in Byzantine fresco style.

✳

ANGLICAN SAINT ANNE has been demoted to "Anne, Mother of the Blessed Virgin Mary" in the feast-day calendar of the *Book of Alternative Services of the Anglican Church in Canada*, first published in 1983. But she still owns July 26, and the *Alternative Services* calendar still honours Saint Mary the Virgin's holy days, sometimes naming her the Blessed Virgin Mary. Some holy days commemorating early saints and martyrs now bear New World names: "October 19 — Jean de Brébeuf, Isaac Jogues, and their Companions, Missionaries and Martyrs in New France, 1642–1649; April 30 — Marie de l'Incarnation, Educator and Spiritual Teacher in New France, 1672," and others "whose lives have reflected the mystery of Christ."[21]

✳

During the Methodist and Presbyterian church services the North West Mounted Police held at La Roche Percée, Mary of Canada may have been on standby near the huge rock shrine, perhaps hoping either or both of them might be noticed. Patiently waiting beside La Roche Percée, Mary already knew that its petroglyph prayers — likely designs of deeply carved hooves within circles — would be obliterated by wind, rain, and graffiti cut by General Custer's U.S. Seventh Cavalry, the NWMP, and other plains newcomers before the stone-set symbols of the endlessly turning divine wheel in all creation could be treasured by anyone except their Assiniboine makers. The twentieth-century summer lightning that would split the arched rock might also have been on her mind.

After four days rest by the Souris River at La Roche Percée, the North West Mounted Police marched on. Half the men, wagons, and animals staggered north to Fort Edmonton; the others moved, too slowly, farther west. One good, late summer day in a Cypress Hills coulee (probably Chimney Coulee at the east end of the Cypress Hills) — fresh antelope and deer meat, sweet water, bellies full of berries — couldn't stave off winter. Horses died and half-frozen recruits went hungry before police work took hold in a chaotic west. Plains Indians life patterns meant to last forever were fragmented by fear and sorrow as fur traders, whisky, and missionaries created staggering changes. Settlers soon followed the police onto the plains. From the 1880s onward, one of history's largest, fastest population shifts filled the Canadian prairie with homesteaders from all over the world, ranchers first, then farmers.

Familiar, sometimes ancient, Virgin Mary forms and traditions travelled into Canada's west with eastern Canadian, American, and overseas settlers. Poland's Black Madonna, whose shadowed, thousand-yard stare had started out from Byzantium when Christianity was young, now watched over the making of justly famed moonshine as well as spiritual matters for Alberta and Manitoba homesteaders.

*While the eyes were uplifted in prayer,*
*Imploring the Lady of Sorrows, the*
*   mother of Christ,*
*As pain brimmed over the cup and the*
*   will was called*
*To stand the test of the coals ...*

From "Brébeuf and His Brethren,"
by E. J. Pratt

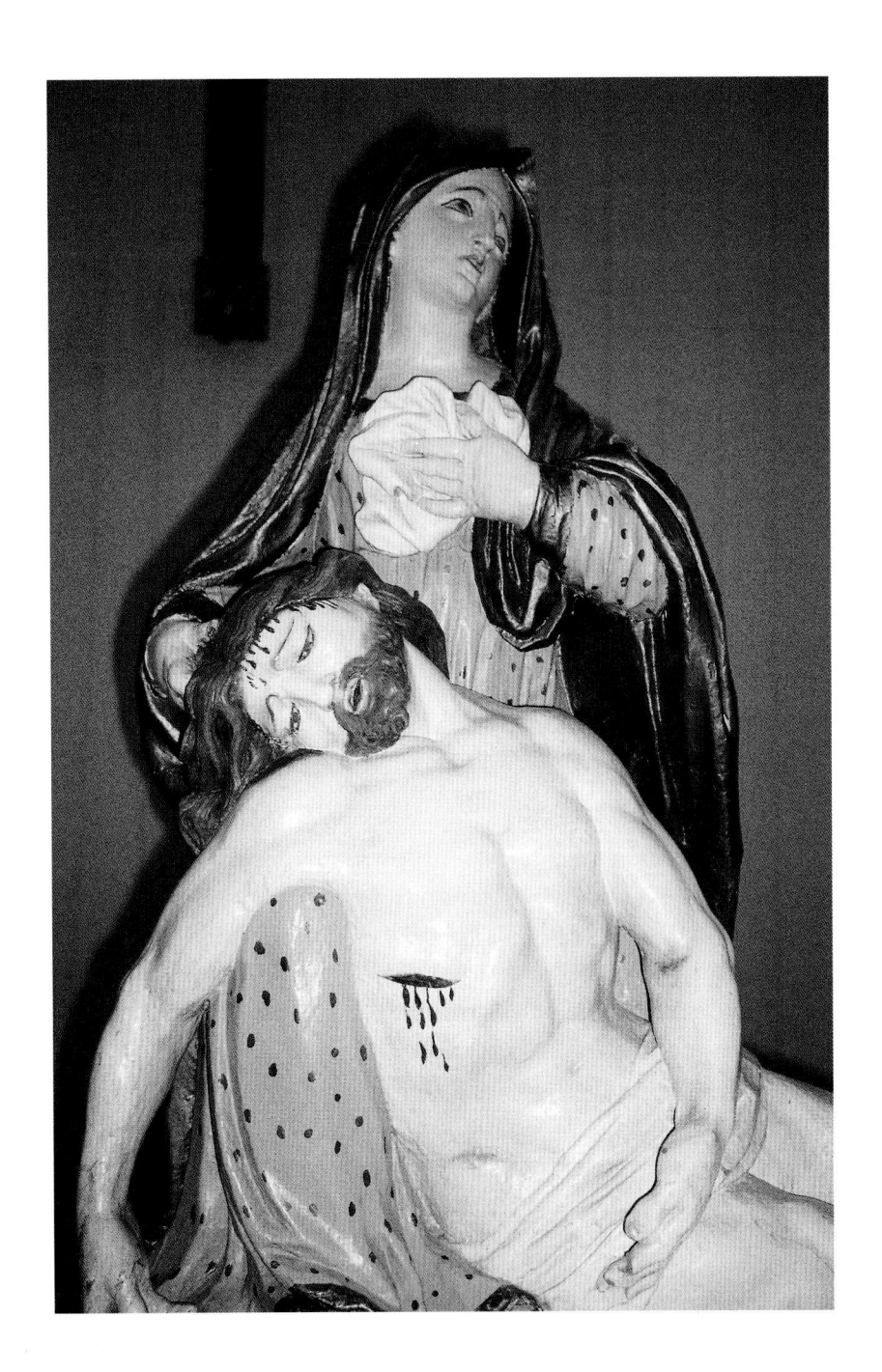

y Three ✱ Venezuela: Our Lady of Coromoto ✱ Mary, Mother of God ✱ Mary, Queen of Hearts ✱ Miriam of Nazareth ✱ Mirror of Justice ✱ Mother of Christ ✱ Mother of the Ch

Borne in immigrants' memories, Marian images and prayers from every country in Europe, and some from the Middle East, became part of the Mother of Consolation who already knew the hearts and minds of people living in the farms, bush camps, villages, and ports of Ontario, Quebec, the Maritimes, and the north as well as in the eastern cities. The always changing Mary who is enriched by prayers was being transformed by the needs and hopes of people working ground never before fenced or broken by the plow.

✻

ONE OLD-WORLD MADONNA whose delicate features bely her sturdiness made a journey to the prairies as long and perilous as any of the western settlers. In 1907, a French cleric, who could scarcely have imagined the huge, sweet-scented wheel of grassland surrounding the village of Pontiex in Saskatchewan, sent a heartening gift to people in the far, far country.

*Notre Dame d'Auvergne*, an almost life-sized fifteenth-century white oak *Pietà* Madonna had been out after dark and around the block long before she ever set out for Canada. For more than four hundred years, she sorrowed over the dead Christ sprawled in her lap while she listened to pilgrims, and saw to more than a few answered prayers. During the French Revolution, her twenty-four-carat gold edges were smeared with *goudron* — pitch, or perhaps lamp black — while she was hidden from angry mobs. (A three-hundred-year-old French painting of the Virgin's Annunciation found in a Nova Scotia barn in 2001 may have been smuggled into Canada during the Revolution.) During the nineteenth or early twentieth century, the Auvergne Madonna was changed by her times again, sanded down and repainted in a style and colours probably very different from the original choices.

Securely wrapped and crated, *Notre Dame d'Auvergne* embarked from the Normandy port of Le Havre, the same Le Havre de Grace where les filles du roi had boarded ship for New France as prospective brides for habitant soldiers, farmers, and trappers in the 1600s. Almost three centuries later, *Notre Dame d'Auvergne*, too, was bound for the New World along with other passengers and cargo.

Some days out, a fierce Atlantic storm pounded the ship. The vessel pitched. She slammed from side to side. She rolled, hesitated, returned, and her hull cracked. When the sea not only sluiced the decks, but also seeped in below, certain of the passengers, seized by uncontrollable terror and superstition as Pontiex parishioners still tell themselves, proposed that the storm might abate if *Notre Dame d'Auvergne* went over the rail. No record remains to suggest whether the act was to be considered as a sacrifice, a way for Mary to rejoin one of her oldest mythological forms, or a version of No Women at Sea. The captain, who must have had other matters on his mind, detailed two sailors to guard Our Lady. The wind and waves eased. *Notre Dame d'Auvergne* and everyone else made port in Montreal.

She didn't turn up with the other boxcar freight at the Canadian National Railway station in Swift Current, though. For months, the shipping company misplaced her in the cargo holds of various ships. Mary, *Notre Dame d'Auvergne*, a.k.a. Stella Maris, in part descended from Aphrodite-Mari, and Sea-Mother Mari, the ocean herself, put in more sea days on the Atlantic inside her dark crate, waiting for human need and daylight to warm her again.

In her new Saskatchewan home at last from 1909 onward, *Notre Dame d'Auvergne* survived the 1923 fire that destroyed the Pontiex church. She knows the shifting ground of lost homes and long, hard journeys to unknown places on which all Canadian immigrants stand, and are changed. Removed from her first French shrine, disguised, hidden, recovered and repainted, threatened, lost, and found, then smoke-stained and cleaned, the much-travelled and transformed *Notre Dame d'Auvergne* is at home now, living in clear white light pouring out of a prairie sky.

After almost eighty years in Canada, Our Lady in a half-millennium-old white oak tree caught wind of troubadour music and tales from the time and place of her first making. Vancouver's Expo 86 entertainment included Pierre Imbert of Lyons, France, performing fifteenth-century songs of the wolfish magic that once haunted Auvergne's forests with his *vielle à roue*, the medieval wheeled viola, a.k.a. hurdy-gurdy. Imbert's medieval wolves who stalked an Auvergne vielle à roue musician through dark woods until he played wildly enough for them to dance appeared on the Millennium Canada CD *How Music Came to the World*, produced by CBC Radio and the Vancouver Storytellers Guild. Pierre Imbert fused jazz with the vielle à roue tunes known to *Notre Dame d'Auvergne* before he died in Vancouver, his adopted hometown.

*Notre Dame d'Auvergne, La Vierge, Sainte Marie* always knew those insistent, madly dancing wolves, and the Auvergne musician who was said to become one of them some full moon nights, were formed from human fears. The loup-garou — werewolf — who haunted Europe in the Middle Ages, then shipped out to New France and the Cajun Acadian bayous in Louisiana, belonged to villagers, townspeople, and farmers uneasy about the shape-shifting quality of human wildness and lust in themselves, and about any creature — highwayman, wolf, or freelance fur trader — who made a living beyond the boundaries of cleared land and organized communities.

An urgent need for the Virgin Mary's protection from a human transformed to a wolf appears in a Metis story translated by Maria Campbell in *Stories of the Road Allowance People*. "Rou Garous," set down as transcription of spoken memory, includes both a native heritage of shamanic shape-shifting and the role of "dah Prees ... He say dat dah *Rou Garou* he don like dah Jesus and dah Virgin Mary." The tale of tall, beautiful Josephine (called Josephine Jug of Wine because she came from the city, even though she didn't drink); the black wolf hit by a car, and George L'Hirondelle, who had to call on the Virgin Mary for the first time since the World War I trenches, is a many-folded mystery. And a source of

*Bless us, O Lady of the Fields
And this prairie vast and wide
We've come to know a mother's love
In our hearts you will reside*

From "Prayer to Our Lady of the Fields," by Trudy Levasseur, imprimatur Peter Mallon, Archbishop of Regina

valuable information for non-Metis: "Me I nearly forget. Dem rou Garous when dere in dah peoples body / dey like to play poker / Dats right / Dey like to play poker."[22]

Sainte Marie, Mary of Canada is not on record as supporting a French Canadian werewolf tradition *The Canadian Encyclopedia* gloomily notes as, "A person could fall under suspicion of being a werewolf if one had not made one's Easter duty for seven years in a row."[23] Neither is Pierre Esprit Radisson.

✸

AT L'ÉGLISE NOTRE-DAME D'AUVERGNE DE PONTIEX in Saskatchewan, Mary and the dead Christ in her arms are displayed in an open space before the altar. Visitors can walk behind the figures to see a nameless carver's more than half-a-millennium-old knife and adze marks chunked into a much older oak tree trunk untouched by decoration, colour, or gilt.

These thousands of small, rough cuts in raw wood, rather than the delicacy of the statue's modern repainting, root Our Lady of Auvergne in the grain fields near her cathedral windows, in nearby Val Marie, and in Our Lady of the Fields, whose prayer, written by Trudy Levasseur of Pontiex, Saskatchewan, ends, "Bless us, O Lady of the Fields, And this prairie vast and wide." Notre Dame d'Auvergne is aware of another lady sometimes called the Madonna of the Prairies: English-born Quaker Elizabeth Chantler McDougall, wife to nineteenth-century Alberta Methodist missionary George McDougall, caregiver to many people.

✸

DURING THE EARLY YEARS of the twentieth century, in the village of Eastend, Saskatchewan, near the Cypress Hills coulee where the exhausted NWMP rested in 1874, and later built an outpost cabin, Mary of Canada,

---

*The land goes out like sea at Frenchman's Creek,*

*...*

*Towns are five-masted here and work the sea —*
*Their boats are out, pinned at the dust-wake's head,*
*Fishing for loaves above the sea-wrack and the sea.*

From "Val Marie," by Eli Mandel in *Saskatchewan Harvest*

as usual, was unsurprised by human beings and doings, or by Canadian churches. Framed by American writer Wallace Stegner's early-twentieth-century childhood in Eastend, *Wolf Willow: A History, a Story and a Memory of the Last Plains Frontier* includes the Pastime Theatre where Catholic mass was celebrated for years. Mary of Canada in the Eastend movie theatre may have been bemused by another Canadian Mary as she flickered, silently, in *Stella Maris*, the 1918 movie starring Toronto-born Mary Pickford.

Cloaked Marian-flowers-in-Canada name references in MGM's mountie musical *Rose Marie*, starring Jeanette MacDonald as prima donna "Canada's own Marie de Flor," would appear on screen in 1928.

Expectations of a connection between Canada and the Virgin Mary survive in the Bethel Publishing (Indiana, USA) Christian RCMP series. In Linda Hall's 1995 *August Gamble*, Constable Roberta St. Marie assists Christian Men's Breakfast Club member Corporal Roger Sheppard of the Chester, Alberta detachment fifteen kilometres east of Calgary. The sad-eyed girlfriend of a murdered drug dealer who may or may not have been led to the Lord before his death is Madeline, a name descended from Magdelen, the supposedly former hooker who became penitent Saint Mary Magdelen. Alberta's Madeline Westmier is penitent to the point of wanting to change her name: "She was thinking of Mary or Madonna — Madonna was nice, it was a real name, someone told her. Mothers actually named their daughters Madonna ... She had finally settled on Madonna Juliet — not the rock star Madonna, but the mother and baby. She had a picture in her mind, remembered from some magazine's long-ago December cover, of a sad-eyed young woman shawled in blue and holding a sad-eyed baby."[24]

✼

THE VIRGIN MARY IN EASTEND c. 1914–21 may have been charmed when her earliest Orthodox, or perhaps Coptic Christian, images began cheerfully attending the United Presbyterian Sunday School, borne there in the consciousness of nine children newly come from Syria. Stegner says, "The United Church ... served a collection of Presbyterians, Methodists, Baptists, Lutherans, Congregationalists, Dutch Reformeds, and others, who, like the Syrians, were not denominationally choosy."[25]

Anglican Mary stood steadfast in Eastend, even though Wallace Stegner remembers that, "The Anglicans were a faintly superior group of exclusives, especially after they had a church built for them as a war memorial by the Girls Friendly Society of Huntley, diocese of Chichester, Sussex."[26]

Mary of Canada in the Anglican Church will have known that soon enough, over in Maple Creek, the cowboy town at the other end of the Cypress Hills, she would encounter other British-based challenges to loving your neighbour as yourself.

The British Israelite sect took hold in Maple Creek, Saskatchewan, and many other Canadian communities — Canada's current British Israel addresses are in Toronto and Windsor, Ontario, as well as at the British Israel Church of God in Markham, Ontario — during the 1920s and 1930s. The *Concise Dictionary of Religion* defines British Israelitism as, "a form of fundamentalism, originating in the eighteenth century, which claimed that the English people were the descendants of the ten 'Lost Tribes' of Israel and therefore heirs to all the Biblical promises made in the Bible to the Jewish people."[27]

St. Mary and Geraldine Fitzgibbon Moodie, Anglican granddaughter of Susanna *Roughing It in the Bush* Moodie, wife of distant cousin John Douglas Moodie, RCMP, retired, both lived in Maple Creek. St. Mary worked at the Anglican church named for her, and Geraldine Moodie was one of Canada's earliest female commercial photographers. Donny White, curator at the Medicine Hat museum, prepared *In Search of Geraldine Moodie* as a collection of her wildflower watercolours, along with photographs of 1891–1920s ranch and town scenes, Arctic land and sea images, Plains Indian, Arctic Inuit, RCMP and family portraits, and a biography. White writes, "In her advancing years Geraldine exhibited, as did many of her contemporaries, an avid interest in the popular British Israelite society ... During the 1930s Geraldine embraced the principles of this movement with increasing conviction. Such an interest seems incongruous with a woman who had lived such an adventurous life and who demonstrated such sensitivity to and understanding of her Native and Inuit photographic subjects." The book's endnotes add the information that the British Israelite's covenant with God usually extended to "pronounced imperialist views."[28]

(Not to mention my inability to decide whether to laugh or weep over the haywire scholarship on which British Israelitism is based. For example: Go to the Old Testament. Remove the *I* from Isaac. Add *son*. Sound it out with *Anglo* in front of it. Now you know who God's chosen people are.)

Geraldine Moodie's strongest, most tender photographs are of Canadian Madonnas, Inuit and Plains Indian women whose gaze into the camera lens combines a measured trust in the photographer with a flicker of long, unknowable distance, and whose bodies incline toward the children in their arms or beside them.

Fortunately for Geraldine Moodie and the rest of us, Mary is familiar, and patient, with Canadians' spiritual, cultural, and historical episodes of selective memory. Neither is she fazed by her sometime consignment to fundamentalist Christian footnotes, or even by her absence from our words and thoughts until urgent needs for mercy or consolation surge in people she hasn't heard from in a while, or ever.

Mary of the long memory is unsurprised by changes of heart about outward forms of faith. Three or four centuries of changing political and economic climates in all nonnative Canadians' old countries, along with earthly and divine love, and hard times around the cabin door in the new land, probably underwrote more changes from one denomination's means of remembering Mary to another, or none, than many Canadians expect from their family histories.

But Mary of Canada expects the unexpected, remembers the past, and stays present. Before, during, and after his baptism, most likely in a

Protestant church, that dapper, thirty-something, draftsman-cartographer who sailed for the St. Lawrence River in 1603, and eventually became the father of New France, would have been in her care. No matter his choice, or change, of denomination, Samuel de Champlain counted on Notre-Dame de Recouvrance to help him wrest New France back from the English in 1630–2, and to comfort him when he lay paralyzed and dying in Quebec City in 1635. She was the chief Canadian beneficiary of his will — five hundred livres for altar furniture at the Notre-Dame de Recouvrance chapel, and four hundred livres for masses to be said there for Champlain's soul.

Another man who counted on Notre Dame came from a mostly Presbyterian Scottish–Canadian merchant family secure enough in turn-of-the-nineteenth-century Toronto to figure Timothy Eaton's store would never last. In accord with his dead mother's wishes, young Athol Murray received a liberal arts education at Loyola College with the Jesuits in Montreal, and at Laval University. He left law studies at Toronto's Osgoode Hall to become a priest.

As the new Wilcox, Saskatchewan, parish priest in 1927, Père Murray's faith in *Notre Dame* of the Prairies' goodwill was not small. Her assistance, and Père Murray's energy, showed up in a successful boys' school begun with no money, running water, or central heat (now Athol Murray College of Notre Dame, linked to the University of Ottawa); in a fiercely ecumenical and devoutly spiritual educational mission (soon extended to girls) that included Plato, Martin Luther, and the legendary Notre Dame Hounds (more than one hundred NHL drafts such as Toronto Maple Leafs' goalie Curtis Joseph, and a Hockey Hall of Fame place for Père Murray); and in a tiny bone (sent along to Wilcox, Saskatchewan, by Pope Paul VI) formerly owned by St. Augustine. But these blessings were only the beginning of Père Athol Murray's confidence in the ways of the Mother of God in Saskatchewan.

Even Notre Dame's astonishing library was just an early sign of Notre Dame of the Prairie's blessings. The library, assembled as various heavenly and earthly opportunities came up (for example, old Father Bacchiocci, working in Swift Current via Corsica, France, New Orleans, and Mississipi River mission postings, left his family's medieval manuscripts to Père Murray and Notre Dame; Father Bacchiocci's family tree had a branch named Napoleon Bonaparte), contains a few good books: a 1535 edition of Martin Luther's Bible; *Flowers of the Saints* with Ignatius de Loyola's 1521 margin notes; the 1492 *Nuremburg Chronicle*; and other medieval manuscript treasures.

Not until Notre Dame College's hockey-playing Hounds, classics curriculum, library, and all else at the school had been ordinary miracles for almost fifty years did Père Murray, aged eighty-two, ask Notre Dame of the Prairies for some serious help. He snuffed out a sixty-five-year cigarette habit as his part of the bargain.

Jack Gorman, Père Murray's biographer, explains, "Since the source of the difficulties in the Middle East was a bitter religious conflict ... the solution must be a religious one. Murray had erected a tower in Wilcox, to the one God worshipped by Christians, Moslems, and Jews and he believed that the Middle East needed a visible symbol making the same assertion ... Père began very methodical research of all the implications to the various countries of the Middle East. His plan included personal calls on the heads of state in Saudi Arabia, Jordan, Israel and Iran, as well as the Pope ... No challenge was too large for Athol Murray."[29]

In 1975, Père Murray visited the Vatican to secure Pope Paul VI's blessing for his Middle East plans, then carried on to Riyadh, Saudi Arabia, for an audience with King Faisal Ibn Abdul Rahman Ibn Faisal Al Saud.

Saudi Arabia's King–Prime Minister–Custodian of Two Holy Mosques had enthusiastically approved the idea, Père reported. But King Faisal was assassinated by his nephew shortly after Père Murray returned home to Wilcox, and the plan for Middle East reconciliation never got as far as Jerusalem or Iran.

Worlds ✳ Cause of Our Joy ✳ Comforter of the Afflicted Consolatrix Afflictorum ✳ Domina ✳ Gate of Heaven ✳ Health of the Sick ✳ Help of Christians ✳ Holy Mother of God ✳ H

Notre Dame of the Prairies, Our Lady of grass, wind, and wide sky on the plains, and possibly Père Murray, soon to die, may not have been entirely astonished that the Saskatchewan college's monument to one God would have to do until the Jewish, Christian, Muslim God's older, higher, holy places on the other side of the world could carry both ancient and new, transformative meanings.

A priest who loved Plato as much as hockey, and who studied the shifting, reshaping revelations carried in the history of ideas, may have known the eleventh-century Platonist prayer to Mary: "Whether thou art Ceres, Mother of the Grain, whether thou art Beloved Venus who first united the sexes in Love, Whether thou art Phoebe's sister who aids women in their confinement, whatever thy name, whatever the rite, in whatever form it is permitted to envoke thee, come to help me. Now. Oh, thou holy one, thou perpetual saviour of Mankind, thou dost give a Mother's sweet affection to the wretched and unfortunate."

Mary as Ceres, Mother of the Grain in Saskatchewan, was pleased to know that in the first years of the twenty-first century, Canada supplied most of the pulse crops — lentils, chickpeas, and beans — to mark Ramadan for the world's 1.5 billion Muslims. When the first crescent moon of the ninth lunar month coincides with Canadian harvest, Ramadan's thirty-day dawn-to-dusk fast to heighten spiritual consciousness and awareness of the world's hungry people has been broken by legumes grown within the reach of Notre Dame of the Prairies.

✸

REDEFINING FAITH'S OUTWARD SHAPE, and changing or discarding ways to remember Mary as an inheritance from earth's mother, is ten-thousand-year-old human cultural news that sometimes still strikes fresh in Canada. In "April Fool's," expatriate Saskatchewan poet Myrna Garanis says, "one look at his Mason ring / swiftly aborted the plan for a family tree / suspiciously grafted from Catholic and Protestant fruit …

but how explain the mockery recounting tales / of Catholic neighbours peeling potatoes same pan / their kids had peed in conversely what about / the great grandchildren their odd attraction to / ritual."[30]

Changing names, Mary's or ours, sometimes rearranges ideas about Mary, Mother of Sorrows, Our Lady of Victory, Virgin of Guadalupe, Madonna of the Americas, Notre Dame, Comforter of the Afflicted, and Sainte Marie.

But the Mother of Consolation by any of her names would always have been watching over that nice Quebecois writer boy who changed his name to reinvent himself as a Montana-born cowboy in early-twentieth-century Hollywood. You know who I mean: the famous Canadian writer-artist whose books, paintings, and movies elevated him to duster sainthood, along with Hoppy, Gene, and a cow horse named Smokey. In the 1920s, Maxwell Perkins, Ernest Hemingway's editor, admired the essays, short stories, and novels written by the young man whose 1930 autobiography was titled *Lone Cowboy: My Life Story*. The Lone Cowboy's name was Ernest, too. Sometimes.

Once upon a time, Joseph Ernest Nephtali Dufault (b. 1892), altar boy and restless dreamer from Ste-Nazaire, Quebec, saw Buffalo Bill Cody's Wild West Show in Montreal. Gabriel Dumont wasn't on the bill that night. He had gladly given up shooting blue glass balls out of the air for Buffalo Bill Cody to keep body and soul together after Batoche.

Even if the true, tragic west had been performed in show-ring sawdust soaked with blood in Montreal, Joseph Ernest would likely have boarded the train to Saskatchewan in 1907 anyway. He was packing a ten-dollar bill, a box of cookies, and a pocketful of Wild West mythology.

The tiny shack where the newcomer sometimes stayed between range jobs sits now in Grassland Park near Val Marie, Saskatchewan. One or two gunnysacks smeared with attempts at painted images still hang over barbed wire near the shack in Mary's Valley. The Cypress Hill cowboy memory inheritance of a kid who drew on bunkhouse walls, sometimes with a pencil stub, sometimes with a horse nail, is part of the story.

Sainte Marie noted that the lad's Saskatchewan homestead application was signed W. R. James, a name that would sometimes become William Roderick James, or Clint Jackson, or Stonewall, or just Bill James. The more fittin' cowboy handles belonged to a moving-on western dreamer, drifter, rodeo rider, cattle rustler, prisoner, movie stunt man, artist, and writer. The invented *Lone Cowboy* autobiography, and the 1934 movie made from the book, had him born on the trail in Montana's medicine line — American-Canadian border — country. When his mother (from southern California, some Spanish blood) died, and his father didn't return from a cattle drive to Texas, why, Trapper Jean Beaupré, "a French Canadian from away up in the far Northwest Country," had to take care of the little feller. Seems like Trapper Jean "had a great lot of religion, only his wasn't of the kind where you kneel and pray and donate, while asking for favors. His was silent and came thru his being and senses at what he seen and felt, and from his heart."[31]

Ian Tyson's "Ballad of Will James" says, "Like the coyote who's always lookin' back / He left no trail behind him,"[32] but the same Sainte Marie who was present at baby Joseph Ernest's baptism in the Ste-Nazaire church, and knew his kitchen-table horse drawings as well as his parents and eight older brothers and sisters did, will surely have been there at the hospital in Hollywood. Joseph Ernest Nephtali Dufault, a.k.a. Will James, western best-seller, movie star, much-collected artist, 1927 Newbery Award for Children's Literature winner for *Smoky*, and alcoholic, died in 1942. Sainte Marie, Our Lady of Mercy who had set Gabriel Dumont astride the horse he called "the best courser in Batoche," and made sure he was carrying "Le Petit," his favourite rifle (and ninety cartridges), knew Will James had always been afraid the Western Mythology Industry would name him an imposter if he had ever admitted he was a Catholic boy from Ste-Nazaire. She knew he always wrote home.

✳︎ *Nicaragua: Our Lady of the Immaculate Conception of El Viejo* ✳︎ *Panama: The Immaculate Conception* ✳︎ *Paraguay: Our Lady of the Miracles of Caacupe* ✳︎ *Peru: Our Lady of M*

✳︎

MARY WHO FLOWS AS A RIVER can flood dry, boundaried human structures, overlapping even the construction of names, hers, ours, and the titles of churches and faiths. Like the sign of the cross Helen Fogwill Porter's "dyed-in-the-wool Protestant" grandmother gestured when she tucked her granddaughter into bed, or set her bread to rise, or blessed "anything else that she wanted to turn out right"[33] on the South Side of St. John's, Newfoundland, a sign or submerged memory of Mary, too, sometimes emerges unexpectedly.

In the West  197

**Magnificat**

1. *My soul proclaims the greatness of the Lord,*
2. *my spirit rejoices in God my Saviour;*
3. *for he has looked with favour on his lowly servant.*
4. *From this day all generations will call me blessed;*
5. *the Almighty has done great things for me,*
6. *and holy is his Name.*
7. *He has mercy on those who fear him*
8. *in every generation.*
9. *He has shown the strength of his arm,*
10. *he has scattered the proud in their conceit.*
11. *He has cast down the mighty from their thrones,*
12. *and has lifted up the lowly.*
13. *He has filled the hungry with good things,*
14. *and the rich he has sent away empty.*
15. *He has come to the help of his servant Israel*
16. *for he has remembered his promise of mercy,*
17. *the promise he made to our fathers,*
18. *to Abraham and his children for ever.*

The Zion United Church in Moosejaw, Saskatchewan, opens its ceiling to the heavens with a beautiful circle of light window, cut and shaped as a petalled rose mandala.

The walls and ceiling of the 1930 United Church at Kitseguecla on the Skeena River are decorated with sponge-painted, eight-petalled roses.

There will always be contradictions. Up in the Ontario bush country of Andrew Pyper's *Lost Girls*, in which memory as well as two teenaged girls may have been murdered, the local historian chose to freeze to death in a snowbank outside our Lady of Perpetual Help church, despite "being a die-hard Presbyterian all his life."[34]

Even Duncan Campbell Scott, "son of the manse" and fifty-two years a federal Indian Affairs bureaucrat, could not resist the idea of a Madonna. Scott presided over steadily increasing departmental appropriations and policies shifting from paternalism to oppressions, such as jailing Kwakiutl chiefs for participating in potlatch ceremonies, while he was deputy superintendent general from 1913 to 1932. His "Onandaga Madonna" "stands full-throated and with careless pose / This woman of a weird and waning race / The tragic savage lurking in her face … And closer in the shawl about her breast / The latest promise of her nation's doom."[35]

✸

FROM TIME TO TIME IN CANADA, it may be as well to get used to finding some sign of the Virgin Mary who lives beyond New Testament gospel references where you least expect her. In United Church services? "No," says Reverend Doctor Gordon Turner in his downtown Vancouver office at St. Andrews Wesley United Church, formed in 1927 from St. Andrews Presbyterian and Wesley Methodist as "the Cathedral Church of the United Church of Canada in the great West." "On the whole, not. The *Magnificat* is used at Christmas time, but that's about all."[36]

On the other hand, an image of the Black Madonna of Czestochowa stands on Doctor Turner's desk, causing the traffic noise on Nelson Street to rise into a long, liquid rhythm, and the room to sway.

✸

I AM LOCKED IN MY CABIN, drawing a diagram of the below-decks factory from the sketch in my notebook. My knees are jammed under a plywood table ridged to catch sliding pens and pencils. The Polish ship is rolling heavily offshore. Every time we hauled today, the ramp dipped low into the sea, pouring water on deck as far as my cabin door, then rose until we looked to be hauling a twenty-ton cod end of hake out of the sky. The ragged blue curtain on a rusted ring swings wildly beside my port-hole. The thin twine cord I am making from a chain of cod end knots has come loose from its mooring on the iron leg of my bunk. I am wearing red socks, dirty jeans, a black sweater, and a jacket crusted with hake scales. My hands are stiff from salt water and rockfish spine cuts. The Madonna from Jasna Gora, the Bright Hill in Poland, is bolted to the bulkhead over my bunk. Except for the worn, gold leaf gleam around her head, she looks not unlike a fisherman. Her face is dark; her eyes hooded, mouth impassive. And her cheek is deeply scarred.

✸

ACCOMPANYING THE PRESENCE of Our Lady of the Unexpected in Doctor Turner's United Church office is the mercy of his undisturbed calm during my minutes-long, silent departure into an ocean dream. His long friendship with Henri Nouwen, the Dutch Catholic theologian and internationally known spiritual writer who lived the last decade of his life as pastor at Daybreak, the Toronto L'Arche community founded by Jean Vanier, is also present. "L'Arche is my spiritual home,"[37] Doctor Turner murmurs.

*Line 1. The Greek has the idea of greatness in the verb, not in the object, and the familiar translation "magnify" expressed this: but it is archaic in this sense. The translation "proclaims the greatness" retains the idea of "greatness" though in a different place in the sentence.*

*Lines 3–6. The punctuation has been brought into greater conformity with that which is found in editions of the Greek text.*

*Line 4. from which the "and" has now been omitted, starts a fresh sentence, and the colon at the end of it shows that the verses which follow give the reasons why Mary is called blessed. At the beginning of line 6 "and," which is in the Greek, has been restored; it improves the rhythm, especially for singing.*

*Line 12. The word "lowly" comes from the same Greek root as lowly in line 3. It seems preferable to "humble and meek," both of which appear to have degenerated somewhat in popular usage.*

*Line 14. The rhythm has been improved by the insertion of "he" and a change in the order of words.*

From *Prayers We Have in Common: Agreed Liturgical Texts Prepared by the International Consultation on English Texts*

*Speed on, speed on, good master!*
*The camp lies far away—*
*We must cross the haunted valley*
*Before the close of day.*

*How the snow-blight came upon me*
*I will tell you as we go —*
*The blight of the shadow hunter*
*Who walks the midnight snow.*

*To the cold December heaven*
*Came the pale moon and the stars,*
*As the yellow sun was sinking*
*Behind the purple bars.*

*The snow was deeply drifted*
*Upon the ridges drear*
*That lay for miles between us*
*And the camp for which we steer.*

*'Twas silent on the hillside,*
*And by the solemn wood*
*No sound of life or motion*
*To break the solitude.*

*Save the wailing of the moose-bird*
*With a plaintive note and low,*
*And the skating of the red leaf*
*Upon the frozen snow.*

*And said I, — "Though dark is falling,*
*And far the camp must be,*
*Yet my heart it would be lightsome,*
*If I had but company."*

*And then I sang and shouted,*
*Keeping measure, as I sped,*
*To the harp-twang of the snowshow*
*As it sprang beneath my tread.*

*And said I, — "Though dark is falling*
*And far the camp must be,*
*Yet my heart it would be lightsome,*
*If I had but company."*

The United Church of Canada, by way of Doctor Turner's kindness and wide spirituality, points me toward the trail to Henri Nouwen's meditation on "divine maternal love, marked by grief, desire, hope and endless waiting"[38] in *The Return of the Prodigal Son*, in which prayer is centred on the love alight in Mennonite Rembrandt's portrait of a Jewish father, and to Jean Vanier's *Be Not Afraid*, dedicated, "These pages I give / to Mary / the silent one / compassionate / and loving / who is not afraid to / say 'Yes' to Love."[39] By the time I see a luminescent Marian symbol, courtesy of a New Brunswick Methodist–born prime minister of Canada, in St. Andrew's Wesley United Church chancel window, I am hardly surprised.

In 1935, four months before a broke, hungry, Great Depression–exhausted country voted Conservative Prime Minister R. B. Bennett out of office in favour of Mackenzie King's Liberals, Bennett commissioned William Morris and Company of England to make the stained glass window above the altar at St. Andrew's Wesley in Vancouver in memory of his sister, Evelyn Bennett Coates. The beautiful window scene showing Christ giving the Sermon on the Mount is surmounted by a smaller, softer-looking "Christ in Glory surrounded by seraphs" framed and extended in crimson and amber glass latticed in a rose design after Mary's rose windows at Chartres Cathedral in France. Yes, the Bennett window is on the west wall of the church.

✺

THE VIRGIN MARY was on Wallace Stegner's mind, if not from any teaching emphasized by his Lutheran mother, if not when he attended Presbyterian Sunday School in Eastend, Saskatchewan, then when he included his short story "Genesis" in *Wolf Willow: A History, a Story, and a Memory of the Last Plains Frontier*. Mary is mentioned three times as an apparent necessity for the "Genesis" characters, cowboys based on men Stegner knew from Eastend's dusty streets and Cypress Hills ranches.

Mary is "Holy Mother!" when Rusty Cullen, greenest, youngest, most English cowboy of all the men on the cattle drive, needs to express his astonishment at being inside western adventure, not dreaming it back in England, even if the wind is starting to howl and the blizzard of 1906 is beginning.

Later in "Genesis," when the cowboys must walk, roped together in the snow, following their foreman, who has the look of "that Spirit Hunter, that Walker of the Snow, one of the shapes with which the country deluded frightened men," four lines of verse from Irish immigrant Charles D. Shanly's poem "The Walker of the Snow" float in the text, unattached to Rusty or any of the other men: "Sancta Maria, speed us! / The sun is falling low; / Before us lies the valley / Of the Walker of the Snow!"[40]

"Sancta Maria, speed us!" will appear once more, italicized and alone in the story's text, before the foreman, Rusty, and the other cowboys, frostbitten and half-dead, find shelter in a wolfer's line shack.

In Stegner's story, Sancta Maria of Shanly's "The Walker of the Snow" is invoked for help when winter's cold silence slows, then staggers the cowboys' footsteps, just as the man hurrying through a cold night calls for her in the poem Stegner remembered from his Eastend school days. Sancta Maria is assumed to belong to a Canadian landscape and its people as much as winter does. If the shadow hunter has been produced by the inhumanly wild, cold Canadian land itself, Sancta Maria, too, has a place in the uncontrollable wilderness.

The 1859 poem in which winter is a shadow companion containing the inevitable meaning of easing into sweet rest wrapped in snow, and Mary speeds stumbling footsteps through the cold much as she hurried Gabriel Dumont to the border on horseback, has travelled a range of Canadian landscapes and traditions. Charles Shanly's poem is "based on an Indian legend,"[41] according to Canadian Heritage's Significant Treasures of Ontario notes for William Blair Bruce's 1988 painting *The Phantom Hunter*. William Blair Bruce, whose picture was painted and exhib-

*And then I sang and shouted,
Keeping measure as I sped,
To the harp-twang of the snowshoe
As it sprang beneath my tread.*

*Not far into the valley
Had I dipped upon my way,
When a dusky figure joined me,
In a capuchin of grey.*

*Bending upon the snowshoes
With a long and limber stride;
And I hailed the dusky stranger,
As we travelled side by side.*

*But no token of communion
Gave he by word or look,
And the fear-chill fell upon me
At the crossing of the brook.*

*For I saw by the sickly moonlight,
As I followed, bending low,
That the walking of the stranger
Left no footmarks on the snow.*

*Then the fear chill gathered o'er me,
Like a shroud around me cast,
As I sank upon the snow-drift
Where the shadow hunter passed.*

*And the otter-trappers found me,
Before the break of day,
With my dark hair blanched and whitened
As the snow in which I lay.*

*But they spoke not, as they raised me;
For they knew that in the night
I had seen the shadow hunter,
And had withered in his blight.*

*Sancta Maria speed us!
The sun is falling low,
Before us lies the Valley
Of the Walker of the Snow!*

From "The Walker of the Snow,"
by Charles Dawson Shanly

ited in Paris, wrote home to Hamilton, Ontario, to tell them his painting had been inspired by a poem "from an old Canadian legend."[42] In the nineteenth century, "The Walker of the Snow," was published in the *Atlantic Monthly*, May 1859, in *Songs of the Great Dominion* 1889, and in *A Wreath of Canadian Song* 1910.

By the time Bliss Carman wrote his poem, "The Vengeance of Noel Brassard: A Tale of the Acadian Expulsion," in 1919, the shadow hunter himself, "who prowls those wintry barrens choked with snow," contained a submerged hint of old devotion when "they say he has a word Sweeter than any save the sea."[43]

In 1948, "The Walker of the Snow" was part of *A Pocketful of Canada*, edited by John D. Robins for the Canadian Council of Education for Citizenship, and was included in *Favourite Scary Stories from Graveside Al*, edited by CBC Radio's Alan Maitland in 1996.

The poem that is also a song with shifting words and musical arrangements reappears in *Shadow Hunter*, a recent collection of Irish music, "with pipes and whistles weaving in and out of its lyrical pattern ... echoing a Northern ghost story."[44]

All along its eastern history, "The Walker of the Snow," with a few word changes, had also been the cowboy ballad "Haunted Hunter," probably sung in the Cypress Hills when the North West Mounted Police, settlers, and Mary enclosed in churches were new. "Haunted Hunter," still occasionally recorded, was a campfire and trail song when the west as wild land was gone.

✴

"Oh, give me a jail where I can get bail / And get out of town by tonight / I'll never exchange my home on the range / For all of your cities so bright." By the time the last Metis families lived in Chimney Coulee, home in paradise west had changed. A round of places sheltering people who knew the land and water as well as they knew their bodies had become a fixed address on a straight line.

Sometimes, the coulee's enfolding peace trembles into a thin, distant loneliness older and more embracing than mine. It is still possible to stand quiet in the snow where the Metis chimneys were, not especially wanting a home fire yourself, but imagining the sound of children's laughter along with the smell of wood smoke and stew, and then, the flat, unclaimed odour of accumulating despair.

Any hope of finding my way to Sainte Marie who knew hard winters, wind-taken chapels, and change with the Metis in Chimney Coulee is suddenly gone, or it was never here for me and only my recognition of its absence is sudden. At 49°34′ N Latitude 108°49′ W Longitude, Saskatchewan, the creek purling past me on its long, inland reach to the sea has to be my stream of possibility for moving toward Mary.

✺

THIS LONG, SLOW, SWEET-WATER FALL of creeks and rivers — down the Cypress Hills height of land, south to the Missouri-Mississippi Rivers and the Gulf of Mexico, or northeast along the North and South Saskatchewan River system draining into Hudson Bay's Atlantic Ocean water through Lake Winnipeg and the Nelson River — bears Mary's sea resonance into the current of old sacred meanings that once moved across an inner landscape common to us all. The seashell amulets lying in the earth of three-thousand-year-old Saskatchewan graves also belong in the stream of lasting human spiritual meanings that takes the ocean, and the colour red, and the west into its flow.

The old, old reasons for red, the universal colour of life that had stained Atlantic coast Beothuk lives and burials rests in the red ochre–marked bones lying in the oldest western plains graves, too, as well as in the Virgin Mary's earlier dress colours. The red clothing Mary wore

*It had been promised in books that if I*
*were good*
*and prayed to the right gods I would*
*find my heart*
*netted in blue pacific light, but I'm*
*perched*
*unsteadily on spindly doubts and*
*can't run.*
*They call me bitter tears, Mary means,*

*without the trace of the sea I hear in*
*Maria like a shell.*
*Only the salt of that forgotten ocean's*
*biography*
*remains a relic of powdered bone,*
*chalk white,*
*Saint Sea who still can make the earth's*
*eyes here moist ...*

From "The Moon and the Salt Flats,"
by Mary di Michele

hundreds of years ago in Titian, Piero della Francesca, and Fra Angelico paintings reappears in the mass-produced reproduction of a probably Eastern European Madonna at the centre of a small townhouse shrine in Eastend, Saskatchewan, and in hand-sized, glossy paper contemporary pictures of *Virgen Maria Auxiliadora*.

The Basque sailors and fishermen who lie in Red Bay, Labrador's cemetery, with their skulls set west, were followed by countrymen who entered the Cypress Hills as cowboys and ranchers like Michael Oxarat, who named his Battle Creek ranch the Pyrenees. But the ones who tenderly turned west the heads of three adults and two small children placed in the earth under Saskatchewan's Bracken Cairn three thousand years ago knew that West as paradise was farther yet. So did Stan Rogers when he sang on his *Home in Halifax* album, "the same ancient fever in the Isles of the Blest / That our fathers brought with them when they 'went West.'"[45]

Ideas of west as a mythical place where souls and bodies could be healed survive in the movies. Johnny Depp knows this. He learned from Gary Farmer, the Canadian actor born on the Ontario Six Nations Reserve who plays Nobody in Jim Jarmusch's 1995 film *Dead Man*. Nobody is a Plains Indian man captured as a child by English soldiers, exhibited in a cage in Toronto, and regularly punished in England until he learned to read William Blake's poetry. Long since escaped to return to a west resembling the Cypress Hills — wolfers, fur and whisky traders, and all — Nobody has to deliver Johnny Depp, a.k.a. Bill Blake, eastern city innocent gone wrong in frontier chaos; a.k.a. William Blake, long-dead poet, back to the spirit realm. He must bear bullet-wounded Bill-William farther west, floating as much as paddling down an easy-riding Columbia or Fraser River until a luxuriously green rain forest enfolds them, then opens to the Pacific Ocean that will receive the dying man like a mother.

*Queen of All Saints ✱ Queen of Confessors ✱ Queen Conceived Without Original Sin ✱ Queen of Families ✱ Queen of Heaven ✱ Queen of Martyrs ✱ Queen of Patriarchs ✱ Que*

✱

The western plains hold pieces of other mythologies. Part of the old goddess of northern paradise story turns real in the entirely nonmetaphorical world of Canadian forage crops. A certain Queen of the World who wore Mary's moon on her forehead when she lived beyond the icebergs on the other side of seven Caucausus mountain ranges in Black Sea tales has recently arranged for Kura clover seed from her legendary orchard garden land to flourish as the west's newest, hardiest forage. Rooted sixty centimetres deep, fiercely winter-hardy Kura clover is named for its homeland by the Kura River in the Caucasus Mountains, east of the Black Sea.

✱

If I still want Chimney Coulee to be a shrine dedicated to home places in a western, once-promised land, I need a litany composed from the French and Latin flowing, filtering root verbs that made the word *coulee*. *Couler* and *colare* are the incantations for streaming around the modern meaning of home, softening its static, straight edges, filtering and straining its grit, reshaping the idea of home to fit its earlier forms again.

Chant *couler, colare* for home in the body as a flesh and bone frame holding life, and for homes only incompletely remembered in moving water. Chant *couler, colare* for home ground in dry land hills that once were islands, and for gently sloped sanctuary at Chimney Coulee.

✱

Prayers for home were made at another western shrine in another coulee, once. A passenger on a moored river steamer with a billiard table and a Gatling gun among its cargo wandered away from the boat, and found the shrine. The river was the South Saskatchewan. The steamboat was the *Northcote*, waiting for General Middleton's troops to board after the Battle of Batoche in 1885. The shrine was an image of Christ pinned to a poplar tree with a tin snap from a plug tobacco box. The poplar tree stood in the coulee where the Metis had gathered daily to meet with Louis Riel during the four-day battle. While the Canadian forces' borrowed Gatling gun, a recent invention firing twelve hundred theoretical bullets a minute, was being tested, a paper image of the Virgin sewn to a cotton banner had flown protection over one Metis meeting house. The new gun was otherwise effective. The billiard table was Gabriel Dumont's, taken from his house upriver at Gabriel's Crossing before all the farm buildings were burned. He never saw it again.

George Woodcock's biography of Gabriel Dumont reports that he said he felt protected on his eleven-night ride into exile across the Montana border, "And I never failed to say to the Holy Virgin: 'You are my mother! Guide me!'"[46] Safely across, Gabriel Dumont knelt to say the rosary in thanks.

✳

"Gabriel's Crossing. One Scow, the Best on the River. The public promptly attended to. May, 1980" were the words on Gabriel Dumont's sign set up on the south branch of the Saskatchewan River system running east with a washload of plains silt into Lake Winnipeg. But for Gabriel, named after the angel who brought Mary news of her annunciation as Mother of God; for Gabriel who slit the coat from a Cree scout's back, then left his own jacket over the man's shoulders to prove he could have killed him, and hadn't; for Gabriel who lies on the hill at Batoche, Saskatchewan, still thinking about Louis Riel's wild eyes, and for Louis, who had written his mother from Regina prison consigning her to Mary's care before he brushed his hair, put on brown pants, a short black jacket, and moccasins, and walked down the hall to be hanged for treason; for Gabriel Dumont and Louis Riel, the Red River in Manitoba runs by the Metis Mary of Canada they trusted.

✺

TAKE THE NO. 62 ST. NORBERT BUS from the Eaton Place stop in downtown Winnipeg. Get off half an hour away at the corner of Avenue de L'Église and St. Pierre, across from the parish church. The Metis wayside shrine to Notre-Dame-du-Bon-Secours is near the bus stop, next to the house with the screened side porch and the basketball hoop out back. The shrine is open to the street, but the neighbourhood noise of power saws and bike-riding children never bothers Our Lady of Good Help. She stands at ease here in a blue cloak and sash beside the ex voto sign for Chapelle du Bon Secours: "Elevated here by the Most Reverend Joseph Noel Ritchot in honour of our blessed Virgin Mary for her very special protection granted during the political troubles of 1869–70."

The chapel is in good repair. The nineteenth-century arched ceiling panels showing translucent coloured scenes of Mary's Biblical life are still in place. One of the eleven blue-glass stars on the back wall is broken, but today there is no sign of the desperate need that caused Metis people from the Red River farms to plead for Mary's help in 1869. The bright, clean shrine contains no reminder of the barricade on the Pembina Trail, built and defended in fear of newcomers who wanted Metis land during "the political troubles," a.k.a. the Red River Rebellion and Louis Riel's provisional government.

The good help Mary gave in 1869–70 provided the inclusion of Metis land grants and language rights in the Manitoba Act when the new province joined Confederation in 1870, but Metis despair and the Northwest Rebellion rose again in the Saskatchewan Valley in 1885. Louis Riel wrote to his mother, Julie Lagimodière Riel, from Regina prison, assuring her that she had been good to him, that he would be brave at the gallows, and that he prayed her beseechings on his behalf would ascend to Jesus

Christ, Mary, and Saint Joseph, "my good protector." Before his body was taken to St. Boniface, the Red River community in eastern Winnipeg where he was born, Requiem mass was given in St. Mary's Regina church. In *Strange Empire: A Narrative of the Northwest,* Joseph Kinsey Howard says, "The church was full; many who knelt in its pews were Protestants and leading citizens of Regina, and they gave reverent attention to the service."[47] Howard also reports that Louis Riel's moccasins were missing.

The only other visitor to the Metis shrine is an elderly East Indian woman with a red dot on her forehead. She kneels long minutes near to Mary, leaves flowers on the altar, and walks stiffly back to the car where someone is keeping the motor running.

A small heap of dried mud and grass is scattered on the chapel floor. Late in the afternoon, two swallows check the broken nest for an instant, ignore the rain-stained four of diamonds lying next to the fragments, and swoop up to the new nest and its hungry occupants hanging near Mary's head. The swallow was sacred long before it became the Madonna's bird, allowed to fly and nest within the great temples at Athens and Ephesus, and believed to migrate to the moon. At Calvary, the swallow tried to fly away with the nails, and, in Russian tales, fluttered around the cross, crying, *Umer, Umer,* He is dead, to persuade Christ's torturers to cease. In Scandinavian countries, the swallow is the Bird of Consolation, who cries, *Svale, Svale,* Console Him, on Mary's behalf.

Mary, Our Lady of Good Help in St. Norbert, looks out her open door toward the Red River, running at peace right now below the dikes. But this Mary's firm mouth implies she knows full well nothing stays the same forever. The waters will rise again. Only a splash of what might be river mud on her skirt suggests the spring 1997 Red River flood, but before that, the river almost destroyed the Earl of Selkirk's Red River Colony on the Red and Assiniboine Rivers in 1826, and drove a hundred thousand people from their homes in 1950.

Mary knows water, as well as other matter, changes form. The river the Cree called *Miscousipi,* Red Water River, from the colour seeping in its deep clay trench, flowed south, not north, before the last glacier receded. A minute or two ago in geological time, the continental divide slid some way south to turn the Red River north into Manitoba. The Red River and its receiving Lake Winnipeg are left over from Lake Agassiz, the glacial lake that used to cover much of Manitoba, northwest Ontario, and parts of eastern Saskatchewan, North Dakota, and northwest Minnesota. Before rivers and lakes, before the ice, Manitoba lay undersea. Lamp shell and sea lily fossils star the marine limestone at Stony Plain, Manitoba.

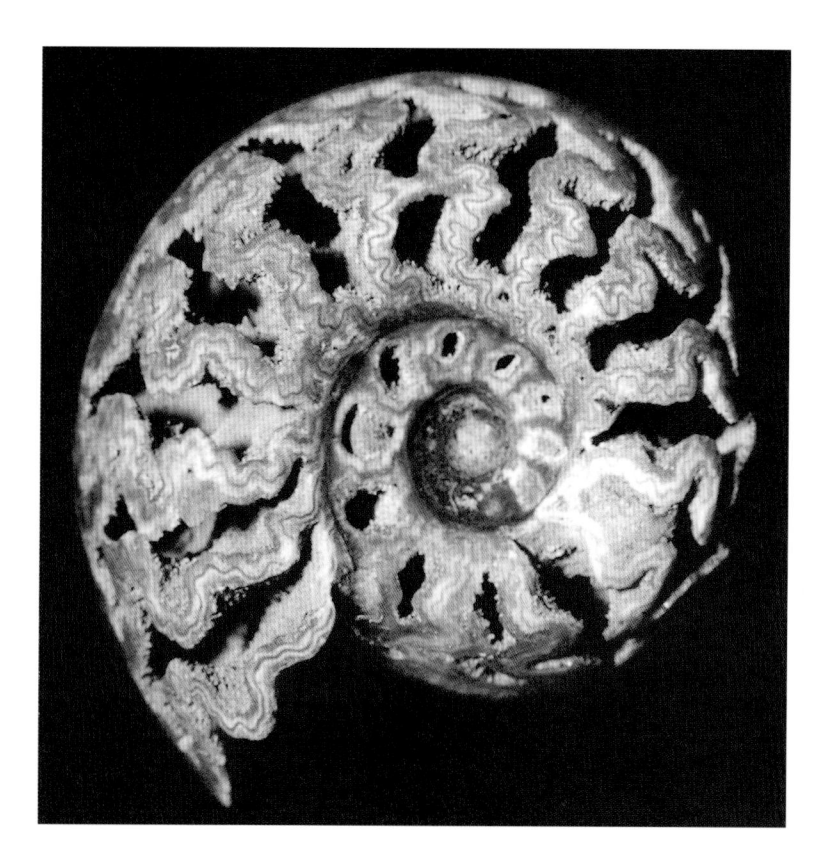

More than river courses and water forms show signs of change here. Mary of Canada who knows single mothers and city streets, and who is

*Kateri, lily of purity, pray for us.*
*Kateri, consoler of the heart of Jesus, pray for us.*
*Kateri, bright light for all Indians, pray for us.*
*Kateri, courage of the afflicted, pray for us.*
*Kateri, lover of the cross of Jesus, pray for us.*
*Kateri, flower of fortitude for the persecuted, pray for us.*
*Kateri, unshakeable in temptations, pray for us.*
*Kateri, full of patience in suffering, pray for us.*
*Kateri, keeper of your virginity in persecutions, pray for us.*
*Kateri, leader of many Indians to the true faith through your love for Mary, pray for us.*

*Kateri, who loved Jesus in the Blessed Sacrament, pray for us.*
*Kateri, lover of penance, pray for us.*
*Kateri, who travelled many miles to learn the faith, pray for us.*
*Kateri, steadfast in all prayer, pray for us.*
*Kateri, who loved to pray the rosary for all people, pray for us.*
*Kateri, example to your people in all virtues, pray for us.*
*Kateri, humble servant to the sick, pray for us.*
*Kateri, who by your love of humility, gave joy to the angels, pray for us.*
*Kateri, your holy death gave strength to all Indians to love Jesus and Mary, pray for us.*
*Kateri, whose scarred face in life became beautiful after death, pray for us.*

present today in the Winnipeg native people's parish named for the Blessed Kateri Tekakwitha, Lily of the Mohawk (1656–80), is very different from the Virgin whom Kateri — Katherine — Tekakwitha was shown at St. Frances Xavier Jesuit mission on the St. Lawrence River.

Even before Montreal voyageurs set out to bear Sainte Marie into the west, the Virgin Kateri Tekakwitha knew as a rigidly defined Mary Immaculate was being re-envisioned as a faithful disciple and teacher in Christ's first church by a practical, loving woman who saw the needs of ordinary people in the city then called Ville-Marie. Marguerite Bourgeoys, founder of the Congregation de Notre Dame, one of the first uncloistered religious communities of women in the Catholic Church, was social worker, teacher, counsellor, and friend to the working people of Ville-Marie, soon to be known as Montreal, between 1657 and 1700. She was made a saint in 1982.

The twenty-four-year-old Turtle clan Mohawk girl, bird-boned from fasting and weakened by self-imposed penances when she died at the mission's chapel door April 17, 1680, is the first native North American to be declared Blessed, and is patron of the environment and ecology. The scars smallpox had given Kateri Tekakwitha in childhood seemed to fade from her face after death. Memories of her gentleness, sometimes an image of her presence, have carried a healing capacity for some visitors to the shrine of Kateri on Mohawk land at Kahnawake, Quebec.

✳

MARY OF MANY CHANGES in Canada doesn't mind that she and Kateri and their sister, Edith, share the woman's role in Leonard Cohen's *Beautiful Losers*. She doesn't even mind that he caught Edith and her lover injecting themselves with liquid from "Perpetual Lourdes Water Ampoules ... and Tekakwitha's Spring,"[48] rather than heroin.

She knows she'll be a mother again in "When Mary the Mother Kissed the Child" — "When Mary the Mother gave of her breast / To the poor inn's latest and lowliest guest / The God born out of the woman's side"[49] by Charles G. D. Roberts; "Mary Tired" — "Through the starred Judean night / She went, in travail of the Light. / With the earliest hush she saw / God beside her in the straw"[50] by Marjorie Pickthall; and in Jay Macpherson's "The Natural Mother."

*Lamb of God, who takes away the sins of the world, spare us, O Lord.*
*Lamb of God, who takes away the sins of the world, graciously hear us, O Lord.*
*Lamb of God, who takes away the sins of the world, have mercy on us.*

*O Jesus, who gave Kateri to the Indians as an example of purity, teach all men to love purity, and to console your immaculate Mother Mary through the lily, Kateri Tekakwitha, and your Holy Cross, Amen.*

*O Jesus, who gave Kateri to the Indians as an example of purity, teach all men to love purity, and to console your immaculate Mother Mary through the lily, Kateri Tekakwitha, and your Holy Cross, Amen.*

*Kateri Tekakwitha, pray for us.*

From the *Litany of Kateri Tekakwitha*

When Mary the Mother gave of her
    breast
To the poor inn's latest and lowliest
    guest
The God born out of the woman's
    side
    …

From "When Mary the Mother Kissed
the Child," by Charles G. D. Roberts


Through the starred Judean night
She went, in travail of the Light.
With the earliest hush she saw
God beside her in the straw …

From "Mary Tired,"
by Marjorie Pickthall


All the soft moon bends over,
All circled in her arm,
All that her blue folds cover,
Sleeps shadowed, safe and warm …

From "The Natural Mother,"
by Jay Macpherson

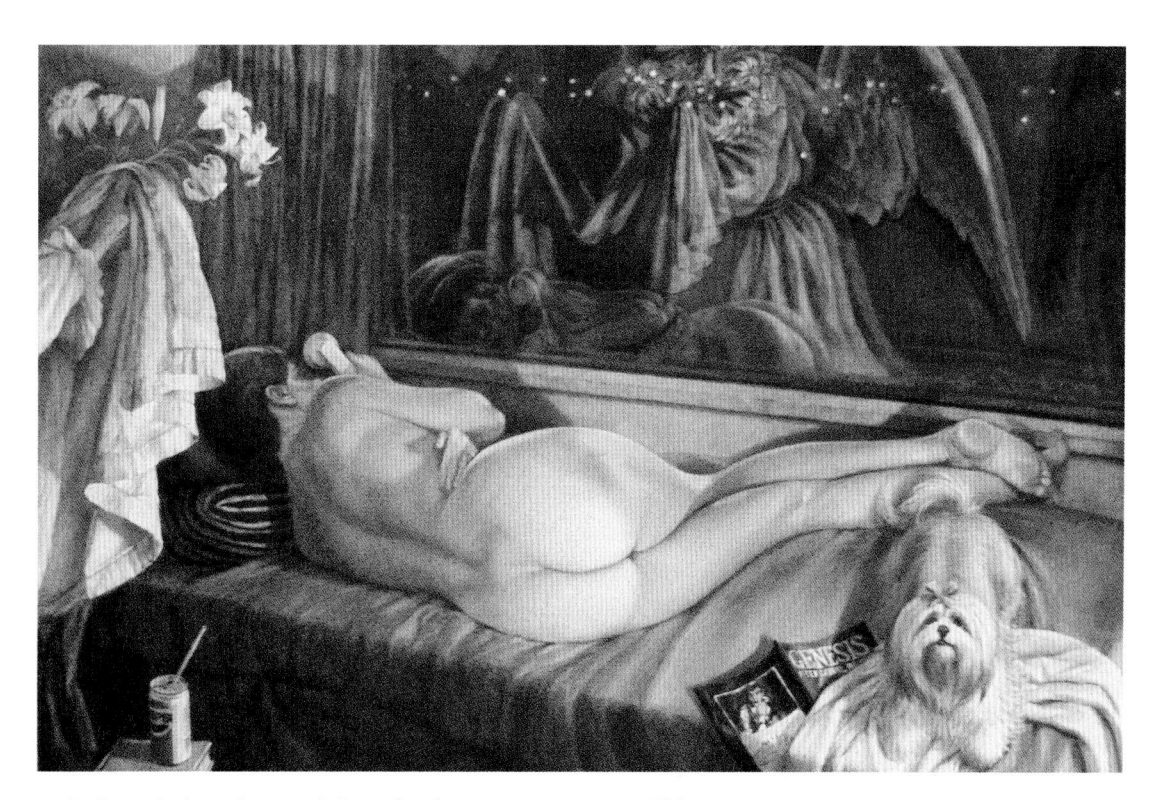

Risk, including the possibility of ordinariness, may attend Mary. She knows we smile, except sometimes in the dark, about the serenely incandescent, white-plastic-robed Virgin Mary night light with the four watt bulb, $1.50 plus GST and PST. Perhaps she smiles to see herself in the Winnipeg phone book, listed with Catholic schools and a cathedral, an Anglican church, a Montessori school, garden centre, dry cleaners, car wash, gas station, and St. Mary's Polish National Catholic Church. She endures being "a simpering puce-mouthed Madonna"[51] in a living room belonging to Rachel Cameron's insistently nice, determinedly Protestant-in-good-taste mother over in Manawaka, Manitoba, in Margaret Laurence's *A Jest of God*.

Winnipeg artist Richard Williams knows a Mary of Canada whose changes have only brought her closer to us. Williams's artist's state-

"Good morning, my great angel
   Gabriel, But you look so sad!"

"Dear God, there's a reason for it.
You remember that you sent me
   to Mary.
Well, I just came back from Nazareth."

"Yes, and what?"

"Mary said 'no.'"

       ...

"Dear God, I had never talked to a
   woman before,
So, last week, I went to earth looking
   for advice.
I met some politicians and religious
   leaders,
And I asked them how they manage
To make people do what they want
   them to do."

"Yes, I know how these people operate.
Gabriel, Mary is a woman of faith,
and there's no need to bribe or
   manipulate her.
Gabriel, I'm sure she has forgiven you.
Wait a month or so, go and talk to
   her again, with respect."

Gabriel followed God's advice, and
   Mary answered:

"I accept the offer."

From "Annunciation," *Here I Sit*,
René Fumoleau, O.M.I.

---

ment for his *Mary Had a Dream* exhibit of contemporary Annunciation drawings and paintings emphasizes her nearness: "My Mary has been removed from a distant past and is shown in the here and now. She is as human as we are, and dreams of better times. Listening to the promise of an angel, she agrees to risk everything in order to help reinvent her world." Williams says his Marys, who are sometimes short-haired, often naked or vulnerable in a torn cloak, and occasionally have a Pepsi (the drink for a new generation), "should not be confused with religious icons ... They try to dismantle the bloodless image underlying the visceral polemics of gender politics. Ancient hatreds may threaten her, but enduring love, generosity of spirit, faith, hope and forgiveness are at the heart of the story."[52]

This Mary of Canada was there in the pub at the hotel on Main Street in the north end of Winnipeg, I thought. She was listening to the man from Conne River near Bay d'Espoir, Newfoundland telling me he was looking for the Virgin Mary, too. "She's about twenty-nine," he said. "She's supposed to be out tonight. Bartender over at the McLaren — he keeps an eye out for her, too — he gave me a call, said she was in there, but she was gone by the time I got down there."

In time, alternating slow speech, pauses, and hurried words, the Conne River man, part Mi'kmaq, told this Mary's story. Hugeness and pain in the night. Pink dresses and new sweaters to reward an eight-, then nine- and ten- and eleven-year-old girl. Sometimes money, sometimes Mae West pies, soft, round, and sweet in cellophane, in return for silence. Now, other rewards from strangers.

"She tries," he said, "for weeks, she tries, but she can't keep out of the life." He looked across the table then. "I tell her," he said, "but she doesn't believe. I tell her she's still the virgin Mary. It was taken away from her. She never gave it up. She's still the virgin Mary."

The Mary who is country-born in Canada makes courage and consolation possible. Notre-Dame-du-Bon-Secours and Our Lady of

Perpetual Help in Winnipeg; Our Lady of Light in the Arctic; Our Lady of Good Counsel in Toronto; and all the Ladies of Help, Sorrow, Mercy, Compassion, Capes, Highways, and Refuges of the Canadian east, west, and northern coasts, and the earth between would do no less.

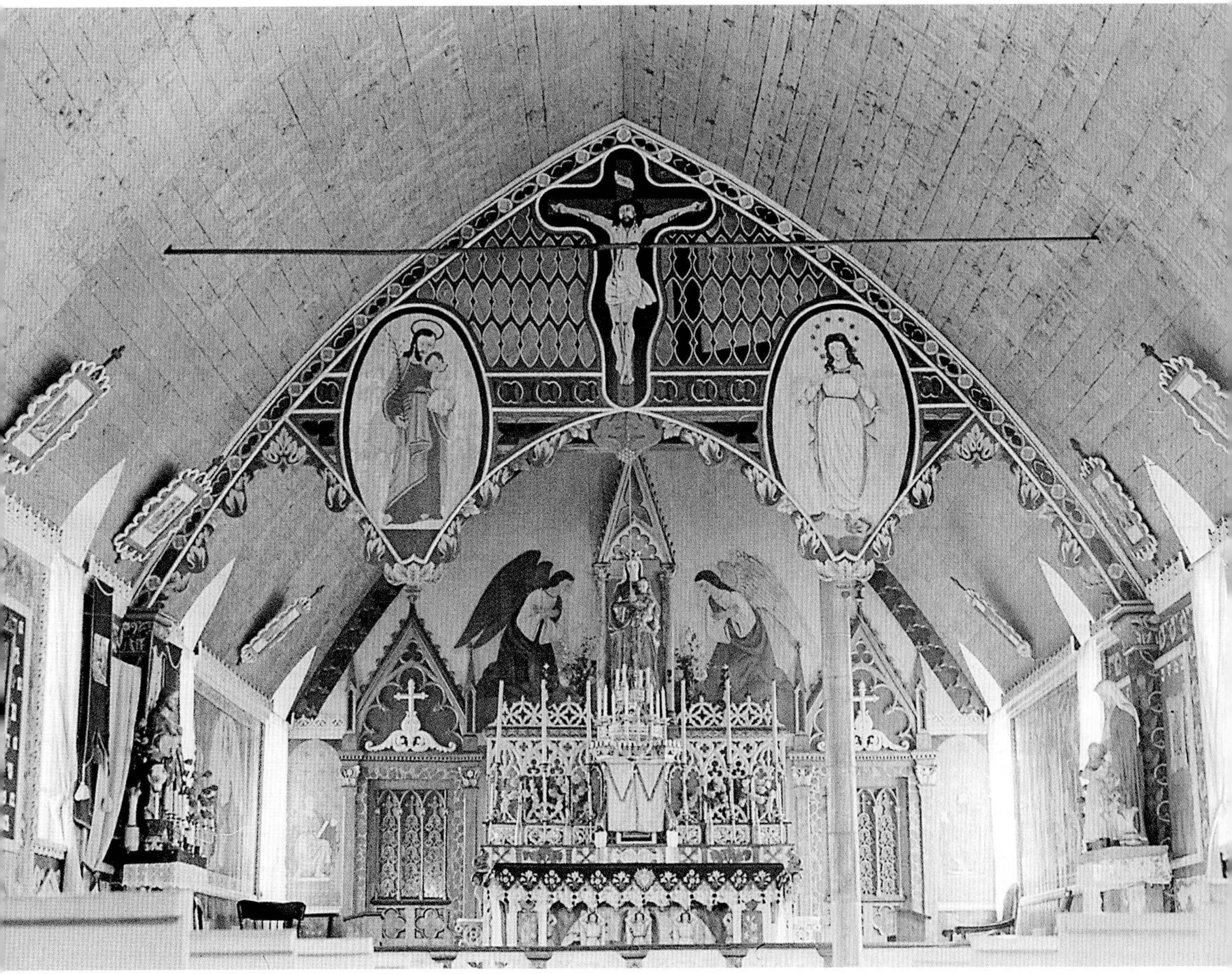

## CHAPTER 7 — *Roads*

I CROSSED SOME DRY GROUND IN SEARCH OF MARY IN CANADA. LOOKING FOR OUR LADY'S HOPE, MERCY, AND GOOD COUNSEL SOMETIMES TURNED UP ONLY MY OWN WEARINESS AND DISAPPOINTMENT.

✴

BY THE TIME I GET OUT OF THE CAR AT OUR LADY OF GOOD HOPE CHURCH ON A DUSTY ROAD AT THE EDGE OF STUART LAKE IN FORT ST. JAMES, BRITISH COLUMBIA, I'M RUNNING ON EMPTY. NOT THE GAS TANK.

My recovery from the belief that running low on gas teaches the car self-discipline, and that the fuel gauge responds to either accusations of duplicity or encouraging words is some years along by now.

Not the belly. Twelve green grapes not yet turned to wine in the summer heat, and the last emergency protein brazil nut, are waiting on the passenger side.

Not even the mind. I still remember that the new church on the Fort St. James Dakelh reserve is Our Lady of the Snows, and that Rudyard Kipling called all of Canada "Our Lady of the Snows" after he visited Quebec City in winter.

The empty vessel here is my heart. My willingness to keep on looking for Mary in Canada has run dry, even though the idea of Canada's Ladies of Good Hope and Help and Light standing by on the edge of the bush or the ice has sustained me against despair through other hard passages during the journey.

✸

Stuart Lake has known Mary, at first as Sainte Marie, since 1805 when North West Company partner Simon Fraser, searching out new fur-trading opportunities, rounded Leon's Point with his voyageurs, who were singing, and a Beaver Indian interpreter, to mark a site for next year's Stuart Lake Post. Sainte Marie was here with Jean Baptiste Boucher, a Red River Metis man who worked at the new post, and while Metis freighters moved furs and trade goods in and out of the lake the hard way, by canoe and barge brigade from McLeod Lake through the Parsnip River, then the harder way, by packhorse train up from Fort Vancouver on the Columbia River.

In winter 1871, when Oblates of Mary Immaculate priests were beginning their work here, Carrier people visiting the mission for Christmas began falling trees across the lake, then hand-skidding logs over the ice to build Our Lady of Good Hope church. One log in the morning, another in the afternoon. Men and women hauling with one-inch ropes. They had already cut trees, pulled stumps, and cleared slash from the land the priests had chosen next to the Hudson's Bay Company post's acreage.

Beams and boards for the church were cut on a sawmill that had been abandoned up on Manson Creek when the Omineca gold rush dimmed, then carried in pieces on pack horses down to the Hudson's Bay fort. Church labour, which went on for years, was unpaid, performed as an offering to the new faith. Beaver, muskrat, lynx, marten, silver and red fox, and other furs were donated to buy bells. Stuart Lake native men cut six hundred cedar shakes apiece for the roof, and Carrier carpenters whose names were recorded in church documents only as "Simon" and "Billy" finished the interior.

The red stained-glass squares, sun-soaked ruby this afternoon, were likely set into the windows some years later. Father Adrien Gabriel Morice, the Oblates of Mary Immaculate priest who had been posted to Stuart Lake in 1885, required Chief Louis Billy Prince, and a man named Fort George Seymour to build the elegantly narrow steeple in 1905. The large globe and beautifully chamfered — bevelled-edge — cross pasted against a bright blue sky was carved by Benoit Prince that same year.

❋

GABRIEL DUMONT WAS CALLED Prince of the Prairies, and contemporary Princes across northern Canada are descendants of Indian trappers and hunters whose skills, strength, and leadership fur traders needed so much they named each of them the "Prince." Princes from Fort St. James and other northern places fought in both world wars, and Winnipeg's Tommy Prince (deceased) is Canada's most decorated native soldier. "Principal hunter" Dick Prince, whose staunch nobility I counted on when I was a child reading R. M. Ballantyne's fur-trade adventure novel, *Ungava*, was closely modelled on real men.

*Lady of Copacabana* ✶ *Brazil: Our Lady of Aparacida* ✶ *Chile: Our Lady of Carmel of the Maipu* ✶ *Columbia: Our Lady of Chiquinquira* ✶ *Costa Rica: Our Lady of the Angels* ✶

✶

AND ROSE PRINCE, gentle always, her body said to be still sweet in a grave made when she died of tuberculosis in 1949, is now attended by pilgrims at the old Lejaq Residential School site on the shore of Fraser Lake, west of Fort St. James in British Columbia. On a quiet day toward fall at Lejaq, it is possible to lie down in the tent near Rose's grave, and see the round sky world through the smoke hole at the height of the tent poles. Within reach of your hand will be the low curved arch of the tent's entrance, a mouth opening into this small container of restfulness, and out into the field, and the lake beyond it.

220   MARY OF CANADA

✹

OUR LADY OF GOOD HOPE'S 130-year-old building on Stuart Lake looks as sturdy as it does in nineteenth-century photographs. The log walls under the siding will last the length of time that passes for forever in British Columbia. Another hundred years. A handwritten sign announces masses for summer months.

Behind the church, the padlocked shed veiled in blackberry branches and alder shoots leans, but still holds. Father Morice's printing press is in the shed, according to one Fort St. James story, or deep in the lake, by another tale. On *abebooks.com*, a bookseller, who was advertising a first edition of A. G. Morice, O.M.I.'s *A Critical History of the Red River Insurrection*, posts: "On a visit some years ago to Fort St. James ... where Morice printed his Carrier and Dene vocabulary, I was appalled to learn that his press had found new life as a boat anchor in the lake facing the town."[1]

Father Adrien Gabriel Morice himself, forced into retirement in Winnipeg from 1908 until his death in 1938, estranged from his order and enclosed within his own authoritarian egotism, vanity, and increasing anti-Semitism, still endlessly publishing books and articles on Dene and Inuit ethnography and linguistics in Canadian, American, and French academic journals, insisted the freighters had smashed his press. Deliberately.

Twenty years ago, when I worked for Fisheries Canada and Prince Rupert's Museum of Northern British Columbia on the Skeena, Nass, and Bulkley Rivers and in their communities, Father Morice was a vague historical figure with heroic possibilities because he had published so much while he worked full time. In my blurred, hopeful imagination, he tramped ahead of me along creeks, a sturdy, black-robed man mapping rivers and ground I knew. He, too, struggled along snowed trails between Fort Babine and Kispiox, maybe, or lurched in wet boots on other hard paths, always keeping enough energy to make notes at the end of a full day's work, being a priest of the order of Oblates Mary Immaculate in still-wild country.

But today, David Mulhall's *The Will to Power*, a Morice biography stowed in the car trunk, and Parks Canada's archives at the restored Hudson's Bay fort along the shore from Our Lady of Good Hope church on Stuart Lake, provide a portrait with no heroic edges.

Mulhall's book, as well as other biographical material based on archival sources rather than on the laudatory "biography" Morice himself wrote under a false name, reveal that his devotion, perhaps clinical obsession, was centred not on his faith, or the Dakelh people, but on his printing press, his international scholarly reputation, and his need for power over others.

No written evidence or oral history indicates that Father Morice, Oblate Order of Mary Immaculate, held a particular place in heart, mind, or spirit for Mary, or any other part of his faith.

Father Morice's mission career in northwestern British Columbia is documented by his frequent use of the lash without the protective blanket, public confession, collective penances, and other extremities — including denial of the sacraments — to enforce the already disturbing (Bishop) "Durieu system" described in *The Will to Power*: "The Oblates appointed Catholic chiefs, captains, and watchmen. The captain was the chief's deputy, and he usually administered the frequent whippings meted out as a form of public penance. The watchmen were spies and policemen who detected and apprehended suspected sinners ... Durieu wanted these Indian aides to help the Oblates to uproot native spirituality and to sow in its place the seeds of Catholicism."[2]

Morice's subjugation of fellow Oblates, and his rebellion against the Order's superiors are documented from France to Fort Babine. Fits of temper, degradation of the Mass, missing money, and machination of fur-trade business were rooted in his need to make the nineteenth-century international academic world aware of his brilliance as an Americanist scholar, and to control his own New World wilderness kingdom.

✸

IN FRONT OF Our Lady of Good Hope's church on the edge of Stuart Lake, look up at the spire now, winding the perfection of its decorative diamonds, stars, and arches into the afternoon sky. Remember Father Blanchet, frail, elderly, leaving the mission door open as he lay on his bed so village elders could enter his room to smoke a pipe with him of an evening. Remember, he was a good carpenter known as "Our dear grandfather" in Fort St. James. Remember that almost all of the mission dishes he lent out for Dakelh feasts were returned, no matter what Father Morice shouted.

✸

ON THE ROADS out of Fort St. James to Highway 16 east awhile, then north, runs more than enough time for me to consider the restlessness growing in my arid interior ground, separating me from any chance of Our Lady of Good Hope. Driving hour after hour into long summer light through an evening lasting near to midnight fails to cool my whiteline fever. Towns, lakes, rivers, and hundreds of kilometres of jack pine and smallish black spruce said to be standing north of Prince George must be flying past the car while I notice only hot wind streaming through the windows, and the fact that I am a pilgrim with no shrine but the road.

Still, goin' ninety I ain't scarey 'cuz I got the Virgin Mary. Except Our Lady of the Highway, tiny on her round metal base, is not so happy on the road, after all. Either she liked the steady shelf life back at the Marian Distributing Centre in Vancouver, surrounded by hundreds of small blue-scarfed Marys dressed mostly in white, occasionally apricot, once a pale raspberry colour, better than escaping from it out here with me, or she needs a stronger magnet. Maybe she would prefer glue. I could use some myself. Always been a bit of a petroleum distillate fan. Mental note, Joan. Don't buy glue.

Parking Virgins and keychain Madonnas ride along in some cars. Mary seems determined to drive. Washington State Police Officer Chico Rodriquez saw her on the road sign at the intersection of Route 241 and the Yakima Valley Highway, and she showed herself a while ago on the rear fender, driver's side of Dario Mendoza's 1981 maroon Chev Camaro in Elsa, Texas.

When the sky is dark enough that my headlights pit-lamp deer eyes into incandescent green globes, the only highway company is the occasional semi-trailer pushing south, and Tom Waits growling, "Hang on Saint Christopher on the passenger side."[3]

❋

SAINT CHRISTOPHER is patron saint of all wayfarers and, nowadays, of drivers. He was a third-century muscleman wanting to serve a mighty master, and disappointed in the powers of both Satan and the local king. Like Gabriel Dumont on the South Saskatchewan, he took to working as a river ferryman. The saint-to-be lived alone by the ford, keeping an eye out for Christ, until the day he staggered under the steadily increasing weight of a child he was carrying across the river. "No wonder," said the child. "You have been bearing the weight of the world. I am the Christ you seek." Christopher, named as the Christ-bearer, was put to death for his faith, but still keeps watch over all travellers.

❋

CHRISTOPHER SHOULD BE STANDING facing forward on my dashboard. Someone in better shape than me, even if only a miniature, magnetized saint, needs to watch the highway in the dark. I'm watching for the sea. Inland, alone at night, I get to expecting it over the next rise.

A familiar, unspoken litany rolls time with the tires' scratched rhythm on the road: I was never this hopeless at sea. Or so tired.

The sea absorbs disorderly human pain. Materia Piper in Ann-Marie MacDonald's *Fall on Your Knees* knew this. When she has become as a stranger in the country of marriage and motherhood, when Our Lady of the Immaculate Conception can't hear her, Materia goes to the sea: "She faced the horizon and listened until she heard what the sea was saying to her: 'Give it to me, my daughter. And I will take it and wash it and carry it to a far country until it is no longer your sin; but just a curiosity adrift, beached and made innocent.'"[4]

Land isn't all it's cracked up to be. Whatever road I travel never finishes the need I'm already building for the next journey.

✳

Some travellers in Canada and other places have restlessness and the need for change that feeds it down to an art. Romani *drom* is the unending road of the *Roma*, nowadays not-so-often called Gypsies, an English word first recorded in 1537 on the already centuries-old assumption that the travellers spreading the fire-magic of forging metals across Europe, along with their music, dances, and fortune-telling mysteries, had started their endless journeying in Egypt.

Egypt might have been the beginning of the trail. Or maybe Chaldea. According to one tale, two Gypsy groups left the land of Babylon and the Tower of Babel a long time ago. Half the people who knew themselves as descendants of Noah walked to Egypt. The others went to northern India. They all carried old secrets, including the fiery skill of working forge and anvil that some of the world's oldest mythologies connect to demons' powers, making metallurgy best done by outcasts or nomads.

Romani mythology about the origin of their wandering sometimes touches *gadjo* — non-Gypsy — traditions. They have to move on forever because they are all cursed descendants of Cain, the Bible's first murderer. Cain is the word for metal worker or blacksmith in Semitic languages. In other tales, the drom will never lead its followers home because a Gypsy smith set up his tent, fire, and anvil outside the gates of Jerusalem, then forged the nails used to crucify Yeshua ben Miriam. And Gypsies are supposed to have refused to help Mary on her flight into Egypt.

✳

MIRIAM-MARY, slumped on a donkey, looks like a woman who needs help in the Art Gallery of Ontario's tiny Rembrandt print called *The Flight into Egypt*. Her features are set in exhaustion and bewilderment. The minute bundle of rags in her arms could be a living child or an infant corpse she can't bear to leave. She looks like a twenty-first-century refugee mother whose hard journey has been forced upon her.

✸

JOURNEYING IS SEASONAL and not always hard travelling for some Canadian Roma now. But like people of the drom all over the world, Canadian Gypsies still hold in memory ancient stories and customs first shaped in India, the Caucasus, the Middle East, Europe, and all the other lands their families travelled for more than a thousand years. Roma storyteller Catherine Philippo was born around, maybe, 1920. She had travelled through Europe with an extended family group until she married a Canadian Rom in Paris and emigrated to Canada. She brought great treasure into the country.

Quebecois anthropologist Chantal Hillaire recorded one of Catherine Philippo's stories, origin unknown, in 1982. "The Enchanted Frog" is the tale of three rich gadjo brothers who once walked the world around searching for wives. At last, they heeded their mother's dying words, and chucked the stones she had given them over their shoulders to find wives where the stones fell. Yeah, the youngest brother had to marry the enchanted frog sitting on his stone. Now the local emperor's demands for magnificent gifts from the brothers' new wives can be satisfied thanks to the beautiful girl who must be a Gypsy because she can breathe diamonds and other matter into being when she appears at night minus her frog skin. After the youngest brother promises never to look at his wife's feet when she is in human form, the frog skin can be burned. The story ends with eating and drinking and happiness.

*Upstairs in the Public Rose Tavern ... Reminded suddenly of her convent days by a sensibility still too conscious of the past, Héloïse decided to take down the lascivious photographs that had been hung all over the walls of her room. Since her eyes were still lowered, Héloïse was unable to make out anything of those naked, crouching figures bathing in the moonlight, offering in the quiet of their white hands, like pairs of lambs in some snowy retreat, immense white breasts, also victims of their own candor, over which, like the chaste locks of the Madonna, there tumbled heavy golden tresses, unsullied symbols, like the breasts, of an innocence about to be lost, a beauty soon to be consecrated in debauchery. Héloïse was unable to make out anything in this depraved fairy landscape but the chaste foot of a girl who was depicted as spurning a pool full of toads — as in other pictures she had seen the Virgin spurn the head of a malignant serpent ...*

From *A Season in the Life of Emmanuel*, by Marie-Claire Blais.

✹

"UP AND DOWN the staircase runs this tale. Ducats on thy forehead! Go a smooth trail!" I am only remembering this Kosovo Albanian, perfectly promised, beginning-again ending to transformation tales because I myself have transformed Highway 97 North into a stoney staircase called a road outside the mountain city of Pec — Peje in Albanian — in the Serbian province of Kosovo. In 1997, already apprehensive Albanian Muslim people and their old, old stories lived there in the company of the Roma — Gypsies — nut trees, and roses, as well as the Virgin Marys in both the fifteenth-century Bajrakii mosque in Pec, and the even older churches along the mountain roads at the Serbian Orthodox Patriarchate and Decani monastery.

If I can turn this stoney track back into a slightly frost-heaved Canadian highway again, I will know that it is possible to form a prayer for people, nut trees, old-fashioned roses, and the remembrance of long-travelled tales in a now burned and bloodied countryside even without perfect certainty of the prayer's destination.

✹

ALL FROGS ARE SHAPE-SHIFTERS, amphibious icons of metamorphosis and transformation. Their connection with enchantment, and perhaps Gypsies, probably began in Egypt, where frogs' resemblance to the human fetus, as well as their ability to grow from water-bound tadpoles into legged land creatures made them sacred to Hekit, crone-goddess midwife to the Egyptian gods. The tiny frogs whose appearance signalled the Nile spring flood added fertility and regenerative aspects to Hekit's frog magic.

Twenty-one species of frogs and toads, order *Anura*, live mostly in southern Canada, except for the wood frog that prospects the Yukon's forested river valleys inside the Arctic Circle. In current climate-changing times, when fire runs wilder than ever in the bush and fields, and during such dry spells as the 2001–02 Alberta-Saskatchewan drought, you can ask for rain from any frog you meet, or any Romani woman you are lucky enough to find. Since Nile River days, and maybe before, frogs have been rain charms. Well into the twentieth century, Gypsy women earned a little money performing prayerful and ancient fecundity rituals dancing for rain on behalf of European farmers in need of a sky change.

Change in the weather of worship came, too, for Hekit, the Egyptian aged-woman divinity who minded birth, along with the unborn still swimming in darkness, and the Nile delta's water-born fertility. She was transformed, first into Greek Hekate, moon goddess of crossroads as signs of choices and undertakings. She also guarded the birth gate and came to be known as a form of Persephone called Queen of the Underworld, darkened soon enough to Queen of Witches in Christian times. Hecate, lead witch, appeared onstage in the first performances of Shakespeare's *Macbeth* about three hundred years before her name was given to a forty-sea-mile stretch of open water in Canada. Hecate Strait between British Columbia's north coast and Haida Gwaii, Queen Charlotte Islands, is a piece of water the Roma, knowing wind or any puff of air as the devil's breath, need to avoid.

✹

Hecate Strait and the deep-sea trawl fishing area north of the fifty-fourth parallel were the waters of transformation in *The Good Companion*, a picture book I dedicated to the British Columbia trawl fishermen whose boats and stories I had come to know on Canadian groundfish observer trips:

In the night the *Good Companion* moved restlessly on her anchor chain, pulled by the tide rushing from the bay to the wild ocean outside. The tide slacked before dawn, and the girl awoke in her foc's'l bunk. She put her hand on the bulkhead beside her, as if to be sure that the waters of the bay were truly almost still.

She slept again. In the stillness below the waterline, she dreamed the same dream as the captain, the cook, the engineer and the two deckhands in their cabins up top. The shared dream carried the fishermen and the red-headed girl together on a boat which became a bird flying high above a storm, then floating easily on the great swells of the sea.[5]

Pages later, when the trawler lies, heeled over, hesitating in the waves' trough on open sea west of Haida Gwaii, Queen Charlotte Islands,

The world of waves and wind, of night sky and distant land, stopped for the men on the *Good Companion*. They could no longer hear the sound of the storm. To them, the heaving sea seemed almost still. They waited to go down.

The captain heard the beating of great wings behind him on the flooding starboard deck. He saw only the deep water almost touching the deckrail, then he felt the *Good Companion* rolling slowly upright, bow into the wind. The sea still surged high, but when the captain took the wheel again, his boat rode the heavy swells like a bird.[6]

✳

LIVING ROMANI MYSTERIES and traditions still weave Canadian modernity with the far past where mythology, Hinduism, Christianity, and Islam were born. The Rom can thrive in the technology- and consumption-laced Canadian culture, while keeping deep in memory a stream of prayers and practices threading back to the oldest divinities.

Once upon a time, charms and spells not unlike Romani earth magic stitched the web of a daily enchanted world for the forebears of every

Canadian immigrant from Lief Erikson to tomorrow's airport arrivals. Some Ontario Mennonites may still be using the Fire Letter their families brought here from Europe, a charm set down from the words of a Gypsy king, said to be from Egypt, who talked down a huge fire in half an hour to save himself from being hanged in Konigsberg, Prussia, 1715: "We welcome you, Fiery Guest, don't take more than you have, this I count you, Fire, for a penance in the name of the Father, Son, and Holy Ghost. I command you, Fire, by God's power, to cease. As the true Christ stood in Jordan where he was baptized by John, the Holy Man. This I count you, Fire, for a penance in the name of the Holy Trinity. I command you, Fire, in the power of God, to lay down your flames."[7] Build this charm into your house, or keep it in the Bible. You are now safe from lightning strikes, too.

Not to mention the endless enchantment the rest of us have always received from the Rom's sturdy, time-out-of-mind inheritance of the ol' "Need-a-good … tinsmith-horse-song-spell-rain-car-dance-new roof-diamond-lucky card-girl-winning number-time-fortunetelling?" trade.

※

THE GYPSIES used to have not bad camp gear, old loggers still murmur when they're rambling through their Vancouver-bright-lights-between-bush-camp memories. Sometimes. On Skid Road days. Caulk boots, gloves, whatever. When you're broke because … go two streets over. Look in the between places … Look in the alcoves.

※

LOOK ANYWHERE IN CANADA. Now, or before the Rom moved on from your hometown. Margaret Atwood's *The Robber Bride*, Zenia, was a Gypsy in one of her incarnations and Ancestor Noah had family in

*I have seen the stone-carved sheilagh-na-gig under the eaves of the church at Kilpeck, in Herefordshire. A skeletal hag (the Winter Hag), she sits, knees wide, in the birthing position. She pulls her labial folds apart to display the door to life and death, to heaven and hell. I have seen pictures of other sheilagh-na-gigs, fecund, with leaves and vines growing out of their vulvas. They represent what men fear and hate in the power of women. The priests pushed her out of the church, but the people of the villages stubbornly insisted that she continue to live, half-hidden, under the eaves. The sheilagh-na-gig is Atargatis out of Araby, Kali out of India. She is Demeter, Morgana, the dark side of Mary. On Hornby Island, off the Pacific coast of Canada, I have come to know a New World version, carved in the rock, under a waterfall. In winter the petroglyph is hidden by the falling waters, but in summer, when there is only a trickle, one can see the outline of a woman — legs wide apart, knees bent. She is swimming (or is she dancing?) up the rock face. Not vines, but a salmon, issues from her vulva.*

From *The Crack in the Teacup: The Life of an Old Woman Steeped in Stories*, by Joan Bodger

Eastend, Saskatchewan, even before the Masonic Lodge and the Free Mason Song ("Old Noah he being righteous in the sight of the Lord / He loved the free masons and he kept the secret word"[8]) moved west.

At the southeast edge of Eastend sometime before 1920, Wallace Stegner spied on ragged outsiders camped for a few days near the town dump: "That stretch of the river was a favourite campsite for passing teamsters, gypsies, sometimes Indians. The very straw scattered around those camps, the ashes of those strangers' campfires, the manure of their teams and saddle horses, were hot with adventurous possibilities."[9]

The Roma traditions that have meandered across most of the country are blended with a measure of Canadian multiculturalism in the Roma Community and Advocacy Centre's book of Canadian Romani poems and ballads. The Roma's goddess of fate or patron saint, Sara, a.k.a. Kali Sara, is the cover girl for *Kanadake-Romane Mirikle — Canadian Romani Pearls*. Sara la Kali, or "the black woman" and/or "the Gypsy woman" is likely a descendant of Kali, the Hindu goddess who shows primal, fierce female energy as both destructive and creative force in the world's last, still worshipped, manifestation of fundamental, undiluted Nature.

Sara Kali of the Gypsies shares the Catholic tradition of Sara the Egyptian, loving handmaid to Mary Salome, Mary Jacobe, and Mary Magdalene, who sailed from the Holy Land to Saintes-Maries-de-la-Mer on the coast of France after the Crucifixion, a legend already ancient when it was documented in the fifteenth century.

Until 1912, only Gypsies held the right to enter the crypt where Sara's bones lie beneath France's Chartres Cathedral in a grotto once sacred to the Druids, inside the hill the Celts had called the Womb of Gaul. Timothy Findley's weary, immortal *Pilgrim* knew this: "The earth above which he now knelt had been dedicated to the pagan 'miracle' of a virgin giving birth. *Virgo paritura*, Pilgrim muttered. And then: *Ava Maria, gratia plena, Dominus tecum* ... Hail Mary, full of grace, the Lord is with thee."[10]

Mary the Mother of God (De Develski — Divine Mother, or Sunto

Mario — "ancestor Mary" in some Roma traditions) and Black Sara drew closer together, and nearer to Sara la Kali's incarnation as Saint Sara of the Gypsies, some time back when Sara la Kali, nobly born container of secrets, was chief of the metalworking Gypsies living at the Mediterranean mouth of the Rhone River.

Once a year, then, the Rhone River people entered the sea to receive its blessing, bearing on their shoulders a figure of Ishtar-Astarte, the great Middle Eastern goddess who, like Kali, like Nature, constantly created, preserved, and destroyed. On the day when Gypsy chief Sara la Kali saw her vision, other holy women appeared at the Rhone River delta. The saintly women who had been with Jesus when he died were in a skiff tossing in rough water off the river mouth.

✱

NOW THE SEA WILL BE WILD, pushing Sara la Kali under, filling her mouth, swallowing the foundering boat and its passengers, tilting them up again more waves away. Sara's long skirt will drag its weight through her strokes and her breath before she gets it off, and twists it into a drenched rope to pull the saints ashore. Christian baptism will be her reward.

✱

AFTER JOURNEYING FOR THOUSANDS OF YEARS, Kali-Sara had no problem immigrating to Canada. She had family connections here already, through the Kwakiutl Tsunoqua, fierce woman of the woods, and other Indian and Inuit wild female spirits, and through a Breton lady named Anne, who knew a thing or two about rain and long-ago powerful incarnations herself, and whose sainthood was spelled with a capital *S* and enshrined at Beaupré, Quebec. Among the shrine's most joyful celebratory feast-day visitors are Montreal and other Canadian Roma who approach the altar at Beaupré bearing shimmering strands of a memory

---

*Black Mary stands*
*back firm against*
*the bare brick spine*
*of the chimney*
*that climbs*
*from the base*
*of the basement suite*
*straight on up and through*
*into the heart of your apartment*
*in the house that you call home.*

*Black Mary is a mannequin*
*immaculate reproduction*
*futuristic, full-of-grace*
*hollow, hollow, holy icon*

*… but Mary, like Kali*
*can hear the rhythm*
*of your heart*
*can rise serpentine*
*within you, wake*
*your female*
*counterpart*

*…*

From "Black Mary," by Andrea Thompson in *Blueprint*

cord connecting Saint Anne with Queen Ana, who descended into a dark fairy land deep in the earth the other side of the Garden of Eden.

Kali Sara made it to the Pacific in May 1998 when the Roma carried her statue into the sea at the First Canadian Romani Congress and Symposium in Vancouver.

✳

THERE IS NO SEA HERE in northern British Columbia, only Highway 97 and a river somewhere in the night. On the left. Out the driver's side window of the car. West?

When hunger comes at last, I remember a truck driver somewhere on another northern summer road before the Skeena and Nass River time. I was hungry and tired then, too, driving the '67 Valiant into the night. Until it ran out of gas. He gave me some gas and a butter tart, then told me to rest in Hotel Valiant until daylight. In the morning, two martens, one large, one small, were drinking and washing in snowmelt pouring off a rock ledge by the car. I drank and splashed my hands and face after they left.

It was this trucker, or another man in a truck somewhere that summer, who said he, personally, always let Mary ride shotgun after dark. I had forgotten this until now. But if I stopped the car, if I shut the engine off and found the flashlight, I could search the Yukon map and figure out where that rock ledge is. Was.

Probably not. Probably I couldn't find that rock ledge—marten fountain road with the map, and the look of the land in noon light tomorrow anymore than I could decide where to stop on Highway 5 south of Lethbridge, and start walking to find the juncture of St. Mary's River and the Old Man at the bottom of Alberta fifteen hundred kilometres back. Anymore than I will be able to find the place where Fort St. Mary's used to be at the junction of the Smoky River and the Peace, if I ever come south of here again.

St. Mary rises in Montana's glacial lakes and joins the Blackfoot, Cree, and Stoney peoples' Old Man, grandson of the north wind, on the Blood reserve south of Lethbridge. That tricky, fast-talking, storytelling one who shifts shape, and the ground of all human assumptions, sends the Old Man River out of a certain cave in the Rockies. There, at the river's beginning, stand cairns made from stones Plains Indians placed on the Old Man's playing ground each time they entered the mountains. Those travellers would have known exactly where they were going, and why, and who was in the cave.

Another St. Mary's River runs fast in the Kootenay system this side of the Rockies. François St. Mary and other Kootenai chiefs were present at the 1923 opening of the Kootenay Park highway. And farther west northwest, English St. Mary of the Fraser River gold rush minds the Lillooet museum's shipped-from-England, packed-up-the-trail remnants of the 1861 St. Mary's Anglican Church, and looks south to Our Lady of Guadalupe in Mexico. They both know how absorbing newcomers' gold lust and Indian sorrow connects them to each other. The Marys are all connected. You just can't drive to the intersection of their fusion.

But keeping the car moving softens my unease about finding a possibility of Mary's presence more often in rivers than in churches. Road sign: "160 km to Fort Nelson." Only 160 kilometres to an attainable goal, which will be signalled by heavy equipment yards and gravel side roads appearing in the bush at intervals, then closer together, followed by a gas station. There will be a sign: "Entering Fort Nelson." Even if I drive through town without stopping, I will have completed a measurable act. Come and gone from Fort Nelson. Look around you. Wherever you go, there you are. Maybe driving is only a detour around disappointment in my search for mercy, even if the grapes and the brazil nut are long gone and there's nothing left to eat in here.

There is no Madonna of Disappointment, though when I wrote to Les Sóeurs de Miséricorde in Montreal to check on the merciful Virgin Mary who had been present at Edmonton's old Misericordia Hospital when I

Roads  235

*lupe* ✸ *Argentina: Our Lady of Lujan* ✸ *Bolivia: Our Lady of Copacabana* ✸ *Brazil: Our Lady of Aparacida* ✸ *Chile: Our Lady of Carmel of the Maipu* ✸ *Columbia: Our Lady of*

was a girl, Sister Liliane Theriault kindly sent me pictures of Notre-Dame de la Vie Interieure and La Vierge du Sourire, along with archival photographs of the hospital chapel. Perhaps she rightly sensed that I needed Madonnas of smiles and the interior life, as well as mercy.

Or I need another kind of Saint Mary right now, probably the one who's already adrift on this road with me, riding as flotsam floating on an interior groundswell also carrying Father Morice, Gypsies, and a general, permanent need to be sorry for not being a better girl. "By Marry Gyp!" Robin Hood swore to invoke his beloved Mary Gipsy, meaning Saint Mary of Egypt, listed under "penitent" in the *Penguin Dictionary of Saints*. Mary, the saint who had been the seventeen-year-old whore of Alexandria before she worked her pilgrimage passage toward Jerusalem by serving the ship's crew, used to be known for her patience with sexual sins.

When Mary of Egypt saw the Virgin's face at the church of the Holy Sepulchre in Jerusalem, she knelt to promise her repentance, then crossed the Jordan River to enter the desert as an anchorite who passed forty-seven years alone, being sorry.

The legendary penitence attributed to Saint Mary of Egypt because she had been a prostitute was expected of British Columbia Coast Salish people for being themselves when the Oblates of Mary Immaculate named their Fraser River mission and residential school after St. Mary of Egypt in 1861. Thirty-one-year-old Brother Gabriel Morice, newly arrived from France in 1880, completed his training for the priesthood at St. Mary of Egypt's Mission on the Fraser River before going upcountry.

✷

GROUNDSWELLS ARE WIDE, slow-moving ocean swells disowned by the marine weather in which your vessel moves offshore. Storms in some far sea distance have created the groundswells that will last until all the waters between your position and that midocean tempest you never knew

Roads 237

have subsided. Flotsam is a wrecked ship's still-floating cargo or its broken hull and fittings, scraps more than one crew has needed to gather and patch together into a fragile vessel that may yet make home port. Four months after Vitus Bering and his crew named the not-yet-Yukon mountain they saw from the North Pacific on Saint Elias's day in 1741, storms forced the *Sviatoi Petr* onto the rocks off one of the Komandorskiye Islands before the open waters now called the Bering Sea. Before he died on the island, Bering ordered his men to rebuild their ship. The *Sviatoi Petr* eventually lurched into the Kamchatka harbour known, almost forty years later, to the *Discovery* and the *Resolution*, who called in to leave word of Captain Cook's death in Hawaii. From this same harbour in Petropavlovsk, named Peter and Paul's city after Bering's ships, the Russian factory vessels set out for Canadian waters when I worked as a foreign fisheries observer. The comfort of this small circularity belongs somewhere on navigation's Great Circles, in which the shortest distance between any two points at sea lies on the circumference of the circle that joins them and is itself centred in the middle of the earth.

✳

THE CAR RUNS ALONG a straight enough line on a hard surface, even though my steering wheel is looking for the point-to-point course forever being pushed into a curve by the tide off the west coast between Cape Caution and Milbanke Sound. My shoulders are eased down now that I can steer from the dodger up top on some small, wood-hulled fishboat, making minute, automatically repeated corrections on the wheel while water, air, and sky move through ceaseless changes around me.

Only when the Prophet River runs close to the road at last, pouring north to the Liard about Mile 250 on the Alaska Highway, is it possible to remember that Mary of the sea and the second-hand store, is in the back seat. The store might have been off the highway the other side of Prince George. Inland, anyway, which caused Mary's pale celluloid form and downcast eyes, redeemed by the lovingly glued seashells under her tiny bare feet, to stand out on a shelf crowded with rusted small-animal traps and serving bowls hairline cracked across English countryside flower patterns.

The glass net float that came with her, six dollars for both of them, is sister to the small, clear hill of solidity that surfaced in *Lana Janine*'s liquid world, making a forty- or fifty-year voyage from Japan until the engineer dip-netted it out of the offshore Pacific for me.

THE FAMILY ROSARY HOUR — DARRO

Christ the King of Kings

Mary shows up once in a while at Value Village and other thrift shops as the Mary part of a night light, minus plug and bulb. It is still possible to find the eight-sided cardboard basket, sometimes plastic covered, made from Mary images carefully, lovingly, blanket-stitched onto an octagon base, usually a picture of Mary watching over someone saying the rosary. In a Saskatchewan thrift shop, I found a framed reproduction of a sturdily pregnant Mary wearing late-nineteenth-, early-twentieth-century Eastern European farm clothes. The knot in her slipped-down yellow shawl, the frayed edge of her skirt, and the oyster shell in her lap were my favourite parts. And the intent calm expression of an out-of-the-picture daydream on her face.

✳

The Petrocan in Fort Nelson sells butter tarts, listed in the *Canadian Oxford Dictionary* as a Canadian noun, "with a filling of butter, eggs, brown sugar and usu. raisins."[11] The born-in-Canada butter-tart-pastry icon also qualifies under the Road Food Rules: Fuel your body where you fuel your vehicle. Food must be available within fifty metres of the highway, and be possible to eat out of one hand while the other is on the wheel. Limited exceptions for food consumed while crouching beside creek or river. Absolutely no campfires. Food preparation must involve only the knife and itinerant spoon living in the glove compartment. No forks. Forks are not roadworthy.

Ideally, road food would be named after people who then become imaginary driving companions. For example, the Breton cracker, named by a Dare Foods Ltd. Canadian contest-winning employee who looked for a word to suit both French and English, and recalled that most New France settlers were Bretons. For example, Jos Louis, the *festin chocolat* — chocolatey feast — born in the 1930s in a Magic brand baking-powder lid inside a woodstove at Sainte-Marie-Beauce, southwest of Quebec City, now satisfying Canada's sweet needs a hundred million times a year.

### Sweet Marie Bars

½ c. peanut butter
½ c. corn syrup
½ c. light brown sugar
2 ½ c. crispy rice cereal
½ c. roasted peanuts

*In a saucepan, mix together the peanut butter, corn syrup, and brown sugar over low heat. Add the crispy rice and peanuts and stir until coated. Press into an 8" x 8" pan. Ice the bars with the melted chocolate chips.*

Country Bulk Store, London, Ontario

A pink drink labelled Virgin was on sale at a Shell station somewhere behind me, but road food named Mary is harder to find, except for Sweet Marie bars — 60g With Lots of Fresh Roasted Peanuts *Avec Une Profusion d'Arachides Fraîches Roties* Guaranteed by Cadbury Chocolate Canada, Toronto, Ontario — Marie biscuits, and Notre Dame Fromage Brie and Camembert from Quebec. Pets de sœur — nun's farts, tiny cinnamon rolls with maple sugar — angel food cake, and products distributed by Santa Maria Foods Corporation don't count. In 2001, Santa Maria paid a hundred thousand dollars in fines for tampering with expiration dates on Italian meats and cheeses sold in Canada.

The Virgin Mary herself gets to eat cherries in the old English Cherry Tree carol, and dates provided by Allah in the Maryam chapter of the Koran: "And when she felt the throes of childbirth she lay down by the trunk of a palm-tree, crying: 'Oh, would that I had died and passed into oblivion!'

"But a voice from below cried out to her: 'Do not despair. Your Lord has provided a brook that runs at your feet, and if you shake the trunk of this palm-tree it will drop fresh dates in your lap. Therefore eat and drink and rejoice.'"[12]

✴

AT THE GAS STATION IN FORT NELSON, ferocious fluorescent lights illuminate my reluctance to give up driving forever to northern rivers as much as they sharpen map lines dotted with butter-tart crumbs, and the blue teardrops of paper lakes.

On the roads south and east of Fort Nelson, I never come to the ruins of the fur-trade post Hudson's Bay Company governor George Simpson called "the lost Fort St. Mary,"[13] at the juncture of the Smoky River and the Peace, only to a river barge, then a long dirt road ending in head-high grass beside invisible river waters murmuring to themselves.

*lp* ✱ *Our Lady of Good Hope* ✱ *Our Lady of the Highway* ✱ *Our Lady of the Iceberg* ✱ *Our Lady of Peace* ✱ *Our Lady of the Prairies* ✱ *Our Lady of the Presentation* ✱ *Our Lady*

I am only able to find Our Lady of Guadalupe because she has run away with the circus at Dawson Creek, where The Mexican International Circus — "No Animals! Supporting the SPCA!!" — has set up a huge tent in the mall parking lot. The road and daylight are abandoned while I sit, enchanted by sparkling glamour in the dark, until, at last, the clown playing a poor man scarcely able to comprehend the beautiful dark-haired trapeze artist flying above him is covered with red roses spilling from the aerial girl's fluttering, unfurling blue cape.

✳

THE VIRGIN MARY REAPPEARED as a circus performer in Vancouver's Leaky Heaven Circus Christmas 2002 show *Birthday Boy (A Nativity)*. She wore striped tights and a bewildered innocent-clown smile, while the Angel Gabriel sported silver tights and Las Vegas attitude.

✳

AT DUNVEGAN, ALBERTA, Our Lady of the Peace faces the broad, glassy river. She might be made from the substance Mario at Ital Decor back in Burnaby, British Columbia, calls "cultured marble." Ital Decor casts many a garden Mary in steel-reinforced concrete, grey or stained antique white. Full sized, hands outstretched, and head inclined down to us from her pedestal, or head and shoulders, holding the child, she keeps company with Venus, Diana, Cupid, and Apollo beside the traffic on Hastings Street.

Even Michelangelo's Mary, in part, may be placed on site, any site, nowadays. Mary's twenty-three-kilogram stone head, made from a mould of Michelangelo's *Pietà*, stamped Edzioni Musei Vaticani, 560,000 lira (about US$250) is available from the Vatican Museums mail order catalogue.

Our Lady of the Peace holds quieter ground. Her crown and the half-globe of the world on which she stands are subdued by her braids and

*Our Lady of the Assumption* ✽ *Our Lady of Good Counsel* ✽ *Our Lady of Grace* ✽ *Our Lady of the Navigators* ✽ *Our Lady of the Sacred Heart* ✽ *Our Lady of Victory* ✽ *Our Mot*

bare feet. Bare foot. Only the right foot shows under her robe, and it is a curiously familiar-looking foot. This Mary's model and I both have a second toe longer than our big toe. Sure sign of a witch, someone said when I was a child. But Our Lady of the Peace has a rose lying at her foot, as part of the statue, and more growing down the riverbank before her, mixed with brown-eyed susans.

Mother of Consolation ✦ Panagia (All-Holy Queen Assumed into Heaven) ✦ Queen of Angels ✦ Queen of Apostles ✦ Queen of All Saints ✦ Queen of Confessors ✦ Queen Conceived

✹

AFTER DUNVEGAN, I'm driving faster, searching the fields ahead, once in a while looking back over my shoulder, right, left. Nothing. Only Alberta in summer heat.

In time, between Grande Prairie and Valleyview, I know I'm trying to drive away from somewhere that was never on this northwestern Alberta road, or any other highway, because it is a piece of time years ago, not a place, and it only burns as if it were happening today when my memory is strip-mined by hot days after July 12.

✹

THE RIVER THERE WAS THE JALA, from the Greek word *halos* for salt. For twenty-five centuries, salt had been mined near the river, first by Neolithic people, then by Celtic Ilyrians, Romans, Slavs, the Ottoman and Austro-Hungarian Empires and their successors in the 1918 Kingdom of Yugoslavia, and the post–World War II communist state.

By its taste of life matter made sacred in blood, sea water, and uterine fluids, salt blessed the oldest altars. Melting winter with road-salt-consecration only makes Canada the world's largest per capita salt consumer. I didn't know this, then.

There were other things to know in the crowded tents on the runways at Dubrave Air Base on the other side of the Jala River trickling through the city of Tuzla in northeastern Bosnia. One woman in the tents dreamed she was back at her own stove making a cup of coffee for her youngest son. She had four sons, before, she told me. One died at the front when the war first started. Soldiers in the same company as the second son last saw him, kneeling, unmoving, beside the body of his brother, the third boy, after an attack. The only surviving son was sitting with her in the kitchen at home in Srebrenica when they came. He tried to run. She was forced onto a bus. The buses sat for hours in the afternoon heat. She heard someone say her son's name. He had hanged himself after he was captured. Now the buses started down the dusty roads from Srebrenica, stopping once when the teenaged girls were taken, and halting at the confrontation line in Kladanj. After a long, heat-sick time, other buses carried her and thousands more of Srebrenica's displaced women and children and a few old men to Dubrave Air Base.

While a Bosnian soldier was hiding in the forest the other side of Kladanj, he dreamed the dead men in his troop had come to life. They were all children again and the trees could speak.

Some nights in Tuzla, I dreamed I was anaesthetized, able to feel, but not move. A man with bloody eyes was kissing me. His kisses landed on my mouth like punches from a cold fist.

Awake, there was a legend. The eight thousand or more men missing from Srebrenica still lived. Their bodies had likely already been ladled into mass graves, but the legendary men and boys were alive and on the march. Slow march. They were travelling in their thousands late at night, moving down into the Drina River valley from the mountain woods where they had been hiding. Radio Tuzla broadcast daily the voices of women reciting their names, and the names of the men they were looking for.

The legend grew. The men from Srebrenica were said to have reached an enormous, mythically huge collective I.D.P. — internally displaced person — centre downtown. In July 1995, they were being registered as some of the 247,741 displaced people temporarily settled in camps and collective centres within forty kilometres of Tuzla.

So would I take this man's name and find him?

✴

I AM DRIVING THE ROAD to other legends now. At Lac Ste. Anne, Mary is a child at her mother's knee in the white statues on the grass and at the shrine altar. Saint Anne's legend includes motherly care for her daughter's body and soul. Soul-tending included teaching Mary to read

los Remedios ✶ Mystical Rose ✶ Mater Dolorosa ✶ Seat of Wisedom ✶ Spiritual Vessel ✶ Stella Maris, Star of the Sea ✶ Theotokos (God Giver) ✶ Vessel of Honour ✶ Virgin Most

the psalms and prayers in Hebrew scriptures. Images of a seated Saint Anne often include a little girl on one knee and a book balanced on the other. Although Anne is the protectress of birth, and patron saint of midwives and miners as well as grandmothers, she may have been overlooked as a literacy model.

In Canada, appeals to Saint Anne's concern for grandmothers sometimes emerge as an expletive. In Donna Morrissey's Newfoundland novel, *Kit's Law*, Kit's grandmother leaps into action when a child is threatened: "Then Shine grabbed a young boy by the ankles, and whilst everyone watched in stunned horror, he held him upside down and started swinging him towards the smoking boughs ... 'Mother of the Blessed Virgin, he's gone mad this time,' Nan cried out, shoving the bag of groceries into my arms and lunging towards Shine."[14]

The tradition of Anne and Joachim as Mary's parents, along with endearing Marian childhood details like early walking (seven months), first birthday party invitations for the whole people of Israel, angelic baby food deliveries, and a toddler's ecstatic dance on the temple altar steps are rooted in *The Book of James*, a first- or second-century apocryphal or "hidden" gospel. The unknown writer or translator, possibly a Greek Jew, probably drew on sources such as the Hebrew Pentateuch — the Five Books of the Torah or Teaching — on Egyptian and Syrian religious rites, and then-current Greek and Roman customs as well as marketplace and dockside reports of the new Christianity. Neither this first apocryphal gospel, its much-later Latin translations, nor the texts derived from them have been absorbed into the New Testament, though some modern Bibles include the Apocrypha as a separate book. Devotion to Saint Anne, Hanna among the Ethiopians, Anne among the Bretons, beloved inheritor of some of the oldest earth mother's fertility aspects, and infinitely patient parent and grandparent, endures despite Biblical scholarship.

    Reaching her Alberta shrine meant an almost nineteen-hundred-year journey for Saint Anne, travelling times during which a stormy Atlantic voyage on board a fishboat headed for Canadian cod grounds was by no means the toughest excursion. Anne's expedition to Canada began in Brittany, where she had once been Ana, the Celtic goddess who was both the meaning of plenty, and the first figure of the female trinity who tended the cauldron of fate.

    Once upon another time in a faraway country called Brittany/Bretagne, there lived a duchess whose kindness matched her luminous beauty, and who had come to be known as Anne. At peace amid the love of her people, Duchess Anne suffered only one sorrow, her husband's distaste for children. When Anne's belly swelled, the Duke of Brittany cast her out. Alone, the grieving duchess wandered as far as the Baie de Douarnez on the Breton coast, where a white ship stood at anchor, seemingly waiting for her.

When Anne set foot on the deck, the ship made ready to sail. Which course would the vessel take? Bound for what port? How long the voyage? And why? "God's will is in the wind," said the angel in white at the wheel.

After a long-enough voyage, the holy ship made port in a desert land. In Jerusalem, the good Duchess Anne of Brittany, a.k.a. Ana of the Celts, a.k.a. Anna Perenna or Grandmother Time for the Romans, a.k.a. Sumerian goddess Queen Nana, and, now, a.k.a. Christian Saint Anne, gave birth to Mary who would be the mother of Christ.

This Breton form of Saint Anne would one far day make camp in Alberta, more than eighteen centuries after she had become homesick in the Holy Land, yearning for Brittany again once Mary was grown up enough to leave home and approach her destiny.

Saint, formerly Duchess, Anne sailed home on another providential ship, with the angel at the wheel in black this time, because the Duke of Brittany had died while his discarded wife was away on God's business. Anne wanted neither the royal riches she was entitled to, nor proof of her people's adoration. She stayed alone in a hut on the Breton beach, praying for the world. One day when she was very old, she gave her blessing to a radiant young man who visited her not long before he was crucified.

Hundreds of years later in France, statues of this earliest Breton Saint Anne, hauled from the sea in fishermen's nets or found underground, became miracle workers at Ste-Anne-de-la-Palue and Ste-Anne-d'Auray in the western region of Brittany. Saint Anne who knows the sea and the hearts of the poor sailed for the St. Lawrence with the Breton fishermen who had years ago learned the Basque's cod fishery secrets over the odd glass of waterfront wine.

She was there all through the storm in the St. Lawrence, standing on the north shore to guide the battered fishboat to safe harbour. The crew gave Saint Anne their thankful prayers, and named their mooring place Beau Pré, beautiful meadow. The tiny wooden chapel built at Beau Pré in

1658 was the beginning of the world's largest Saint Anne shrine and July 26 feast day pilgrimage.

Among the Beaupré shrine's most joyful celebratory feast day visitors are the Canadian Roma who remember a tradition connecting Saint Anne to complex, unimaginably ancient tales of an underearth queen of the good fairies named Ana, protector of humans from the underworld demons who cause illness and sudden death.

❋

IF THE ROMA GO to Saint Anne in Quebec, if the gravel road here in Alberta drifts warm, clean-smelling dust into the car, if pinto horses are at the fence, if the fields running down to the lake are spread with tents and campers and Indian people, and if breath comes easier just seeing them, this must be the place.

❋

LAC STE. ANNE was first *Manitou Sakahigan*, the Cree Lake of the Spirit, a summer ceremonies place known to be healing, as well as rich with fish, berries, and game, and said to have been kept as safe, neutral ground for all tribes. The Alexis First Nations people now living on the north shore of the lake call it *Wakamne*, God's Lake.

David Thompson called it Manito Lake on the maps he made for the North West Company; the Hudson's Bay traders called it Devil's Lake, perhaps because the water whips up quickly in any wind.

In 1843, Reverend J. B. Thibault, a secular priest from St. Boniface, Red River (shepherded through his Alberta missionary journeys by a capable man who survives in Catholic church records as "his faithful guide, the Metis, Gabriel Dumont"), renamed the lake. *Short Sketches of the History of the Catholic Churches and Missions in Central Alberta* continues, "as a true son of Canada so devoted to the great and good saint whose shrine graces the shores of the St. Lawrence River, he changed the name of this lake and called it 'Lake St. Anne.'"¹⁵ Saint Anne as the grandmother of Christ fit well with the traditional cultural value, and love, First Nations peoples give to grandmothers.

The Oblates of Mary Immaculate took over the Lac Ste. Anne mission in 1856. *Short Sketches of the History of the Catholic Churches and Missions in Central Alberta* continues, "In 1889 ... when the Rev. Fr. Lestanc was Superior of St. Albert, it came to the mind of this pious missionary, who was a native of Brittany, that the good Ste. Anne, who scatters her favours from her Breton sanctuary at Ste. Anne D'Auray and her Canadian shrine of Ste. Anne de Beaupré, could also well grant similar favours in a sanctuary of the North West if only she were solicited for them."¹⁶ The yearly pilgrimage that began more than a century ago was July 21 to 26 in 2001, with ceremonies each day. More than forty thousand people are expected.

✴

STILL, LAC STE. ANNE is a place to rest, lying on the grass, listening to Cree fiddle music, including "St. Anne's Reel," floating from the booths set up in the next field until *Ave Maria* is sung in Cree, and I have to go over there to buy the tape of *Cree Hymns Nisokamawin*, sung by Johnny Waniandy, Eva Ladouceur, Beatrice Calliou, and Darlene Starrs.

✴

THE CANADIAN MUSIC CENTRE's catalogues show Canada's classical musicians composing, scoring, and arranging music for *Ave Maria* as *motets en français*; in Latin for men's voices; in Latin for a cappella women's voices; in Latin for mezzo-soprano and chorus; in Latin for mezzo-soprano and choir; in Latin for mixed voices, five parts, unaccompanied; *en français et latin pour deux ténors, basse et orgue avec le clavier; en latin pour soprano et guitare*. *Ava Maria Stellis*, the ninth-century Star of the Sea hymn Jacques

*Kesewatisiyan Marie*
*Ki pakusihitin*
*Mekwatch e pimatisiyan*
*Wi kanaweyimin.*

From "Merciful Mary," a Cree hymn

Cartier's crew and the North West Mounted Police recruits sang, has been arranged for elementary piano by a Canadian composer. Canada's most frequently performed contemporary classical vocal work is *The Confession Stone: Songs of Mary*. The music was composed by Robert Fleming (1921–76) for Maureen Forrester as song cycles from Owen Dodson's words in *Beyond the Blues — New Poems by American Negroes*.

Mary hears something of herself in the Toronto rock band Our Lady Peace, though she doesn't count on making pop music charts as often as she did when Leonard Cohen was writing "Our Lady of Solitude" ("And her dress was blue and silver / And her words were few and small / She is the vessel of the whole wide world / Mistress, oh mistress, of us all"[17]) for his *Recent Songs* album, or "Song of Bernadette," sung by Jennifer Warnes on her *Famous Blue Raincoat* collection of Cohen's music, the ballad for the child who saw the Queen of Heaven and kept the vision in her soul ("No one believed what she had heard / That there were sorrows to be healed / And mercy, mercy in this world"[18]).

Toronto's *Shift media-entertainment-technology mag* did provide Tori Amos with a Mother Mary night light in April 1996, so the interviewer could ask her, "What does that invoke?"

Amos's answer: "The lies. They hold this in a sacred way, but you know, Mother Mary had other kids besides Jesus."

*Shift* interviewer: "She was fooling around afterward, you mean?"

Amos: "She was enjoying herself. She had a life that no one wants to talk about."[19]

"Dashboard Mary," "ready ... on a nicotine fuse," in Ryan Knighton's words with music by Peter Alan, surges out of The Jelly Roll Blues Band's performance on the CD accompanying *Why I Sing the Blues, Lyrics & Poems*, edited by Jan Zwicky and Brad Cran. A few tunes along on the CD, The Bill Johnson Blues Band performs "St. Mary Blues," a Winnipeg elegy by Patrick Friesen: "sitting here on a dime / watching the trains slide away / there's nowhere else I'd rather stay / than st. mary at the dying of the day ..."[20], with music by Bill Johnson.

Sarah MacLachlan wrote the music and words for an ambiguous Mary who is "faded / a shadow of what she once was," but able to "lead you through the fire / give you back hope,"[21] by the end of the song on the album *Fumbling toward Ecstasy*. Her Nettwerk music sister, Lily Frost, claiming Welsh, Gypsy, and Metis family background, as well as Mary's moon and sea, in the title of her first CD, *Lunamarium*, makes love in the ruins of a church until "Mary Magdalene smiled with chagrin,"[22] in "St. Augustine."

✸

Because so many people on the field at Lac Ste. Anne share their bannock and coffee, and kindness with me, I keep thinking I must know their brothers, or daughters, or someone else in the family from up the west coast. But I don't. These pilgrims are Blackfoot, Chipewyan, Cree, Dene, Ojibwa, Saulteaux, Sarcee, Stoney, and other First Nations and Metis people from across Canada, along with some from the States.

The Fort Chippewyan Seniors are here. And Bill from Fort McMurray, on his fortieth pilgrimage. And the people he says walked here from Cold Lake. Eva from Grande Prairie, whose mother used to bring her and her sisters and brothers here every summer, says she visited a friend in Calling Lake a couple of weeks ago, and heard about the two hundred people walking down from Fort Smith. They'll be here in a day or two, keeping a family vow made for Saint Anne's sweet help with a niece's dangerously late delivery. The help was given. All is well with a new mother and baby in Fort Smith, Northwest Territories, 750 kilometres northeast of here, as the pilgrim walks.

Eva is carrying red roses. They're for Mother Mary, she says, and I am reminded of an old friend whose first home was the Salish village at Mount Currie in B.C. She always looks mildly surprised when Mary is spoken of by any name besides Mother.

Together, we all move slowly across the campground field toward the huge open-sided shrine for a dusk candlelit procession down to the water. Day still lights an arc of western sky.

On the altar, votive candle flames tremble at Saint Anne's feet. Discarded crutches, canes, and hardworn braces hang in the shrine as signs of gratitude for her help with easing illness and pain. Her images here, as well as in the tiny mission church at the entrance to the pilgrimage grounds, and in the white statue on the grass, show a slightly sharp-nosed woman with intently focused eyes. She looks to me as if she wouldn't suffer fools gladly. Even the two burned-out bulbs in the halo around the outdoor Anne's white marble head can't diminish her dignity.

A sombre, deerskin-jacketed Christ with braided black hair surveys us all from above the altar. Saint Anne with her left hand on the child Mary's shoulder, her right hand pointing to the book Mary is reading, is flanked by the Blessed Kateri Tetakwitha, Lily of the Mohawk, and the Mexican Virgin of Guadalupe. This Madonna of all the Americas is the Mary of Canada who knows the place she is sometimes given in Cree sacred pipe rituals, and in the dance for the ancestors at Fox Lake, Alberta, in the Little Red River area, are among her truest forms. Mary sees herself as a Canadian Indian woman with her head bowed in grief, beside a tormented Christ with a broken eagle feather fastened to his braids in native artist Alex Twin's stained-glass windows at the church on the Ermineskin Reserve in Hobbema, Alberta.

The shrine benches fill as daylight fades. Stereo speakers pour out Cree hymns: *Saint Anne n'okuminan ki sakihitinan, Pe natamawinan kitchikaskihuyak*. "Saint Anne, our beloved grandmother, Come to us. Help us and free us." Maryka and Andrina from Saint Theresa Point Reserve, and Theresa from Wasagamack Reserve in the same Island Lake region of Manitoba, whisper their translations to me, worrying because Cree can be translated in many ways.

Holding our unlit candles poked into pink paper, scallop-edged Venetian lanterns, we wait for the ceremony to begin. Coyotes are calling in the mustard and hay fields east of the shrine, and the grasshoppers plaguing prairie crops are here, too. The soft night air smells of woodsmoke and lake water and afternoon rain. In other years, Saint Anne drenched drought and put out forest fires with that rain, just as she subdued winds whipping up barn fires in the Rivière Ouelle St. Denis and other Quebec parishes well into the twentieth century.

The altar is being smudged now, scented with the smoke of burning sweet grass. Thunder rolls all through *O Canada*. Lightning cracks into our prayers. We are in a tornado-watch area, but it won't be tonight. Bic lighters and wooden matches come out for the candles.

Slowly, slowly, the procession of light snakes across the field down to the lake. The lanterns cast a peach-coloured glow. The only other illumination is the cool, white gleam of the cross atop the shrine. Then, a red amplifier light winks through the door of a tent near the lakeshore, and the musicians onstage in the gospel tent wail out Hank Williams's "I Saw the Light" while rebel pilgrims, including me, reel out of the procession, clapping and stomping. Fortunately, I had foxgloves on my fingertips, and they make you invisible at twilight. (Take it easy with this one. Foxglove magic may not work for all adults on all occasions. Lac Ste. Anne was an exception.)

While I'm fooling around with Hank, the lake has been blessed. Eva is already in. "She's been seen," she told me in the parking lot this afternoon. Saint Anne, Eva means. "The story goes, she stood on a rock in the lake. Her footprints are on the rock. They fit whoever stands in them. They fit me, then my sister. She's only size six."

Half a dozen or more huge rocks show themselves within reach of the shore. The lake water is low in this drought year, knee-high a long way out, cool and sweet-tasting. For days in the car, hot wires have been strung through my fingers, wrists, and elbows, so I lay these parts into the water, and look at them, pale and shimmer-edged under the surface in the last daylight.

As it happens, Saint Anne's own wrist is not far away. A minute fragment of bone, encased in a steel circle and glass covered, is embedded into the stones supporting her statue back up on the grass. The rest of a portion of her wrist is at Beaupré on the St. Lawrence, sent from Rome in 1892.

Roads 259

I don't want to climb any of the rocks, even the likely looking one. I don't want to know if my feet won't fit into the footprints.

Saint Anne seems to startle when I pass her white statue on my way back from the lake with wet feet. It was probably only the kids throwing glow sticks up behind her. When I turn around for a last look from the edge of the field, she is settled again for the pilgrims touching the hem of her robe or lifting their hands before her, cupped, ready to receive any blessing at all.

✳

IN THE CAR AGAIN, driving slowly through the warm night, not sure which road I want when the gravel ends, Hank Williams, not Saint Anne, is on my mind. Hank Williams, a.k.a. Luke the Drifter, a.k.a. the leader of sometime bands always called the Drifting Cowboys. Known, too, to be so hooked to the road, among other things, that he married Audrey Mae Sheppard at a gas station in Andalusia, Alabama, in 1944, eight years before he died from alcoholic heart failure in the back seat of a car.

Hank Williams owned "The Lost Highway" — "I'm a rolling stone all alone and lost / For a life of sin I have paid the cost / When I pass by all the people say / Just another guy on the lost highway"[23] — and untreated spina bifida. Lac Ste. Anne would have helped. He probably wouldn't have come. Unless he knew about the music in the gospel tent. He probably wouldn't have left the tent to go into the lake. If Hank Williams went into Lac Ste. Anne, he wouldn't have climbed up on that rock, either.

Jack Kerouac, sometime, brief time, seafarer, would have travelled to Lac Ste. Anne of the Bretons via his autobiographical novel *Vanity of Duluoz: An Adventurous Education 1935–46*. Here's scullion Jack, on board a World War II U.S. merchant ship bound for Greenland, pretending to keep a "seamenlike" log for at least a few lines: "'As I write tonight, we are passing thru the most dangerous phase of our journey to that mysterious northern land ... we are steaming ahead in a choppy sea past the mouth of the St. Lawrence River in a crystal clear Moonglow.' (Good enough for a Duluoz, descendant of the Gaspe and Cape Bretons.)"[24]

Like this, Ti-Jean would have come to Lac Ste. Anne:

Far from the sea far from the sea
of Breton fishermen
...

VII
by roar of river
where now *Ti-Jean* alone
(returned to Lowell
in one more doomed Wolfian attempt
to Go Home Again)
gropes past the Twelve Stations of the Cross
reciting aloud the French inscriptions
in his Joual accent
...

And a very real tear drops
in the Grotto
from the face
of the Stoned Virgin ...

From "The Canticle of Jack Kerouac" by Lawrence Ferlinghetti[25]

✸

I MADE ONE MORE PILGRIMAGE on the roads back to the west coast, a few steps into a field in the Chilcotin plateau range land where the Coastguard Loran — LOng RAnge Navigation — tower stands in grass threaded with wild daisies and fireweed. This far inland from Bella Coola and Burke Channel the other side of the Coast Mountains, the sea is only imaginary. An act of faith is necessary to believe the tower's transmissions of minute, steady 100 kHz low frequency pulses will reach Loran receivers on salt-water vessels where the transmissions' timing will be measured, corrected for sky-wave reflections, then set down as latitude and longitude on electronic charts.

The Loran tower in this sweet-smelling field would have marked *Lana Janine*'s last position hundreds of land kilometres and sea miles west of here. I imagine Mary remembers the *Lana Janine*. She would have been there, Monday, March 16, 1992, about eight in the morning on the west coast of Haida Gwaii, Queen Charlotte Islands. I imagine she saw, perhaps she felt, the flames flying out of the engine room and across the main deck. She would have heard the shouting, have heeled with the boat one last time to slide the lifeboat off the deck. She would have seen, I hope, the Fisheries patrol vessel *Arrow Post* steaming full speed over an otherwise empty sea to pick the raft, and the men known to me — the deckhands, the cook, the engineer, and the captain — out of the choppy water.

If the top deck lasted until *Lana* went under, the Mary in the storage-locker chapel by the wheelhouse ladder is four hundred fathoms down now, lying on her side, while the chapel door, surely burst from its latch again, stirs back and forth in the dark water. If the plaster Mary burned with the superstructure of the boat, her dust is there, in the sea.

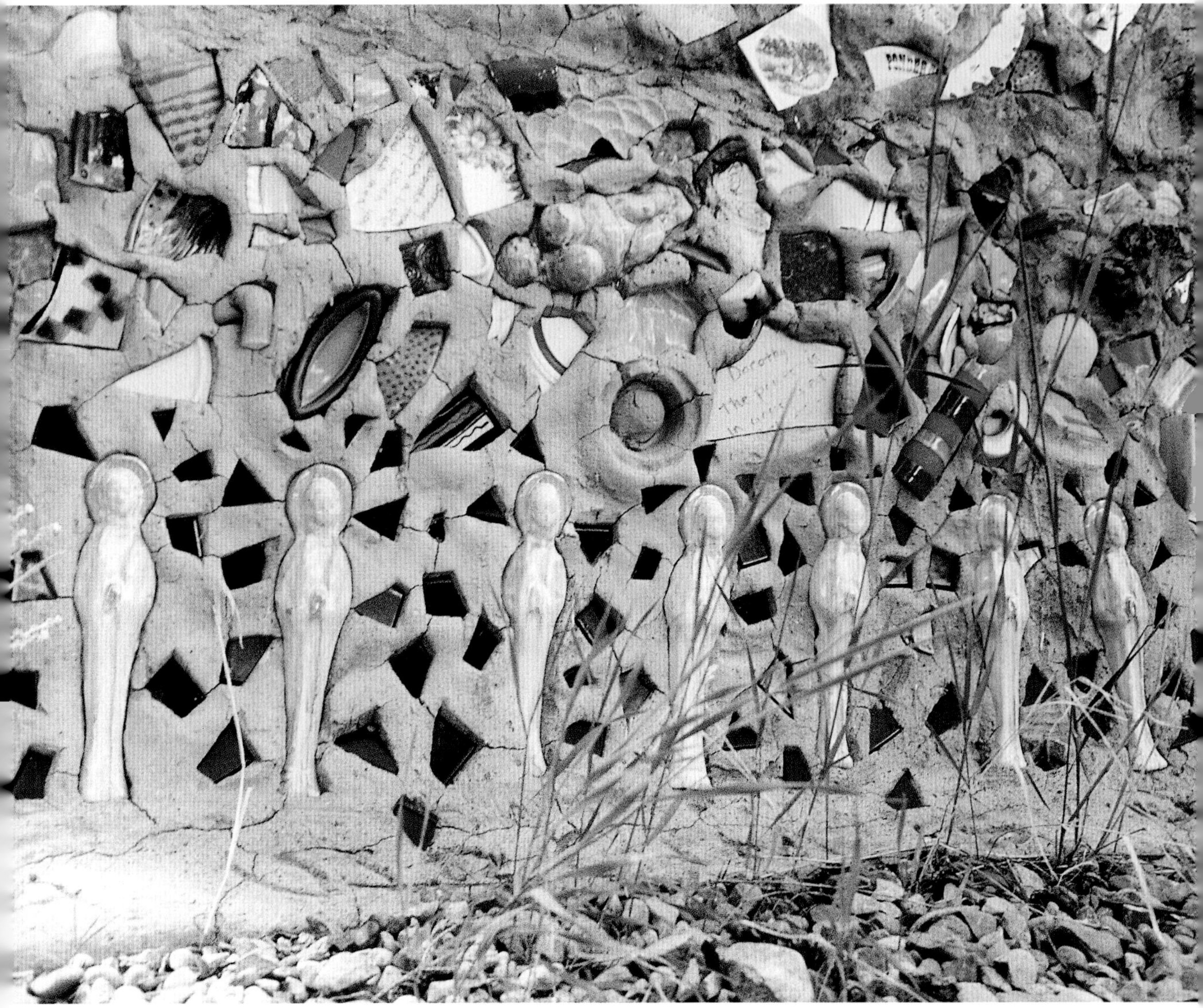

✳ CHAPTER 8 ✳

# *Common Ground*

FROM TIME TO TIME, MERCY (MISERICORDE) MAY TAKE A WINDING, RIVERINE COURSE, BUT THE STREAM OF SECOND OR THIRD OR FIFTIETH CHANCES RECEIVED AS BLESSINGS FROM MARY OR OTHER WELLSPRINGS STILL RUNS IN THE WORLD. MERCY TRICKLES AMONG US, EVEN WHEN ITS NAME IS GIVEN TO A TORONTO FASHION LABEL ADVERTISED AS AVAILABLE AT "SELECT HOLT RENFREW STORES"; EVEN WHEN THE BLESSED VIRGIN MARY, *eiparthenos (Ever-Virgin)* ✳ *Ark of the Covenant* ✳ *A Mercy for the Worlds* ✳ *Cause of Our Joy* ✳ *Comforter of the Afflicted Consolatrix Afflictorum* ✳ *Domina* ✳ *Gate of Heaven* ✳

*Dear Mary,*
*My boyfriend likes it when I make noises when I'm having an orgasm. But I prefer to quietly focus on what's happening ... I've taken to faking it for him while I get my real fix by myself ... for my next performance, I need other lines I might blurt out instead of "Yes, Yes, Yes!" and "Oh God!"*
*Quiet Zone*

*Dear Quiet Zone,*
*"Oh Jesus in the breadbox!" "Sweet mother of God!" or "Christ on a crutch, don't stop!" are always Good ones to blurt out if you're a repressed Catholic. But only if you want to ... All that screaming and hollering can leave you exhausted and a victim of chronic dry-throat syndrome. P.S. "Oh blessed virgin Mary, stander on the head of snakes!" is always a good one, if you're really stuck.*

From "Ask Mary," by Mary Walsh, *Elle Canada*, March 2002

crowned and gazing straight ahead, holding a Christ Child of similar aspect, appears on a Dolce & Gabbana dress, US$435, and when Mary also resides within her own soap, as an alternate to the Dirty Girls' bar; even when Demeter Fragrances' "Holy Water" can be found at Ogilvys in Montreal; even though Divine is an Edmonton clothing shop, and Heaven 27 belongs to Sofia Coppola in Los Angeles; even when Imitation of Christ is the New York clothing line favoured by Hollywood starlets who may accessorize with a rosary necklace, hand-enamelled.

Mercy may be all that can water the drought of despair. The Madonna della Misericordia, Our Lady of Mercy, who gathers all humanity into the protection of her star-spangled cloak, was first formed in Italy from late- thirteenth-century prayers and paintings made by people beset with fear. The freezing storms, crop failures, and famine of the Little Ice Age had already begun. By the time the Black Plague was burning through the fourteenth century, killing a third of the population between India and Iceland, and shattering every belief and act belonging to an ordinary day, the Madonna of Mercy was an enormously strong, grave-faced, monumental figure. In Pierro della Francesca's 1445 painting, she stands alone in a red dress, holding open her black, brown-lined cloak to encompass kneeling men and women, one of whom is hidden under the black hood worn by the few brave religious and lay people who dealt with the Plague dead. The human beings in della Francesca's painting come about knee-high to the Madonna. She was cut down to size at the Catholic Church's Counter-Reformation Council of Trent, 1545–63, and isn't seen as often in a red dress now (though the Virgin Mary's fifteenth-century miraculous protection from the Black Plague for the Italian village of Pratolo is remembered in a yearly London, Ontario, street procession), but nothing else has changed about the human need for mercy, Mary's capacity to give it, and the ambiguity between receiving divine or earthly mercies, and being merciful ourselves.

✶

IN HUMILITY ON COMMON GROUND, the Latin *humus* from which the word is made, the net of connections containing the world can be seen. The mesh leaves no one on earth, and no place, apart from the rest, immune from shock and fear. When a piece of the sky is Mary-blue one minute, then crossed with flames and falling buildings and bodies the next, the contrasting web strands strung through mercy tighten. Only helpless need can ask. Only love can give. And only recipients of mercy in any of its abundant, uncalculated courses, rising in Mary the Mother's patient grace, or a stranger's, or an enemy's, or a sister's compassion, can recognize its sweetness and may be covenanted to continue its flow.

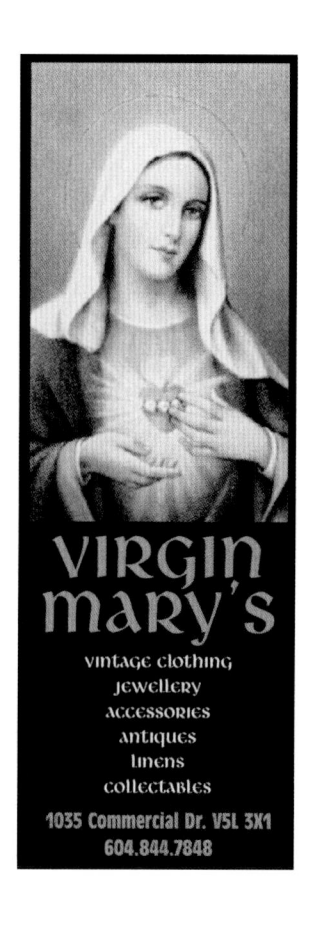

The possibility of receiving, recognizing, withholding, or giving mercy is folded with contradiction, as is the timing of the gold-on-blue American Eid stamp, issued September 2001, to honour Islamic calligraphy, as is Mary's own Afghanistan-born blue dress. The Renaissance Italian painters and their patrons wanted to use the most expensive pigment in the world for her garments. A faraway mountain country's lapis lazuli, ground into luminous blue stain, was more costly than gold leaf.

After September 11, 2001, wanting to bear with contradiction, wanting to hold onto my belief in the oldest Afghan proverb — "The world is a travellers' inn" — and wanting to remember mercies received in Muslim countries, I attended Friday afternoon prayers at the mosque on West 8th Avenue in Vancouver.

In the basement of the mosque, floor-length blue curtains enclosed a space for three women, wearing the hijab to hide their hair, and me, only partly hidden in a peach-coloured shawl. A speaker system broadcast the imam's Arabic exhortations from the main floor. Traffic noise floated in from Heather Street. The concealing curtains stirred in the warm wind flowing through the mosque when latecomers opened the front door upstairs. Closed white venetian blinds clicked at the window. Nothing felt familiar, at first.

I sat cross-legged on the floor, staring at a thin beige-and-blue-striped carpet until the softly chanted prayers, and my body's imitation of the Ethiopian woman almost imperceptibly swaying from side to side next to me, resurrected one hot day in the middle of the war in Bosnia.

Old men whose hard, scarred hands tenderly smoothed my bangs under a headscarf took me into Tuzla's Many Coloured Mosque. Inside was a place for a non-Muslim stranger in the circle of men and women passing a rope of apricot-sized carved beads from hand to hand.

Each bead represented one of Allah's names, murmured to mourn a dead man I didn't know. For a moment or two, the lifting and falling litany of names and the slight left–right rocking of those who spoke them sent a current of consolation beyond the mosque, into the mortar-broken city and the camps crowded with displaced people in the countryside. The scent and flavour of the rose-petal candy that was a funeral gift from the dead man to sweeten his memory has lasted so long in my senses that I have only to smell an old-fashioned rose to stand again, for an instant, on the steps of the Many Coloured Mosque in Tuzla after the ceremony.

✷

I DIDN'T ENTER the fifteenth-century Bajrakii mosque in Pec, Kosovo, in 1997, only sat by the heart-of-the-flame pink rose bush outside, reading a poem written by an Islamic mystic born in September 1207, when Balkh, Afghanistan, was part of the Persian empire:

> The wind is the Holy Spirit.
> The trees are Mary.
>  …
> The scent of Joseph's shirt comes to Jacob.
> A red carnelian of Yemeni laughter is heard
> by Muhammad in Mecca.
>  …

From *The Essential Rumi*, "Spring is Christ," translated by Coleman Banks and John Moyne[1]

✷

WHEN SERBIAN PARAMILITARY GANGS were shelling and burning Pec, I was dreaming in my sleep upstairs in a house on a Canadian west coast island. Mary — it must have been her with her back to me in the dark, dream smoke — was climbing down from her place on the western edge of the prayer niche in the ruins of Bajrakii mosque, feeling her way along the blackened walls with her hands.

✷

AFTER THE LAND SURVEY for the Virgin Mary in Canada, her mercy seems real and distinct and daily to me when the heat of the days after July 12 summons Srebrenica and Bosnia again, but slightly apart from me now, not in my body and mind as if it were all happening again in the present.

✷

I RECEIVED A RESPONSE to my need for mercy to drench the arid memory of driving north to escape Father Morice's history and my own emptiness at Our Lady of Good Hope's Fort St. James church. I was given a chance to learn that bitter disappointment is an unfinished work, not a black entity with bound edges, as I had thought, but a matter that may yet loosen, diffusing at least a portion of itself into an accompanying, sidelong grace. A crack of watery, uncertain light opened around a Dakelh Dene bear-hunter legend known to me since I had read anthropological research notes recording its structure more than twenty years ago when I worked along the Skeena River.

Bears are for knowing as creatures not far from us, I have believed since those river times when I met up with them now and then. When bears and humans lived on the same ground, they hunted and gathered the same animals, fish, root vegetables, fruit, and green plants. Bears standing on their hind legs, or skinned, look human. In Europe, Russia, Asia, and here, wherever people shared their lives with bears, they knew each other as spirit and shape-shifters, and a star bear walked across the night sky.

On the ocean at night, rolling into an unseen horizon; in countries where dancing bears belonged to the Roma whose oldest legends allowed the occasional virgin to give birth to a bear who could work like a man, and along all of the roads to Mary in Canada, I had remembered the Athabaskan-speaking peoples' bear hunter.

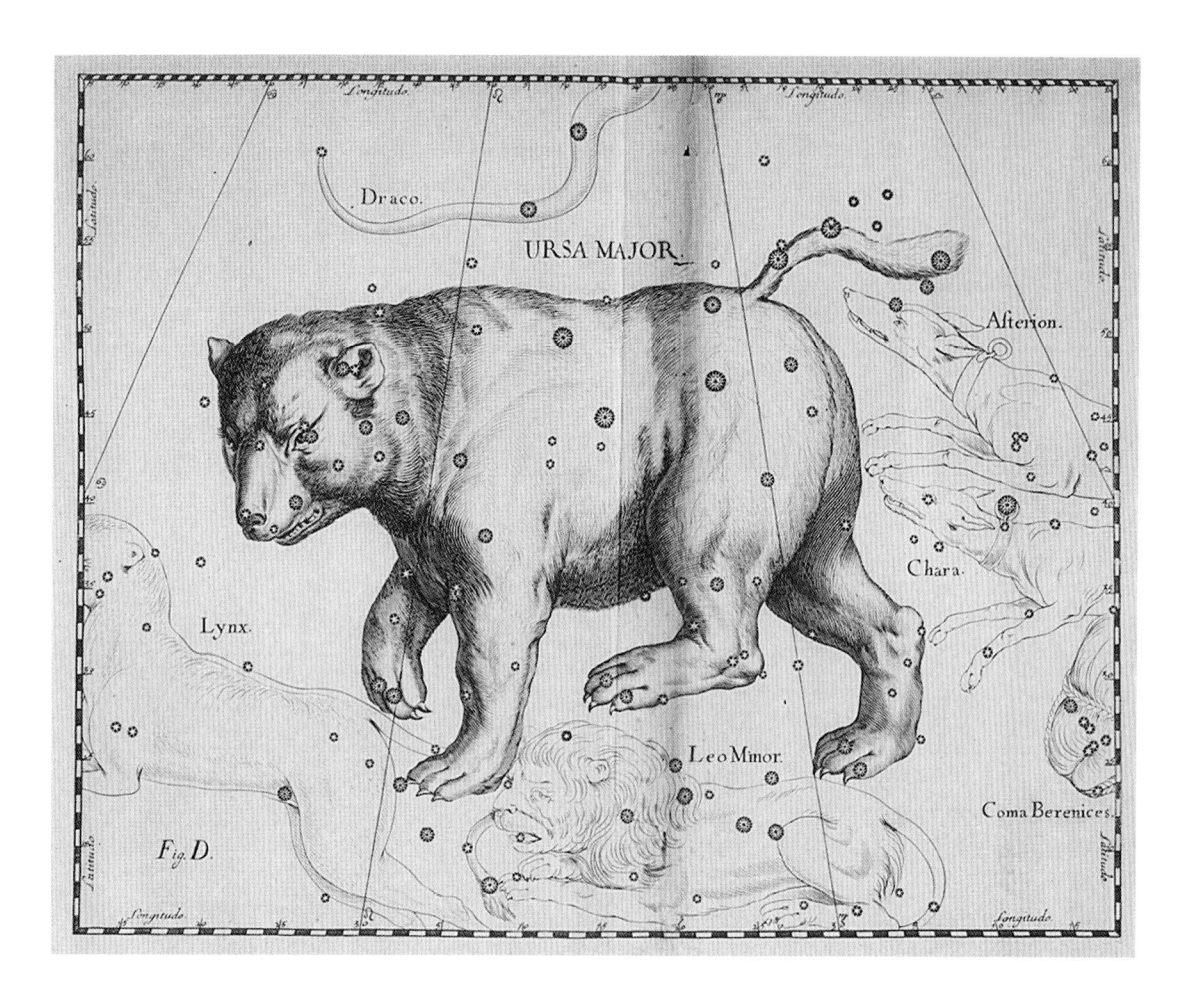

Now, empty-hearted on dry ground again, with no northern runaway roads to drive, I set down the mythic frame of the hunter's story, with details of Dene tradition from that time when bears shared British Columbia's northern forests with the Dakelh people.

One night in early spring, a young hunter slept wrapped in a black bear skin, his body curved like a new moon around the circle of his fire. Late frost stiffened the hides he had hung over his lodge entrance and his breath clouded the cool air as he slept.

When pine wood snapped in the flames, the young man woke to stare at the night sky rounded in the roof opening above his fire. He got up and stepped into the night. Yoehta, star-shape of the Great Bear, hung overhead. The bright, sharp points of Yoehta's eye stars looked down on the dark blur of the northern forest, on the lodge where a thread of smoke rose from the roof hole, on the dogs sleeping outside the lodge, and on the young bear hunter looking back at the Great Bear in the sky.

Yoehta had walked only half his journey across the night. Dawn was still far away, so the young man who longed for morning wrapped himself in his bear skin robe again to sleep curled around his fire.

Once more, he woke suddenly, and stepped outside. But Old Yoehta seemed to stand as still in the heavens as the hunter was standing on earth. He threw more wood on his fire and lay down again. Behind his closed eyes, the familiar, beloved hunt began in his dreams: the trail; the dogs running beside him; the bear, still winter-sleepy and blundering; the sure arrow shot. Even in his sleep, the hunter smiled a little, proud of his own skill and strength.

Once, and once again, he woke and went out into the night to see if Old Yoehta had moved toward morning. The bear stars, still far from their journey's end at the edge of the sky, stared down at him.

"How slowly you move, Yoehta!" the young man shouted. His voice splintered into laughter, "You are old indeed ..." His cries faded into the cold, quiet dark.

The hunter sat by his fire then, until his dogs stirred at first light. He called to them and set out on the hunting trail. His feet moved quickly, lightly, and his eyes flashed, seeking bear signs: a broken branch; the small, dry droppings that mean a winter-sleeping bear is newly awake; a print on frosted ground. Far ahead of him, the dogs barked. He ran toward them, certain they had found a bear.

But the dogs were crouched at the feet of an old man sitting on a stump in a small clearing. His white hair lifted in the wind, and his sharp, bright eyes shone from a face slashed with streaks of vermillion red paint. He held a walking stick before him as he looked hard at the young hunter. "Come here to me," he called. The hunter did not want to leave the sheltering, green woods he knew to walk on open ground, but, in time, he came forward.

"You laughed at me," the old one said. "You cried out in the night, saying I am so old I walk across the sky too slowly for you." The red-painted man's mouth clouded no breath into the cool air as he spoke. The hunter tried to look away from his shining eyes, but he could not. "Still ..." the old man continued, "Still, each night I walk the distance you have travelled this morning while the world was made small for you. Now, you will learn how long your journey home will be."

"Your home trail is not marked," the old voice went on, "so perhaps ..." He was silent a moment, then, "Perhaps if you take my staff, and use it as I tell you, the trail you find will bring you home." He held out the long spruce pole, but the young man did not reach for it. Instead, he whistled to his dogs, but they stayed still at the old man's feet. Their ears did not even twitch to his whistle.

The hunter wanted only his homeward trail, but the path he had travelled from his lodge that morning was already gone. Trees enclosed him in the clearing now. He looked again at the old man with red-slashed cheeks and bright eyes, then he reached out and grasped the stick.

"Let no other hand touch it," the old one said. "When no bears come to you, when only hunger finds you, and you see no certain trail, stand this spruce staff on the ground before you, holding it straight between earth and sky. Let go.

"If it falls to the rising or setting sun, bears, male and female, wait for you on that path.

"If it falls the north wind's way, only famine lives there. Walk on another way and try again.

"Go carefully when the stick falls south."

The young hunter turned away from these words. He was already hungry, and he wanted his own fire in his own lodge. When he looked back, the old one was gone. So, the hunter set out again, certain his home trail must be near by.

But night after night, Old Yoehta looked down on a tired young man asleep in a tangle of brush. Every step the hunter ran in the woods showed him how far and long he had yet to travel. His home stood on the other side of a world an old man with red-slashed cheeks and bright eyes had made small for only one morning.

The young hunter ran for days, slashing the pole through branches and bushes in a forest strange to him. No bears came. No clear trail appeared. His belly tightened with hunger. His steps slowed at last, and he carried the spruce pole over his shoulder.

When days and days and days had rolled past, he remembered the old man's words about the stick. He crouched to hold it straight between earth and sky, then let it fall. When he walked the trail leading into the sun's path, or following it, bears, male and female, came to him, giving themselves to his arrows. His hunger eased, and he walked on, carrying the pole in his hand.

When a moon had grown round and full, then thinned through the nights to a fingernail, and fattened again, the trail showed itself to the south. The young hunter followed, and searched long on wide, open ground that frightened him before bears both larger and smaller than any he had known came to him, and the trail appeared again. He walked on, carrying the stick.

When moons had rolled into winter, the spruce pole fell the north wind's way, and he followed it. Bears sleeping deep in hidden dens stirred in their dreams when the hunter staggered near death from hunger and weariness in the north. He fell to his knees and the stick dropped from his hand, pointing a clear trail away from the cold at last. Too weak to rise alone, the hunter took hold of the spruce pole to help him to his feet. He walked on, leaning on the stick.

When winter moons had rolled into spring, Old Yoehta looked down from the night sky to see bears, large and small, male and female, crossing the trail where the hunter slept. Their furred shapes — coloured black or white or many kinds of brown, and sometimes silvery grey — blurred into forest shadows. The hunter saw them in his dreams. In the morning, he used the spruce pole as a walking stick, and went on.

When all the seasons had rolled into time, and time had turned into the rhythm of the soft, repeated sounds the hunter made every day with his footsteps and his walking stick on the trail, Old Yoehta looked down some nights to see the shape of a bear sleeping on the hunter's home trail.

When the sounds of the hunter's footsteps and his stick touching the trail were as familiar to him as the small wind of his own breath, when he and the bears moved together in the same dreams at night, he saw his home, small in the far distance ahead.

The hunter's steps were slow, now, so he leaned heavily on the spruce walking stick while he watched his old home grow larger as he walked toward it. When he reached his lodge in the evening, he saw that its roof had been broken with the weight of many snows. The house poles were leaning, and overgrown with moss.

The hunter set the spruce walking stick straight between earth and sky at the entrance to his lodge, then he cleaned leaves and pine needles from the circle of fire stones. He made a fire, curved his body like a new moon around it, and slept.

The night sky covered the roofless lodge and the sleeping hunter. The wind stirred his white hair and the firelight striped his cheeks red. Old Yoehta, the Great Bear in the stars, looked down on him, and saw how easily he and the bears moved along the trails in their dreams. He walked on, slowly, across the night sky.

✳

For months afterward, the earth-round trail of transitions between humans, animals, stars, and sacred beings unfurled. Until the bear legend entered the making of this book, I didn't know that Artemis the Great She-Bear, Mother of the Animals — Ursa Major — was also the great bear in the sky, or that the word *arctic* was formed from *arktos*, the Greek term for Ursa Major.

I knew that Panagia, the Byzantine title meaning Holy Queen Mother, was the name of the Virgin Mary in some of the oldest churches in Constantinople-Istanbul and Greece, as well as in Greek Canadian places like the café in Eastend, Saskatchewan, where Angela Doulias thinks a portion of her possibilities can be found in all women. I knew Panagia was also an Arabian mare, beautiful grey, high-headed mother to Pakistan and greatgranddam of Palestyna, Paladin, and others in a line of European champion horses. But I didn't know that in Crete, where Artemis was worshipped as the divine she-bear, the Virgin Mary is Panagia Arkoudiotissa, Goddess or All Holy Queen of the Bears. I didn't know the Ursuline nuns took their name from a mythical Saint Ursula, originally Ursel, the Saxon bear goddess, or that the Basque fishermen who carried Pyrenees Virgin Mary memories and prayers on their Terra Nova cod voyages were also certain of their eternal connection with the bear stars above them in their liquid, tilting world.

And, until I had to search an old file for the name of the church decorated with Mary's roses at Kitseguecla up the Skeena River, I didn't remember who had made the field notes for the Dakelh bear story that had borne me along for so many years.

There was no miraculous Seeing the Light in the papers at the back of the Skeena file. The Goodnight Irene Miracle remains my only experience that meets the Catholic Church's definition of "a truth above reason but revealed by God."[2]

Resurrected from my own field notes in a Rite-in-the-Rain book that still smells like fish:

2333: Northern offshore areas: winds westerly two five knots, rising to three zero overnight; seas two point one metres, northwesterly swells.

Here is an irrational, even modestly insane, act taking place in the radio room on board a stern trawling ship registered in Gydnia, Poland, and fishing hake in waters within Canada's headland to headland two hundred sea mile limit off the west coast:

(Surely to God we are still in Canadian waters. We could have changed course for the Gulf of Mexico while I was below decks in the factory, but the ship's engines never hurried their beat under my boots, so we are still here. Here is out of sight of land.)

Neither the captain and third officer, on bridge duty outside the radio room until midnight, nor the ship's radio officer, nor the marine operator on land, if there is still land, will find cause for alarm because the fisheries observer is making a brief ship-to-shore call. She will not touch the transmit button on the radio handset until the three minutes between thirty and thirty-three minutes after the hour have passed. On every ocean, these minutes, and the three after the hour, are saved in silence. The silence is for the possibility of a voice threading through distance and static from a vessel in distress.

The ship's Polish name is pronounced correctly for the marine operator. Her port of registry — Golf Yankee Delta November India Alpha — proceeds through the air without pause. Her call sign is recited clearly: Juliet Sierra Hotel Uniform.

When the phone is answered in another world, only a few words are spoken. No charges have been incurred by the vessel, which is beginning to plunge on a long groundswell.

2240: Even when the companionways on a ship carrying a hundred men are empty, a person's bewildered consideration of her own behaviour can become humiliation in the minutes needed to go down three decks, slowly, for once, to the main fishing deck.

Tomorrow, someone listening to song request messages on a CBC Radio 800 number will hear my voice saying, "Goodnight Irene." The words callers are supposed to say about themselves and the song will not be on the message tape. I may have said, "Ship." I may have muttered, "Sea."

The irrationality, or more, lives in the inescapable, known-to-me-all-along fact that if CBC Radio sees fit to play "Goodnight Irene" tomorrow afternoon, or any other afternoon of the next forty or more days, I will never hear it. The fitful shortwave radio rigged in my cabin works best, if at all, at night. Its brief afternoon performance today was an anomaly, as was my presence beside it. Afternoons, I am on deck with the bosun and his crew if we are hauling fish, or on the bridge checking the fishing and factory production logs, or down in the factory counting the by-catch — twenty or so yellow-tail rock cod, maybe a few coppers every ton of hake right now — and grabbing fish off the conveyor belt for biological sampling.

I'm halfway across the wide wooden fishing deck on my way to the portside factory ladder when the hammer-hard voice waltzes "Now I wish the Lord I'd never seen your face. I'm sorry you all was born. Irene, goodnight," into the smooth, heavy rhythms of the sea and the ship's engines.

I'm going to stand here now, facing the stern and the wind long enough to stop my rambling, and my gambling, and settle down by my fireside bright, before I turn around to see if "Goodnight Irene" is real.

2245: Nope. Ferociously uttered Polish words have already swallowed, "I'll love her 'til the sea runs dry." Now I need coffee courage to face the factory.

When I walk up the slanting deck to find the kettle in the crew's messroom, Roman, the fishing bosun, and Franek, and the others on duty tonight are dozing in front of a scratchy video screen. A Polish-dubbed version of Huddie Ledbetter's life is roaring forth into the wind on deck. Every word of the movie is smash-dubbed into Polish except for the songs. Lead Belly sang "Goodnight Irene" in Canada's offshore Pacific fishing area for himself.

✹

IN MY TWENTY-YEAR-OLD FILE, faded 1979 photocopies mailed to me from the National Archives in care of the Fisheries office in Prince Rupert are filled with right-slanting, evenly formed, black ink handwriting. The events of the bear hunter's story are recorded in perfect English: his shouted fury in the night, his dogs, the strange old man in the clearing, and the hunter's long walk around the earth to reach home. An explanation of the Great Bear Star—old man's vermillion face paint is included. ("This was done by scratching off with the fingers part of the vermillion wherewith the face was originally covered.") The notes may have been considered, then eventually not used, for academic papers published in *Transactions of the Royal Society of Canada, 1892*, and *Transactions of the Canadian Institute, 1895*.

The papers are labelled, in the same handwriting, "Dene myths-[indecipherable word, perhaps "Rev."] Father Morice. 1892." Father Adrien Gabriel Morice had provided me with the spirit lines between earth, stars, and bears through which the Dakelh people's bear hunter moved on his long homeward trail. Only the hunter's earthbound humility makes his transformations possible. By now, I know I need bears and stars and willingness more than dogma to stay on watch for the eternal interconnectedness of all life and matter. Trust in the Mary who still knows older, wilder, divine mothers while she moves and changes in this world allows me, now, to see the bear hunter's story in the light widely diffused from her aspects of earthly humility and divine compassion.

If I could recognize the Good Hope trickling down from Fort St. James so long after my blank despair of meaning in the search for Our Lady there, I might be starting to know the Virgin Jacques Cartier never doubted would adapt to life beyond church walls in the New World. Her simultaneous aspects as both mother of the world, with intimate knowledge of every human failing and bright possibility, and willing, teenaged bearer of "that holy thing which shall be born of thee ... the son of God,"[3] in Luke's Gospel, are present not only in the oceans and rivers where I first looked for her, but also in Canadian earth, rock, and snow. Before she was ever listed in the *Novalis Guide to Canadian Shrines*, she inhabited capes, bays, islands, rivers, mountains, streets, and towns named for her coast to coast. She enters into living water and cedar trees of life.

✱

MARY HAS SOMETIMES BEEN TRANSFORMED by Canada's geography. As the world's only portage and iceberg Madonna, she is within the matter of a specifically Canadian world. Her place in Canadian culture as the mother of God, sometimes just mother, comfort in a blue cloak, lies even deeper. The Virgin Berg of St. John's harbour, June 24, 1905, reappears not only in Wayne Johnston's 1999 Newfoundland memoir *Baltimore's*

*Mansion*, but also as Rex Murphy's cloaked, irresistible reference in his May 11, 2002, *Globe and Mail* column: "Every fluffball from second-rate sitcoms and B movies was willing to do a walk on the ice 'to save the seals.' The day that Brigitte Bardot, Madonna of the ice-fields, came trailing clouds of glory, and linking her expertise to the agitated consciences of the animal-rights brigade, we knew the game was over."

The Virgin Mary had to travel a long way past scriptural and liturgical references in Canadian Catholic and Protestant churches, and Muslim mosques before Nova Scotia's Larry Gorman could make a song called "Matt and the Anchor" about how well she understood a working man's troubles. In *Folklore of Canada*, Edith Fowke explains:

> Larry also went fishing with ... Matt Howard. Early one season Matt lost an anchor; his wife, when he told her, said she would pray every day to the Blessed Virgin Mary for its return. Months later, he and Larry hauled in their nets and, sure enough, there was the anchor, corroded but still recognizable. We can imagine the transports of joy and thanksgiving at home when Matt reported his luck to his wife, because sometime later someone asked Larry how the day's fishing had gone and he replied: "'Tis to the Virgin we must pray / And every day must thank her; / Matt went out to fish today / And caught his little anchor."[4]

Mary of Canada had to move even further from formal religious structures, and deeper into our common memory storage, before one Canuck lesbian could ask another, "Do you know why the Virgin Mary looks sad in so many of her pictures?" Answer: "Because she really wanted a girl."

It's possible to see the sweetly rhymed, ordinary-dayness of Larry Gorman's extemporaneous song, and even the joke, as signs of the wide ground Mary owns in Canada, as well as evidence of how often, from the beginning of Christianity onward, she escapes the theological box to flow in the larger, non-Catholic, sometimes nonchurched, congregation of human beings who need mercy and other blessings.

Canada herself is blessed with the presence of Indian people who know spiritual traditions in which divine creation is now, and before, and forever, in all beings, and may, without contradiction, include Christianity, and Mary. In *Le Christ est amerindien — Christ Is a Native American —* Achiel Peelman O.M.I., professor of theology at Saint Paul University in Ottawa, offers: "The Amerindian religious experience is profoundly mystical and sacramental ... The Great Mystery is not situated 'above' nature or the cosmos, but is an intimate dimension of it. The total reality of nature or the cosmos can therefore be conceived as an immense iconography which contains concrete signs of the Great Mystery ... It is important to insist that this mystical dimension of the Amerindian religious experience did not disappear after the native religions had contact with Christianity."[5]

Peelman's book includes his interview with Father Paul Hernou, who had worked among the Cree in northwestern Alberta:

> While performing my ordinary duties as a priest (for example, in the field of the sacraments), I have also had the opportunity to participate in the field of religious ceremonies of the Cree and I have observed that the Cree themselves have started to integrate Christ into these rituals. For example, in the ritual of the sacred pipe, Christ is often addressed as "our elder brother." Even the Virgin Mary, "our mother," and Saint Ann, "our grandmother," find a place in these rituals. Frank Cardinal, one of the elders who taught me a lot, often prays in this manner.
>
> In 1984, the Dogrib Indians of the North West Territories prepared for the papal visit to Fort Simpson with an impressive sacrifice ceremony to the ancestors. The statues of the Virgin Mary and the Sacred Heart occupied a central place in this ritual ... Last year, I participated in a dance for the ancestors at Fox Lake in the

Little Red River area (Cree). On the main drum I saw a picture of the Virgin Mary.[6]

✸

THE RHYTHMS OF CONSOLATION I found in the Virgin Mary's ocean inheritance have surged some way across the map of inland Madonnas in Canada. Travelling a spiralling, labyrinthine trail across earth, sea, and sky, and into myself, will always be a pilgrimage. I will always be looking for the lighted place where the hope implicit in the continuously created natural world joins the stream of compassion running inside the contradictions organized religion, history, and culture give to Mary.

This Mary who holds the spirit lines of so many divine legacies gladly moves within the long, continuous resonance of native spirituality. She shares the synchronicity of her everlasting freshness and her fluid possibilities with the pregnant, Aztec fertility-sash-wearing Guadalupe Madonna of the Americas; with the Virgin Mary who appeared on a blue wall at Indian Brook, Nova Scotia, not as Mary Immaculate, alone, but holding the child to her shoulder, and, surely, with that adaptable Virgin of the movies who stands by Moony Pottey and her friends in *New Waterford Girl*. Adaptability and possibility are Mary's middle names in Canada. She gives her full consent to snow and ice, to fresh and salt water, to cities and cedar trees — eastern white and western red — to change, and to us.

---

*Who is she then who knows each
 creature's pain
and how it makes an opening for light?
All things to her are different and
 the same:*

*This dust is mother of the
 orphaned rain,
a full moon wears the barn owl's face
 in flight.
She knows each beast and every
 secret name.
All things to her are different and
 the same.*

From "Who is She, Then?" *Apochrypha of Light*, by Lorna Crozier,

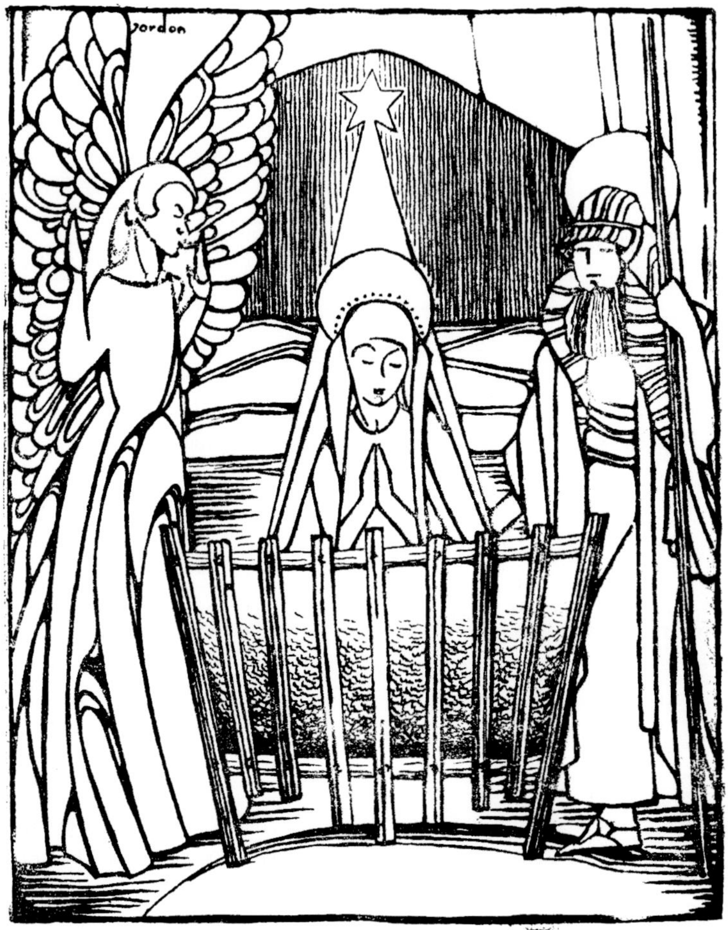
Gordon

# ✴ ENDNOTES ✴

INTRODUCTION

1. Jean Vanier, *Be Not Afraid* (Toronto: Griffin House, 1975).
2. Carol Dallaire, *Les Lieux Communs / Commonplaces* (Walter Phillips Gallery, 1995).

1 ✴ AT SEA

1. Alexander Carmichael, *Carmina Gadelica Hymns & Incantations: Collected in the Highlands and Islands of Scotland in the Last Century* (Edinburgh: Floris Books, 1992).
2. *Vinland Sagas: Norse Discovery of America*, trans. Magnus Magnusson (New York: Viking Press, 1965).
3. Author's interview with Alberto Ruy Sánchez.
4. Edward Haies's account of Sir Humphrey Gilbert's voyage to Newfoundland in the Modern History Sourcebook, located at www.fordham.edu © Paul Halsall, August 1998. Original source is *Voyages and Travels: Ancient and Modern, with Introductions, Notes and Illustrations* (New York: P.F. Collier & Son, c. 1910), The Harvard Classics, ed. C.W. Ellot (Vol. 33).
5. *The Bible*, authorized King James version.
6. W. M. Valgardson, *Sarah and the People of Sand River* (Toronto: Groundwood Books, 1996).

2 ✴ MAP-MAKING

1. Jean Chrétien, *Straight from the Heart* (Toronto: Key Porter Books, 1985).
2. Marian Engel, *The Glassy Sea* (Toronto: McClelland and Stewart, 1978).
3. Alberto Manguel, *Reading Pictures: A History of Love and Hate* (Toronto: Alfred A. Knopf Canada, 2000).
4. *The Hanging Garden*. Dir. Thom Fitzgerald. Goldwyn Films, 1998.
5. Joyce Marshall, ed. and trans., *Word from New France: The Selected Letters of Marie de l'Incarnation* (Toronto: Oxford University Press, 1967).
6. Ibid.
7. Ibid.

8   Marina Warner, *Alone of All Her Sex: The Myth and the Cult of the Virgin Mary* (New York: Random House, 1983).
9   Robert Ward, *Virgin Trails: A Secular Pilgrimage* (Toronto: Key Porter Books, 2002).
10  Marina Warner, *Alone of All Her Sex: The Myth and the Cult of the Virgin Mary* (New York: Random House, 1983).
11  Northrop Frye, *The Bush Garden: Essays on the Canadian Imagination* (Toronto: House of Anansi Press, 1971).
12  Katherine Govier, *The Immaculate Conception Photography Gallery* (Toronto: Random House Canada, 2000).
13  Deborah Porter, *Flowers & No More Medea* (Toronto: Playwrights Canada Press, 1994).
14  Colleen Curran, *Sacred Hearts* (Toronto: Playwrights Canada Press, 1997).
15  Denise Boucher, *The Fairies Are Thirsty* (Vancouver: Talonbooks, 1982).
16  Ibid.
17  Erika de Vasconcelos, *My Darling Dead Ones* (Toronto: Alfred A. Knopf, 1997).
18  Ibid.
19  *Westminster Larger Catechism*. "The Larger Catechism; agreed upon by the Assembly of Divines at Westminster, with the assistance of commissioners from the Church of Scotland, and, as a part of the covenanted uniformity in religion betwixt the churches of Christ in the kingdoms of Scotland, England, and Ireland. And approved anno 1648, by the General Assembly of the Church of Scotland, to be a directory for catechising such as have made some proficiency in the lnowledge of the grounds of religion, with the proofs from the Scripture. Edinburgh." Located at www.reformed.org/documents/index_docu.html
20  Don Gillmor, *The Desire of Every Living Thing: A Search for Home* (Toronto: Random House Canada, 1999).
21  F.W. Lindsay, *Outlaws in British Columbia* (Vernon: Interior Printers, 1963).
22  Douglas Barbour and Stephen Scobie, eds, *The Maple Laugh Forever: An Anthology of Canadian Comic Poetry* (Edmonton: Hurtig Publishers, 1981).
23  Statistics Canada Internet Site located at www.statcan.ca. Statistics Canada information is used with the permission of Statistics Canada. Users are forbidden to copy the data and redisseminate them, in an original or modified form, for commercial purposes, without the expressed permission of Statistics Canada. Information on the availability of the wide range of data from Statistics Canada can be obtained from Statistics Canada's Regional Offices, its World Wide Web site at http://www.statcan.ca, and its toll-free access number 1-800-263-1136.
24  1871 Canadian Census Index located at www.KindredKonnections.com © 1998-2003 Fficiency Software, Inc.
25  Robert Service, *The Collected Poems of Robert Service* (New York: Dodd, Mead & Company, 1940).
26  Margaret Atwood, *Cat's Eye* (Toronto: McClelland & Stewart, 1988).

## 3 ✳ MARY IN CANADA

1   An account of Jacques Cartier's second voyage, taken from his log books and probably written by a crew man, was first published in 1545, and then absorbed into Marc Lescarbot's 1609 *Histoire de la Nouvelle-France*. Sources: *Dictionary of Canadian Biography* and Early Canadiana Online located at www.canadiana.org © Canadian Institute for Historical Microreproductions.
2   Ibid.
3   Roy Kiyooka, *Transcanadaletters* (Vancouver: Talonbooks, 1975).
4   Margaret Atwood, *Wilderness Tips* (Toronto: McClelland & Stewart, 1992).
5   Alissa York, *Mercy* (Toronto: Random House Canada, 2003).
6   James W. Nicol, *Sainte-Marie Among the Hurons* (Toronto: Playwrights Co-op, 1977).

7. Brian Moore, *Black Robe* (New York: E. P. Dutton, 1985).
8. Joyce Marshall, ed. and trans., *Word from New France: The Selected Letters of Marie de l'Incarnation* (Toronto: Oxford University Press, 1967).
9. Stephen Clarkson and Christina McCall, *Trudeau and Our Times: Volume 1, The Magnificent Obsession* (Toronto: McClelland & Stewart, 1990).
10. Peter C. Newman, *Caesars of the Wilderness: Company of Adventurers Volume II* (Toronto: Viking Penguin Books Canada, 1987).
11. Traditional song.
12. Hugh Durnford and Peter Madely, "Birchbark Brigades," *Great Canadian Adventures* (Montreal: The Reader's Digest Association [Canada], 1976).
13. Charles Lillard and Terry Glavin, *A Voice Great Within Us: The Story of Chinook* (Vancouver: New Star Books, 1998).
14. H.C. Holling, *Paddle-to-the-Sea* (Boston: Houghton Mifflin Co., 1969).
15. "Rupert's Land," *A Dictionary of Canadianisms on Historical Principals*.
16. 1871 Canadian Census Index located at www.KindredKonnections.com © 1998-2003 Fficiency Software, Inc.
17. Ibid.
18. Andrew Shiels, *The Witch of the Westcot: A Tale of Nova Scotia in Three Cantos and Other Waste Leaves of Literature* (Halifax: Joseph Howe, 1831). Located at http://toroprod.library.utoronto.ca © University of Toronto Libraries, 2003
19. David Trumble and Glen Ellis, *The Road to St. Ola and Other Stories* (Don Mills: J.M. Dent & Sons, Canada, 1978).
20. Helen Fogwill Porter, *Below the Bridge* (St. John's: Breakwater Books, 1979).
21. Ibid.
22. Leonard St. John, *The Novalis Guide to Canadian Shrines* (Ottawa: Novalis, 2002).
23. Author's interview with Carmen Bizet-Irigoyen.
24. Terry Glavin, "Miracles and Lies Still Flourish Around the Virgin." *Georgia Straight* (June 27–July 4, 2002): 28.
25. Lynn Coady, *Strange Heaven* (Fredericton: Goose Lane Editions, 1998).
26. Leonard St. John, *The Novalis Guide to Canadian Shrines* (Ottawa: Novalis, 2002).
27. Acadian Geneology located at www.acadian.org/acadflag.html courtesy of Yvon Cyr.
28. Antonine Maillet, *La Sagouine*, trans. Luis de C'espedes (Toronto: Simon & Pierre, 1985).
29. William Kirby, *The Golden Dog (Le Chien d'Or): A Romance of Old Quebec* (Toronto: McClelland & Stewart, 1969).
30. Katherine Govier, *The Truth Teller* (Toronto: Random House Canada, 2000).
31. Mary Woodbury, "Not in Front of the Virgin." *Prairie Fire* 135–43.
32. Melissa Hardy, *The Uncharted Heart* (Toronto: Alfred A. Knopf Canada, 2001).
33. *Leolo*. Dir. Jean-Claude Lauzon. Les Productions du Verseau and Flach Film with The National Film Board of Canada, 1992.
34. Madonna House Apostolate, Our Lady of Combermere, © 2000 Madonna House Publications.
35. Robertson Davies, *The Lyre of Orpheus* (Toronto: Macmillan, Canada, 1988).
36. Barry Callaghan and Bruce Meyer, eds. *We Wasn't Pals: Canadian Poetry and Prose of the First World War* (Toronto: Exile Editions 2001).
37. Ibid.
38. The Bible, authorized King James version.
39. Alberto Manguel, *Reading Pictures: A History of Love and Hate* (Toronto: Alfred A. Knopf Canada, 2000).
40. Author's e-mail correspondence with Marianna Gartner.
41. Robert Service, *The Collected Poems of Robert Service* (New York: Dodd, Mead & Company, 1940).
42. Diane Schoemperlen, *Our Lady of the Lost and Found* (Toronto: Harper Flamingo Canada, 2001).

## 4 ✳ EASTERN SETTINGS

1. William R. Gray, *Voyages to Paradise: Exploring in the Wake of Captain Cook*, photo. Gordon W. Gahan (Washington, D.C.: National Geographic Society, 1981).
2. *Book of Common Prayer and Administration of the Sacraments and Other Rites and Ceremonies of the Church According to the Use of the Church of England in the Dominion of Canada* (Toronto: Oxford University Press). Inscription: B. M. Anderson, May 9, 1929.
3. The Bible, authorized King James version.
4. Amy Barratt, "Holy Mary! And Mary and Marie and Maria and …" *Montreal Mirror* (January 4, 2001): Theatre section. www.montrealmirror.com © Mirror 2001.
5. Shirley Sterling, *My Name is Seepeetza* (Vancouver: Douglas & McIntyre, 1992).
6. Cyrus Macmillan, *Canadian Wonder Tales*, being the two collections *Canadian Wonder Tales* and *Canadian Fairy Tales* collected from oral sources, (London, Sydney, Toronto: Bodley Head, 1974).
7. Marius Barbeau, *The Tree of Dreams* (Toronto: Oxford University Press, 1955).
8. Idries Shah, comp. "The Algonquin Cinderella," *World Tales: The Extraordinary Coincidence of Stories Told in All Times in All Places* (New York: Harcourt Brace & Company, 1979).
9. *Notre-Dame-du-Cap* shrine pamphlet, Cap-de-la-Madeleine, Quebec.
10. *Catholic Encyclopedia* (New York: The Encyclopedia Press, 1917).
11. The Bible, authorized King James version.
12. "The Magdalene Laundries," lyrics by Joni Mitchell, Crazy Crow Music & Sony/ATV Music Publishing, 1994.

## 5 ✳ NORTHERN BLESSINGS

1. R. M. Ballantyne, *Ungava: A Tale of the Esquimaux Land* (London and Glasgow: Collins Clear-Type Press, n.d.).
2. Hilary Stewart, *Cedar* (Seattle: University of Washington Press, 1984).
3. Winton D. Thomas, ed., *Documents from Old Testament Times* (New York: Harper & Row, 1961).
4. Frank L. Baum, *The Wonderful Wizard of Oz* (1900).
5. Lizette Hall, *The Carrier My People* (Prince George: Papyrus Printing, 1992).
6. The Bible, authorized King James version.
7. Ibid.
8. Northrop Frye, *The Great Code: The Bible & Literature* (Markham: Penguin Books, 1990).
9. George MacDonald, *At the Back of the North Wind* (London: Strahan & Co., 1890).
10. John Buchan, *Sick Heart River* (Oxford: Oxford University Press, 1994).
11. Ibid.
12. Ibid.
13. "Fifty Mission Cap," lyrics by Gordon Edgar Downie, Songs of Peer Ltd., 1992.
14. Benedict Freedman and Nancy Freedman, *Mrs. Mike* (New York: Coward, McCann & Geoghegan, 1968).
15. Ibid.
16. Ibid.
17. "Revelation of Art in Canada," *Canadian Theosophist* (July 1926).
18. Aurias Diamonds advertisement, *Fashion Magazine*, Vancouver Edition (June 2003).
19. Robert M. Hamilton and Dorothy Shields, eds., *The Dictionary of Canadian Quotations and Phrases* (Toronto: McClelland & Stewart, 1982).
20. Henry A. Larsen, *The Big Ship: An Autobiography*, co-op. Frank R. Sheer and Edvard Omholt-Jensen (Toronto: McClelland & Stewart, 1967).
21. Ibid.
22. Author's interview with Aimé Anhegona.
23. Marina Jimenez, "Spiritualities can co-exist. I am a true believer in Nuliajuk." *Globe and Mail* (August 25, 2001): B3.
24. Samuel Hearne, *A Journey from Prince of Wales' Fort in Hudson's Bay, to the Northern Ocean … in the Years 1769, 1770, 1771 and 1772* (London: Strahan and Cadell, 1795).

25  George Elliot Clarke, *Whylah Falls* (Vancouver: Polestar, 1990).
26  Three-thousand-year-old prayer.

## 6 * IN THE WEST

1   Traditional American folk song.
2   W. G. Sebald, *Austerlitz*, trans. by Anthea Bell (Toronto: Random House, Canada, 2002).
3   Wallace Stegner, *Wolf Willow: A History, a Story, and a Memory of the Last Plains Frontier* (Toronto: Macmillan Canada, 1967).
4   Sharon Butala, *Wild Stone Heart: An Apprentice in the Field* (Toronto: HarperCollins, 2000).
5   Northrop Frye, *The Great Code: The Bible & Literature* (Markham: Penguin Books, 1990).
6   Traditional prayer.
7   Donald Atkin, "The March West," *Great Canadian Adventures*, Hugh Durnford and Peter Madely, eds., (Montreal: The Reader's Digest Association (Canada), 1976).
8   Scott W. See, *Riots in New Brunswick: Orange Nativism and Social Violence in the 1840s* (Toronto: University of Toronto Press, 1993).
9   Ibid.
10  Marius Barbeau, *Folk Songs of Old Quebec* (Ottawa: National Museum of Canada, 1964).
11  Winston Churchill, *The Birth of Britain* (New York: Dodd, Mead & Company, 1956).
12  Alexander Carmichael, *Carmina Gadelica: Hymns and Incantations Collected in the Highlands and Islands of Scotland in the Last Century* (Edinburgh: Floris Books, 1992).
13  Traditional English.
14  *Book of Common Prayer and Administration of the Sacraments and Other Rites and Ceremonies of the Church According to the Use of the Church of England in the Dominion of Canada* (Toronto: Oxford University Press). Inscription: B. M. Anderson, May 9, 1929.
15  Author's interview with Reverend Doctor Richard G. Leggett.
16  "The United Church of Canada: Our History, Life and Work" located at www.ucan.org/ucc/History.
17  *The Three Voyages of Martin Frobisher Vols. I and II*, Vilhjalmur Stefansson and Eloise McCaskill, eds. (London: The Argonaut Press, 1938).
18  Ibid.
19  Author's interview with Reverend Doctor Richard G. Leggett.
20  "The United Church of Canada: Our History, Life and Work" located at www.ucan.org/ucc/History.
21  *Book of Alternative Services of the Anglican Church in Canada* (Toronto: Anglican Book Centre, 1985).
22  Maria Campbell, *Stories of the Road Allowance People* (Penticton: Theytus Books, 1995).
23  *The Canadian Encyclopedia* (Edmonton: Hurtig Publishers, 1985).
24  Linda Hall, *August Gamble* (Elkhart: Bethel Publishing, 1995).
25  Wallace Stegner, *Wolf Willow: A History, a Story, and a Memory of the Last Plains Frontier* (Toronto: Macmillan Canada, 1967).
26  Ibid.
27  Irving Hexham, *Concise Dictionary of Religion* (Leicester: Inter Varsity Press: 1993).
28  Donny White, *In Search of Geraldine Moodie* (Regina: Canadian Plains Research Centre, University of Regina, 1998).
29  Jack Gorman, *Père Murray and the Hounds: The Story of Saskatchewan's Notre Dame College* (Sidney: Gray's Publishing, 1977).
30  Myrna Garanis, "April Fool's," *NeWest Review* (October/November 1995).
31  Will James, *Lone Cowboy: My Life Story* (New York: Charles Scribner's Sons, 1932).
32  "Will James," lyrics by Ian Tyson, Slick Fork Music, 1984.
33  Helen Fogwill Porter, *Below the Bridge* (St. John's: Breakwater Books, 1979).
34  Andrew Pyper, *Lost Girls* (Toronto: HarperCollins Canada, 1999).

35  Duncan Campbell Scott, *Selected Poems* (Toronto: Ryerson Press, 1951).
36  Author's interview with Reverand Doctor Gordon Bruce Turner.
37  Ibid.
38  Henri Nouwen, *Writings Selected: With an Introduction by Robert A. Jonas* (Maryknoll: Orbis Books, 1998).
39  Jean Vanier, *Be Not Afraid* (Toronto: Griffin House, 1975).
40  Wallace Stegner, *Wolf Willow: A History, a Story, and a Memory of the Last Plains Frontier* (Toronto: Macmillan Canada, 1967).
41  Significant Treasures, Ontario, Art Gallery of Hamilton, located at www.cffm-fcam.ca/Significant_Treasures/English © 1999 Canadian Heritage Information Network.
42  Lisa Chalykoff, "Tracing C.D. Shanly's 'The Walker of the Snow'," *Canadian Literature: A Quarterly of Criticism and Review*, No. 160 (Spring 1999): Opinions & Notes section. Located at www.canlit.ca/archive/ © 2003 *Canadian Literature*.
43  Bliss Carman, "The Vengeance of Noel Brassard: A Tale of the Acadian Expulsion," (Cambridge: The University Press, 1919).
44  From a review by Oliver P. Sweeney, *Hotpress*, located at www.taramusic.com © Tara Music Company Limited.
45  Stan Rogers, *Home in Halifax*, a live concert recorded by the CBC from the Rebecca Cohn Auditorium in 1982, Fogarty's Cove Music, 1994.
46  George Woodcock, *Gabriel Dumont: The Metis Chief and His Lost World* (Edmonton: Hurtig Publishers, 1975).
47  Joseph Kinsey Howard, *Strange Empire: A Narrative of the Northwest* (New York: William Morrow and Company, 1952).
48  Leonard Cohen, *Beautiful Losers* (Toronto: McClelland & Stewart, 1966).
49  Research and Information Services, National Library of Canada.
50  Ibid.
51  Margaret Laurence, *A Jest of God* (Toronto: McClelland & Stewart, 1991).
52  Richard E. Williams's artist statement from the exhibit *Mary Had a Dream* at the Main/Access Gallery, 1993.

7 * ROADS

1  Abebooks.com, an online marketplace for used, rare, and out-of-print books, located at www.abebooks.com © 1996-2003 Advanced Book Exchange Inc.
2  David Mulhall, *Will to Power: The Missionary Career of Father Morice* (Vancouver: University of British Columbia Press, 1986).
3  "Hang On St. Christopher," lyrics by Tom Waits, Jalma Music, 1987.
4  Ann-Marie MacDonald, *Fall on Your Knees* (Toronto: Alfred A. Knopf Canada, 1997).
5  Joan Skogan, *The Good Companion* (Victoria: Orca Books, 1998).
6  Ibid.
7  Blodwen Davies, *A String of Amber: The Story of the Mennonites in Canada* (Vancouver: Mitchell Press, 1973).
8  MacEdward Leach, *Folk Ballads & Songs of the Lower Labrador Coast* (Ottawa: National Museum of Canada, 1965).
9  Wallace Stegner, *Wolf Willow: A History, a Story, and a Memory of the Last Plains Frontier* (Toronto: Macmillan Canada, 1967).
10  Timothy Findley, *Pilgrim* (Toronto: HarperFlamingo Canada, 1999).
11  Katherine Barber, ed. *The Canadian Oxford Dictionary* (Don Mills: Oxford University Press, 1998).
12  N. J. Dawood, trans. *The Koran* (London: Penguin Books, 1956).
13  Sir George Simpson (Governor, Hon. Hudson's Bay Company), *Peace River: A Canoe Voyage from Hudson's Bay to the Pacific* (Toronto: Coles Publishing Company, 1970).
14  Donna Morrissey, *Kit's Law* (Toronto: Penguin Books Canada, 1999).
15  Émile Joseph Léger, *Short Sketches of the History of the Catholic Churches and Missions in Central Alberta* (Western Canada Publishing, 1914).
16  Ibid.

17. "Our Lady of Solitude," lyrics by Leonard Cohen, Sony/ATV Music Publishing, 1979.
18. "Song of Bernadette," lyrics by Leonard Cohen, Bill Elliott, and Jennifer Warnes, Sony/ATV Music Publishing, 1986.
19. Evan Solomon, "Tori Amos: Under the Volcano." *Shift Magazine* (April 1996).
20. Jan Zwicky and Brad Cran, eds., *Why I Sing the Blues: Lyrics & Poems* (Vancouver: Smoking Lung Press, 2001), CD included.
21. "Mary," lyrics by Sarah MacLachlan, Nettwerk Management, 1993.
22. "St. Augustine," lyrics by Lindsey Davis and Chad Horton, Nettwerk Management, 2001.
23. "Lost Highway," lyrics by Leon Payne. Sony/ATV Music Publishing, 1964.
24. Jack Kerouac, *Vanity of Duluoz: An Adventurous Education, 1935–46* (New York: Penguin Books, 1994).
25. Ann Charters, ed., *The Portable Beat Reader* (New York: Penguin Books USA, 1992).

## 8 ✼ COMMON GROUND

1. Coleman Barks and John Moyne, trans., *The Essential Rumi* (New York: HarperCollins Publishers, 1995).
2. Marina Warner, *Alone of All Her Sex: The Myth and the Cult of the Virgin Mary* (New York: Random House, 1983).
3. The Bible, authorized King James version.
4. Edith Fowke, *Folklore of Canada* (Toronto: McClelland & Stewart, 1976).
5. Achiel Peelman, *Christ Is a Native American* (Maryknoll: Orbis Books, 1995). Translation of *Le Christ est amérindien* (Toronto: Novalis, 1995).
6. Ibid.

✷ OTHER SOURCES ✷

*A Dictionary of Canadianisms on Historical Principles*. Toronto: Gage Educational Publishing Company, 1991.

"Ancient painting a mystery." *National Post*, September 10, 2001. A5.

Anderson, Frank. *81 Interesting Places in Saskatchewan*. Saskatoon: Gopher Books, 1989.

Armstrong, Bruce. *Sable Island*. Toronto: Doubleday Canada Limited, 1981.

*Art Book, The*. London: Phaidon Press Limited, 1997.

Attwater, Donald. *The Penguin Dictionary of Saints*. Middlesex: Penguin Books Ltd., 1965.

Atwood, Margaret. *The Robber Bride*. Toronto: McClelland & Stewart Ltd., 1993.

Barry, Bill. *The Dictionary of Saskatchewan Place Names*. Regina: People Places Publishing Ltd., 1998.

Bawlf, Samuel. "Secret voyage to B.C." *Vancouver Sun*, August 5, 2000. B1.

Beck, Horace. *Folklore and the Sea*. Middletown, CT: Marine Historical Association, 1973. Reprint Mystic, CT: Mystic Seaport Museum, Incorporated, 1996.

Bingham, Caroline. *Beyond the Highland Line: Highland History and Culture*. London: Constable, 1998.

Bindoff, S.T. *Tudor England*. Middlesex: Penguin, 1950.

Blais, Marie-Claire. Trans. Derek Coleman. *A Season in the Life of Emmanuel*. Toronto: McClelland & Stewart Ltd., 1966.

Boas, Franz. *Kwakiutl Tales Volume 11*. New York: Columbia University Press, 1910.

Bodger, Joan. *The Crack in the Teacup: The Life of an Old Woman Steeped in Stories*. Toronto: McClelland & Stewart Ltd., 2000.

Brody, Hugh. *The Other Side of Eden: Hunters, Farmers and the Shaping of the World*. Vancouver: Douglas & McIntyre, 2000.

Brown, George Mackey. *Portrait of Orkney*. London: The Hogarth Press Ltd., 1981.

Cahill, Thomas. *The Gifts of the Jews: How a Tribe of Desert Nomads Changed the Way Everyone Thinks and Feels*. New York: Doubleday, 1998.

Callaghan, Morley. *Our Lady of the Snows*. New York: St. Martin's Press, 1985.

Canada Post Customer Service

Caron, Louis. Trans. David T. Homel. *Draft Dodger*. Toronto: House of Anansi Press, 1980.

Carrier, Roch. Trans. Sheila Fischman. *La Guerre, Yes Sir!* Toronto: House of Anansi Press Limited, 1970.

Catholic Encyclopedia. New York: The Encyclopedia Press, Inc., 1917.

Cesca, Stephanie. "March Brings Old Italian Custom to Streets of Downtown London." *London Free Press*, June 8, 2001. News final.

Clebert, Jean-Paul. *The Gypsies*. Trans. by Charles Duff. Penguin Books edition, 1967. Paris: B. Arthaud, 1961.

Cole, Douglas and Ira Chakin. *An Iron Hand Upon the People: The Law Against the Potlatch on the Northwest Coast*. Vancouver and Seattle: Douglas & McIntyre and University of Washington Press, 1990.

Columbo, John Robert. *The Penguin Book of Canadian Jokes*. Toronto: Penguin Books, 2001.

Compton, Wade, ed. *Bluesprint: Black British Columbian Literature and Orature*. Vancouver: Arsenal Pulp Press, 2002.

Comte, Fernand. *The Wordsworth Dictionary of Mythology*. First published in France as *Les grandes figures des mythologies*. Ware: Wordsworth Editions Ltd., 1994.

Cox, Kevin. "Is this the Virgin Mary?" *Globe and Mail*, May 1, 2001. A1.

Craughwell, Thomas J., ed. *Every Eye Beholds You: A World Treasury of Prayer*. New York: Harcourt Brace & Company, 1998.

Creighton, Helen. *A Folk Tale Journey Through the Maritimes*. Cape Breton Island: Breton Books, 1993.

"'Cross' from World Trade Center steel beams becomes rescue workers' symbol of faith." *National Post*, October 6, 2001. A10.

Crozier, Lorna. *Apocrypha of Light*. Toronto: McClelland & Stewart Ltd., 2002

Cullison, Sheila. "Tattoo's Most Beautiful Image, The Virgin of Guadaloupe." *Skin & Ink*, March, 2002, 50-56.

Davies, Blodwen. *A String of Amber: The Story of the Mennonites in Canada*. Vancouver: Mitchell Press Limited, 1973.

Davies, Robertson. *Fifth Business*. Toronto: Penguin Books, 1970.

Delgado, James P. *Across the Top of the World: The Quest for the Northwest Passage*. Vancouver: Douglas & McIntyre Ltd. 1999.

di Michele, Mary. *Mimosa and Other Poems*. Oakville: Mosaic Press, 1981.

Dunn, Richard S. *The Age of Religious Wars 1559-1715*. New York, London: W. W. Norton & Company, 1979.

Fauset, Arthur Huff. *Folklore from Nova Scotia*. Columbus: American Folklore Society, 1931.

Feiler, Bruce. *Walking the Bible: A Journey by Land Through the Five Books of Moses*. New York: HarperCollins Publishers, Inc., 2001.

Fowke, Edith. *Tales Told in Canada*. Toronto: Doubleday Canada Limited, 1986.

Francis, Daniel, ed. *Encyclopedia of British Columbia*. Madeira Park, British Columbia: Harbour Publishing, 2000.

Frazer, Sir James George. *The Golden Bough: A Study in Magic and Religion*. London: MacMillan and Co. Limited, 1959.

Friis-Baastad, Erling. *The Exile House*. Cliffs of Moher, Co. Clare, Ireland: Salmon Publishing Ltd., 2001.

"Frost image draws crowd of curious in Saskatchewan." *Vancouver Sun*, November 7, 2002, A6.

Frye, Northrop. *The Great Code: The Bible & Literature*. Markham, Ontario: Penguin Books, 1990.

Fumoleau, René. *Here I Sit*. Ottawa: Novalis, 1999.

Gadon, Elinor W. *The Once & Future Goddess: A Sweeping Visual Chronicle of the Sacred Female and Her Reemergence In the Cultural Mythology of Our Time*. New York: Harper & Row, Publishers Inc., 1989.

Galashan, Sarah. "Delta firm fined $100,000 for food package tampering." *Vancouver Sun*, August 9, 2001. B1.

*Gisele Amantea: Recent Work* exhibition catalogue with essays by Daina Augaitas and David Joselit. Banff: Walter Phillips Gallery, 1991.

*Gumbo Ya-Ya Folk Tales of Louisiana*. Material gathered by Works Progress Administration Louisiana Writers' Project. Gretna, Louisiana: Pelican Publishing Company, 1991.

Graves, Robert. *The White Goddess: A Historical Grammar of Poetic Myth*. New York and Toronto: Farrar, Straus and Giroux; McGraw Hill Ryerson, 1983.

Giuliano, Bruce. *Sacro o Profano? A Consideration of Four Italian-Canadian Religious Festivals*. Ottawa: National Museums of Canada, 1976.

Halpenny, Francess G., Jean Hamelin, and Ramsay Cook, eds. *Dictionary of Canadian Biography*. University of Toronto Press, 1998.

Hannah, Don. *The Wise and Foolish Virgins*. Toronto: Alfred A. Knopf Canada, 1998.

Harris, Marvin. *Culture, People, Nature: An Introduction to General Anthropology*. New York and Toronto: Thomas Y. Crowell Company, Inc. and Fitzhenry & Whiteside, Ltd., 1975.

Hay, Elizabeth. *Captivity Tales: Canadians in New York*. Vancouver: New Star Books, 1993.

Harvey, Andrew, & Eryk Hanut. *Mary's Vineyard: Daily Meditations, Readings, and Revelations*. Wheaton, Illinois: The Theosophical Publishing House, 1996.

Hildebrandt, Walter and Brian Hubner. *The Cypress Hills: The Land and Its People*. Saskatoon: Purich Publishing, 1994.

*Historic Newfoundland and Labrador*. St. John's, Newfoundland: Newfoundland Department of Development.

Horsfield, Margaret and Peter. *Beyond Bethlehem*. Toronto: CBC Enterprises, 1989.

Hunter, Andrew. *Up North: A Northern Ontario Tragedy*. Owen Sound, Ontario: Thomson Books, 1997.

"Hymns of a Pilgrim," pamphlet, Cree hymns.

Ives, Edward D. *Larry Gorman, The Man Who Made the Songs*. Fredericton: Goose Lane Editions, 1993.

Johnson, Pauline (Tekahionwake). *Flint and Feather: The Complete Poems of Pauline Johnson*. Toronto: The Musson Book Company Limited. 1943.

Johnson, Sister Alice, s.f.c.c. *Marmora, Canada: Is Our Blessed Mother Speaking Here to Her Beloved Children?* Peterborough, Ontario: Amor Enterprises, 1994.

Johnston, Wayne. *Baltimore's Mansion: A Memoir*. Toronto: Alfred A. Knopf Canada, 1999.

Keller, Betty. *Pauline: A Biography of Pauline Johnson*. Halifax: Formac Publishing Company Limited, 1981.

King, Carlyle, ed. *Saskatchewan Harvest: A Golden Jubilee Selection of Song and Story*. Toronto: McClelland & Stewart Ltd., 1955.

Klymasz, Robert. *The Icon in Canada: Recent Findings from the Canadian Museum of Civilization*. Ottawa: Canadian Museum of Civilization, 1997.

Kurelek, William. *A Northern Nativity: Christmas Dreams of a Prairie Boy*. Montreal: Tundra Books, 1976.

Kurlansky, Mark. *Cod: A biography of the fish that changed the world*. Toronto: Knopf Canada, 1997.

Lalonde, Meika and Elton LaClare. *Discover Saskatchewan: A Guide to Historic Sites*. Regina: Canadian Plains Research Centre, University of Regina, 1998.

LaDow, Beth. *Medicine Line: Life and Death on a North American Borderland*. New York and London: Routledge, 2001.

Leach, MacEdward. *Folk Ballads & Songs of the Lower Labrador Coast*. Ottawa: National Museum of Canada, 1965.

Lewis-Harrison, June. *The People of Gabriola: A History of Our Pioneers*. 1982.

Lockheart, Gary. *The Weather Companion: An album of meteorological history, science, legend and folklore*. New York: John Wiley & Sons Inc., 1988.

Longfellow, Henry Wadsworth. *Evangeline: A Tale of Acadie*. London and Glasgow: Blackie & Son Limited, n.d.

Luke, Pearl. *Burning Ground*. Toronto: HarperCollins Canada, 2000.

MacArthur, Mary. "Super Hardy clover ideal for pasture." *The Western Producer*, November 22, 2001, 60.

MacGregor, Roy. "Puck Portents." *Globe and Mail*, November 30, 2002. D28.

MacMechan, Archibald. "The Captain's Boat." *Great Canadian Adventures*. Hugh Durnford and Peter Madely, eds. Montreal: The Reader's Digest Association (Canada) Ltd., 1976.

Macpherson, Jay. *Poems Twice Told*. Don Mills: Oxford University Press, 1981.

McNutt, Linda. *Summer Point*. Toronto: Cormorant Books, 1997.

Manchester, William. *A World Lit Only By Fire: The Medieval Mind and the Renaissance, Portrait of an Age*. Boston, Toronto, London: Little, Brown and Company, 1992.

Martel, Suzanne. *The King's Daughter*. Revised edition. Groundwood Book. Toronto: Douglas & McIntyre, 1980.

Massie, Robert K. *Peter the Great: His Life and World*. Toronto: Random House of Canada Limited, 1980.

Milne, Courtenay (photographs) and Sherrill Miller, text. *Visions of the Goddess.* Toronto: Penguin Canada, 1998.

Miner, Horace. *St. Denis: A French Canadian Parish.* Chicago & Toronto: University of Chicago Press and University of Toronto Press, 1963.

Morley, Patricia. *Kurelek: A Biography.* Toronto: Macmillan of Canada, 1986.

*Newfoundland & Labrador Heritage Guide.* St. John's, Newfoundland: Newfoundland & Labrador Tourism, Department of Canadian Heritage, Museum Association of Newfoundland and Labrador.

Newman, Peter C. *Caesars of the Wilderness: Company of Adventurers Volume II.* Toronto: Viking Penguin Books Canada Ltd., 1987.

Núñez, Luis Manuel. *Santeria: A Practical Guide to Afro-Caribbean Magic.* Dallas: Spring Publications, Inc., 1992.

O'Shea, Stephen. *Back to the Front: An Accidental Historian Walks the Trenches of World War I.* New York: Walker and Company, 1996.

Ostwald, Peter. *Glenn Gould: The Ecstasy and Tragedy of Genius* (New York: W. W. Norton & Company, 1997).

Overvold, Joanne and Alan Clovis, eds. *Our Metis Heritage: A portrayal. Metis Association of the Northwest Territories.* Bulletin Commercial, 1976.

Parkman, Francis. "Martyrs of the Wilderness." *Great Canadian Adventures.* Hugh Durnford and Peter Madely, eds. Montreal: The Reader's Digest Association (Canada) Ltd., 1976.

Phenix, Patricia. *Olga Romanov: Russia's Last Grand Duchess.* Toronto: Penguin Books Canada Limited, 1999.

Pratt, E. J. *Brebeuf and His Brethren.* Toronto: Macmillan of Canada, 1966.

Pratt, Sean. "Month of fasting boosts pulse sales." *The Western Producer,* November 22, 2001. 13.

*Prayers We Have in Common. Agreed Liturgical Texts Prepared by the International Consultation on English Texts.* Philadelphia: Fortress Press, 1975.

Raddall, Thomas H. "The Rover, Private Ship of War." *Great Canadian Adventures.* Hugh Durnford and Peter Madely, eds. Montreal: The Reader's Digest Association (Canada) Ltd., 1976.

Robins, John D., editor for Canadian Council of Education for Citizenship. *A Pocketful of Canada.* Toronto: Wm. Collins Sons & Co. Canada Ltd., 1948.

Rosenbaum, Jonathan. *Dead Man.* London: British Film Institute, 2000.

Ross, Malcolm, ed. *Poets of the Confederation.* Toronto: McClelland and Stewart Ltd., 1960.

Ross, Oakland. *The Dark Virgin: A Novel of Mexico.* Toronto: HarperCollins Publishers Ltd., 2000.

Scott, Sarah. "Putting the pieces together." *National Post,* July 6, 2002. B7.

"Scottish Studies Foundation," pamphlet. Toronto, Ontario.

Sealey, D. Bruce and Antoine S. Lussier. *The Metis: Canada's Forgotten People.* Winnipeg: Metis Federation Press, 1975.

Service, Robert W. *The Spell of the Yukon.* New York: Putnam Publishing Group, 1990.

Setton, Kenneh Meyer, ed., and National Geographic Staff. *The Renaissance: Maker of Modern Man.* Simon & Schuster, 1970.

Sjercic, Hedina, ed. *Canadian Romani Pearls.* Toronto: The Roma Community & Advocacy Centre (O Kanadako-Romano Phralipe), 1999.

Soueif, Ahdaf. *The Map of Love.* London: Bloomsbury, 2000.

*St. Andrew's Wesley Church Reflections 1933-1993.* Vancouver: St. Andrew's Wesley Church and Cunningham Theological Foundation.

Stenson, Fred. *R.C.M.P.: The March West, N.W.M.P.–R.C.M.P. 1873-1999.* GAPC Entertainment Inc., 1999.

Taché, Joseph-Charles. *Forestiers et voyageurs.* Quebec, 1863; rpt. Montreal: Fides, 1946.

Thomson, George Malcolm. *Sir Francis Drake.* New York: William Morrow & Company Inc., 1972.

Tilney, Phil. *This Other Eden: Canadian Folk Art Outdoors.* Vancouver: Douglas & McIntyre, 1999. Hull, Quebec: Canadian Museum of Civilization, 1999.

Tong, Diane. *Gypsy Folk Tales.* New York: MJF Books, 1989.

Tuchman, Barbara. *A Distant Mirror: The Calamitous 14th Century.* New York, Alfred A. Knopf, Inc., 1978.

Urquhart, Jane. *The Stone Carvers*. Toronto: McClelland & Stewart Ltd., 2001.

Vanderhaeghe, Guy. *The Englishman's Boy*. Toronto: McClelland & Stewart Ltd., 1997.

Vardey, Lucinda, ed. *The Flowering of the Soul: A Book of Prayers by Women*. Toronto: Alfred A. Knopf, 1999.

Veillette, John and Gary White. *Early Indian Village Churches: Wooden Frontier Architecture in British Columbia*. Vancouver: University of British Columbia Press, 1977.

"Virgin Vision Blamed on Sap." *Vancouver Province*, December 24, 1996. A51.

Visser, Margaret. *The Way We Are*. Toronto: HarperCollins Publishers Ltd., 1994.

Walker, Barbara. *The Woman's Dictionary of Symbols & Sacred Objects*. New York: Harper & Row, Publishers, Inc., 1988.

*The Woman's Encyclopedia of Myths and Secrets*. New York: HarperCollins Publishers Inc., 1983.

Warner, Marina. *From the Beast to the Blonde: On Fairytales and Their Tellers*. London: Chatto & Windus, 1994.

Weekley, Ernest. *An Etymological Dictionary of Modern English*. New York: Dover Publications, Inc., 1967; Don Mills, Ontario: General Publishing Company Ltd.

Westwood, Jennifer. *Sacred Journeys: An Illustrated Guide to Pilgrimages Around the World*. New York: Henry Holt and Company, 1997.

Whitaker, Muriel, ed. *Great Canadian War Stories*. Edmonton: The University of Alberta Press, 2001.

Wiebe, Rudy. *A Discovery of Strangers*. Toronto: Random House of Canada Limited, 1995.

Winter, Tim. "Pulchra Ut Luna: Some Reflections on The Marian Theme in Muslim-Catholic Dialogue." *Journal of Ecumenical Studies*, Summer/Fall 1999, Vol. 36, 439.

Woodman, Marian with Jill Mellick. *Coming Home to Myself: Daily Reflections for a Woman's Body and Soul*. Berkeley, California: Conari Press, 1998.

FILM

*Alias Will James*. Dir. Jacques Godbout. National Film Board.

*Dead Man*. Dir. Jim Jarmusch. 12 Gauge Productions, Inc. with Pandora film, Frankfort, and with the support of FFA Berlin Filmboard Berlin-Brandenburg/Filmstiftung.

*Conversion* (Part Two in *Before Columbus* series). Dir. Brian Moser. Central Productions in association with the National Film Board of Canada.

*Straight to the Heart: The Life of Henri Nouen*. Windbourne Productions film.

INTERNET SOURCES

http://www.lastdraft.com/alumsample.htm *Gods, Bears, Stones, and Stars*.
http://www.barridoff.com/2002/hartley *Marsden Hartley Roses*
http://www.islamsa.org.za/arrasheed
http://www.parkscanada.pch.gc.ca/parks *L'Anse aux Meadows National Historic Site of Canada*
http://www.saint-mike.org/apologetics *Lazarus*
http://geonames.nrcan.gc.ca *Geographical Names Database*. Ottawa: Natural Resources Canada
http://www.newadvent.org/cathen *Catholic Encyclopedia: Miracle*

INTERVIEWS

Angela Doulias
Don Gillmore
Terry Glavin
Linda Kelly-Smith

✳ IMAGE NOTES ✳

1 ✳ AT SEA

p. iii, 17 Beaded Mary and Child, print, Iroquois, mid-20th century; [AN 8]; newsprint, glass beads, cotton thread, cardboard; 40.6 x 34.3 cm. Collection of Glenbow Museum, Calgary, Canada

p. xiv (top,bottom) also p. 53, "Proposed Water Power on St. Mary River, Alberta," plan prepared by F. K. Beach, Civil Engineer, March 17, 1910, Calgary, Alberta (middle), "St. Mary River below confluence with Spring Coulee, Alberta," 1898, photograph. Courtesy of Glenbow Archives PD-301-15, Calgary, Canada

p. vxiii–xix Map of Canada, by Wendy Johnson, Johnson Cartographics, Edmonton, AB

p. xx, 19 *Our Lady of the Iceberg*, by Thomas B. Hayward. Courtesy of The Archives of the Roman Catholic Archdiocese and the Newfoundland Historical Society, St. John's, NL

p. 4 *The Virgin*, c. 1700-1799, wood with gilt and polychrome, 42.8 x 13.8 x 9.8 cm, unknown artist (Canadian, Quebec). © National Gallery of Canada, Ottawa. Purchased 1971. 16898

p. 10 *Virgen de Guadalupe*. Reprinted with permission of the publisher, from *Artes de México*, No. 29, 1995. The original image is courtesy of the Basílica de Santa María de Guadalupe, Mexico, D. F. Photo by Rafael Doníz

2 ✳ MAP-MAKING

p. 22, 30 *Rose and Queenship of Mary*, stained-glass window, in Holy Rosary Cathedral, Regina, SK, by Andre Rault, Rault Studios, Rennes, France. Photo courtesy of Gordon Domm – Timeless Moments PHOTO GRAPHICS – Regina, SK

p. 29 *Wild rose (Rosa acicularis)*, watercolour, by L. R. Stockelbach, produced for the IXth International Congress of Botany in Montréal, 1959. For the Department of Agriculture and Agri-Food, © Minister of Public Works and Government Services Canada, 2003, Government of Canada. Used with permission.

p. 31 Champlain Rose postage stamp, #1913, © Canada Post Corporation, 2001. Reproduced with permission.

p. 32 (left) Sainte-Marie-aux-Hurons Mission Rosary, c. 17th century. Photo supplied by Sainte-Marie among the Hurons, an attraction of the Ontario Ministry of Tourism and Recreation
(right) "Vicious Cycle" Laundromat, postcard, Vancouver, BC

p. 33 (left) Spiral pathway at the Bethlehem Retreat Centre, Nanaimo, BC. Photo by Joan Skogan
(right), also p. 209, "Goniatites sp," postcard, ammonoid from Morocco, Devonian, 370 million years. Courtesy of Fossilsaurus, Montreal, QC. Photo by Daniel Lussier.

p. 41 *Creche*; cedar, pine, wood, chipboard, straw, metal rods, paint, wire, plastic thongs, fabric braid and light fixture; 1983; by Gordon Law (Canadian, b. 1914). Purchase, 1983. Collection of the Robert McLaughlin Gallery, Oshawa, ON

p. 42 *France Bringing the Faith to the Indians of New France*, attributed to Claude François (Frère Luc), oil on canvas (1997.1017). Collection du monastère des Ursulines de Québec

p. 52 *Mary of God of Canada*, 1992, acrylic and gold on wood panel, artist Slavko Protic, © Canadian Museum of Civilization, artist Slavko Protic, 1992, catalogue no. 94-87, image no. S94-38878. Photo by Merle Toole

3 ✳ MARY IN CANADA

p. 56 *Our Lady of Canada*, 1995, acrylic, wood, muslin, 22K gold, by André J. Prevost, at All Saints Orthodox Cathedral, Edmonton, AB. Courtesy of André J. Prevost

p. 58 "Our Lady of the Highway Shrine," postcard. Our Lady of the Highway Shrine is located east of Vegreville, AB, on the Yellowhead Highway. Photo by Holiday Photo, Vegreville, AB

p. 64 "Notre-Dame de Roc-Amadour," prayer card. St-François d'Assise, Quebec, QC (avec la permission de l'Ordinaire, Quebec, 8 septembre 1987)

p. 66 *Le Premier Pèlerinage au Canada*, 1921, by Antonio Masselotte, at St-François d'Assise church, Quebec, QC

p. 69 Brooch, Métis, mid-20th century; [AR 42 a]; tin, velvet cloth, paper, silk thread, glass; 9.4 x 7.6 cm. Collection of Glenbow Museum, Calgary, Canada

p. 76 *The Holy Family*, early 19th century, painted wood, near Caughnawga, QC, © Canadian Museum of Civilization, catalogue no. 76-191, image no. S83-596

p. 85 *Guadalupe-Tonantzim*, 2000, box art—mixed media, by Carmen Bizet-Irigoyen, from the *Altared Spaces* community exhibition. Courtesy of Carmen Bizet-Irigoyen and Gallery Gachet, Vancouver, BC

p. 86 Sacred Heart tattoo. Courtesy of Jen Asmus

p. 90 *The Holy Family*, c. 1850-1899, wood with polychrome, 31.3 x 20.5 x 10.5 cm, by Jean-Baptiste Côté (Canadian, 1832-1907). © National Gallery of Canada, Ottawa. Purchased 1978. 23182

p. 94 *Our Lady of Combermere*, 1960, bronze, by Frances Rich, located at Madonna House, Combermere, ON. Courtesy of Madonna House Publications

p. 96 *Vladimir Mother of God*, 1874, Russian (with and without the silver/gold riza). Courtesy of Maryhill Museum of Art, Goldendale, WA

p. 100 *Stations of the Cross: Jesus Is Taken Down from the Cross, and Jesus Is Laid in the Tomb*, 1995, oil on panel, 16" x 12", by Chris Woods, in St. David's Anglican Church, Vancouver, BC. Courtesy of Chris Woods and Diane Farris Gallery.com

p. 101 Cartoon, from *The Globe and Mail*, April 4, 2002, A12, by Gable. Reprinted with permission from *The Globe and Mail*, Toronto, Canada

p. 102 (left) *The Virgin Elvis*, photograph. Copyright © 1990 by Shari Hatt. Courtesy of Shari Hatt
(right) *St. Pinocchio*, 1994, oil painting, 36" x 24", by Barbara Klunder. Collection of the Vatican. Courtesy of Barbara Klunder

p. 103 *This Dark Edge of Monkeys*, 1991, acrylic on canvas, 28" x 64", by Marianna Gartner. Collection of the Canada Council Art Bank. Courtesy of Marianna Gartner.

p. 104 *Mary — Aged 7 Years*, 2000, oil on canvas, 48" x 72", by Marianna Gartner. Private Collection. Courtesy of Marianna Gartner

### 4 ✳ EASTERN SETTINGS

p. 108, 119 "The Statue of Notre-Dame du Cap," postcard. Sculpture is located at Sanctuaire Notre-Dame du Cap Shrine, Montreal, QC

p. 111 *The Holy Family*, print on a 1992 calendar from Kelly's Store, Lawn, NL

p. 112 *Our Lady of the World and of Marystown*, Marystown, NF. Photo by Joan Skogan

### 5 ✳ NORTHERN BLESSINGS

p. 124, 145 *Pine Tree Madonna*, 1926, oil on canvas, by Thoreau MacDonald (Canadian, 1901-1989). Gift of the estate of Doris Huestis Speirs, 2001. Collection of the Robert McLaughlin Gallery, Oshawa, ON

p. 130 Virgin Mary square pillow cover, by Trish Tacoma and Julie Higginson of Smoking Lily, Victoria, BC. Courtesy of Trish Tacoma and Julie Higginson. Photo by Rita Taylor and Marni Wilson

p. 134 *St. Mary*, wood sculpture by Ted Bellis, located at St. Mary's Spring, Lawn Hill, Haida Gwaii, Queen Charlotte Islands, BC. Courtesy of Dick Bellis.

p. 144 Interior of St. Bernard Catholic Church, Grouard, AB (on the shores of Lesser Slave Lake), n.d. Courtesy of the Missionary Oblates Grandin Archives (Provincial Archives of Alberta), OB.895

p. 152 *Sea Goddess*, 1971, soapstone, 11.3 x 6.5 x 20.5 cm, by Lymeekee Kakkee [Canadian, Inuit, Qikiqtarjuaq (Broughton Island), born 1937]. Collection of T. Bert and Joanne Rose. Photo by Don Hall, courtesy of the Mackenzie Art Gallery

### 6 ✳ IN THE WEST

p. 158 "Beside Chimney Coulee north of Eastend, site of H. B. Company trading post 1871-1872 and NWMP post 1876-1887," postcard. Photo by Lynne, Eastend, SK

p. 178 *Pilgrims to Ste. Anne de Beaupre*, July 19, 1879, vol. XX, no. 3, 40, artist unknown, record 3496. The National Library of Canada, Canadian Illustrated News. Reproduced from the National Library of Canada's website (www.nlc-bnc.ca)

p. 182 *Notre Dame d'Auvergne*. Sculpture is located at Notre Dame d'Auvergne Parish, Ponteix, SK. Photo by Joan Skogan

p. 186 "Our Lady of the Fields," prayer card. Our Lady of the Fields, Ponteix, SK. Imprimatur: Peter Mallon, Archbishop of Regina, July 16, 2000

p. 193 *Our Lady of the Prairies*, stained-glass window in St. Augustine's Church, Wilcox, SK. Courtesy of Athol Murray College of Notre Dame Archives/Museum

p. 197 Wooden Rose windows. Reprinted with permission of the publisher from *Early Indian Village Churches* by John Veillette and Gary White © University of British Columbia Press 1977

p. 210 Kateri Tekakwitha magnet (prayer card on cut pine). Photo by Rita Taylor and Marni Wilson

p. 212 Virgin Mary nightlight. Photo by Rita Taylor and Marni Wilson

p. 213 *Person to Person*, 1985, oil on canvas, 122 x 183 cm, by Richard Williams. Permanent collection of the University of Manitoba School of Art, Winnipeg, MB. Courtesy of Richard Williams.

### 7 ✳ ROADS

p. 216, 220 "Good Hope. R.C. Church [interior]. 1937," b&w negative by Charles Rowan. Photo courtesy of the NWT Archives

p. 226 *The Flight Into Egypt: Crossing a Brook*, 1654, etching and drypoint on laid paper, 9.4 x 14.5 cm, by Rembrandt

*Image Notes* 301

Harmensz, van Rijn (1606-1669). Courtesy of the Art Gallery of Ontario, Toronto, ON. Purchase 1922

p. 236 (top) "La Vierge du Sourire," prayer card. Petites Soeurs de Notre-Dame du Sourire, Montreal, QC. Imprimatur: (200 jours d'indulgence) Paul-Emile Cardinal Léger, Archbishop of Montreal, September 12, 1953

(bottom) "Notre-Dame de la Vie Intérieure," prayer card. Imprimatur: (100 jours d'indulgence) Paul-Emile Cardinal Léger, Archbishop of Montreal, June 16, 1953

*Mère de Misericord*, 1879, by Louis-Phillipe Hébert, at Chappelle de la Misericorde, Montreal, QC

p. 239 Shell Mary. Photo by Rita Taylor and Marni Wilson

p. 240 Mary prayer card basket. Photo by Rita Taylor and Marni Wilson

p. 243 Leaky Heaven Circus, poster; artist, Marina Szijarto; layout, Nadene Rehnby. Courtesy of Leaky Heaven Circus, Vancouver, BC

p. 245 *Virgin Mary*, stone sculpture, by Ital Décor, Burnaby, BC. Photo by Joan Skogan

p. 246 *Our Lady of the Peace*, Dunvegan, AB. Photos by Joan Skogan

p. 249 "St. Anne," prayer card

p. 256 Stained-glass window, by Alex Twin, located at the Ermineskin Church in Hobbema, AB. Photo courtesy of Todd Korol

p. 258 "Lac Ste. Anne Pilgrimage – Candlelight Procession," postcard. Lac Ste. Anne Pilgimage Office, St. Albert, AB

p. 259 Lac Ste. Anne Pilgrimage paper candle shield. Lac Ste. Anne Pilgimage Office, St. Albert, AB

8 ✳ COMMON GROUND

p. 264 *I Don't Want a Massage, I Want a Miracle*, 1989, site-specific adobe sculpture, 78" high, by Sharon Moodie. Courtesy of Sharon Moodie. Photo by Joan Skogan

p. 266 Mary soap. Photo by Rita Taylor and Marni Wilson

p. 267 Virgin Mary's store advertisement, Vancouver, BC

p. 271 *Ursa Major*, from *Uranographia* (1690) by Johannes Hevelius. Courtesy of Istituto di Fisica Generale Applicata, Università degli Studi di Milano

p. 284 *Virgin Mary*, block print, by Mary Gordon. Courtesy of Joan Skogan

✶ TEXT PERMISSIONS ✶

The publisher gratefully acknowledges the following authors and publishers for permission to reprint material contained in this book. Every effort has been made to obtain permission for text excerpts. The publisher would be pleased to adjust acknowledgements upon reprinting:

From *Be Not Afraid* by Jean Vanier. Copyright © by Jean Vanier. Reprinted by permission of the author and L'Arche-Trosly, France.

From the exhibit *Les Lieux Communs/Commonplaces* at the Walter Phillips Gallery, 1995, by Carol Dallaire. Reprinted by permission of the artist. http://www.ava.qc.ca/creation/carol_dallaire/Carol_Dallaire.html

From *Sarah and the People of Sand River* by W.D. Valgardson. Reprinted by permission of Groundwood Books.

From *The Dark Virgin* by Oakland Ross. Copyright © 2001 by Oakland Ross. Reprinted by permission of HarperCollins *Publishers Ltd*.

From *Virgin Trails* by Robert Ward. Copyright © 2002 by Robert Ward. Reprinted by permission of Key Porter Books.

From *Reading Pictures* by Alberto Manguel. Copyright © 2000 by Alberto Manguel. Reprinted by permission of Alfred A. Knopf Canada.

From "Portraits of a Lady" from *The Exile House* by Erling Friis-Baastad. Copyright © Erling Friis-Baastad. Published by Salmon Publishing, Cliffs of Moher, Co. Clare, Ireland. Reprinted by permission of the author.

From *Word from New France* by Joyce Marshall. Copyright © 1993 by Joyce Marshall. Reprinted by permission of the author.

From *The Fairies Are Thirsty* by Denise Boucher. Copyright © 1982 by Denise Boucher. Reprinted by permission of Talonbooks.

From *My Darling Dead Ones* by Erika de Vasconcelos. Copyright © 1997 by Erika de Vasconcelos. Reprinted by permission of Alfred A. Knopf Canada.

From *Transcanadaletters* by Roy Kiyooka. Copyright © 1975 by Roy Kiyooka. Reprinted by permission of Talonbooks.

From "Isis in the Darkness," from *Wilderness Tips* by Margaret Atwood. Used by permission, McClelland & Stewart Ltd. *The Canadian Publishers*.

*parthenos (Ever-Virgin)* ✷ *Ark of the Covenant* ✷ *A Mercy for the Worlds* ✷ *Cause of Our Joy* ✷ *Comforter of the Afflicted Consolatrix Afflictorum* ✷ *Domina* ✷ *Gate of Heaven* ✷

From *Coming Home to Myself* by Marian Woodman and Jill Mellick. Reprinted by permission of Conari Press, an imprint of Red Wheel/Weiser, Boston, MA, and York Beach, ME.

From *Novalis Guide to Canadian Shrines* by Leonard St. John. Copyright © 1999 by Novalis Publishing. Reprinted by permission of the publisher. Order toll-free 1-800-387-7164 or cservice@novalis.ca.

From *La Sagouine* by Antonine Maillet. Published by Simon & Pierre, an imprint of The Dundurn Group. Reprinted by permission of The Dundurn Group.

From *The Truth Teller* by Katherine Govier. Copyright © 2000 by Katherine Govier. Reprinted by permission of Random House Canada.

From "The Draft Dodger," by Louis Caron. Copyright © by Louis Caron. Reprinted by permission of House of Anansi Press.

From *La Guerre, Yes Sir!* By Roch Carrier. Copyright © 1968 Editions du Jour. English translation copyright © 1970 by Sheila Fischman. Reprinted by permission of House of Anansi Press.

From *Our Lady of the Lost and Found* by Diane Schoemperlen. Copyright © 2001 by Diane Schoemperlen. A Phyllis Bruce Book. Reprinted by permission of HarperCollins Publishers Ltd.

From "Pat and Mike Jokes from Nova Scotia" from *Folklore from Nova Scotia* by Arthur Huff Fauset. Reprinted by permission of the American Folklore Society.

From *The Penguin Book of Canadian Jokes* by John Robert Columbo. Copyright © 2001 by John Robert Columbo. Reprinted by permission of Penguin Books Canada Limited.

From *The Great Code* by Northrop Frye. Copyright © 1982, 1981 by Northrop Frye. Reprinted by permission of Harcourt, Inc.

From *The Englishman's Boy* by Guy Vanderhaeghe. Used by permission, McClelland & Stewart Ltd. *The Canadian Publishers*.

From *Wild Stone Heart: An Apprentice in the Field* by Sharon Butala. Copyright © 2000 by Sharon Butala. A Phyllis BruceBook. Reprinted by permission of HarperCollins Publishers Ltd.

From "Val Marie" by Eli Mandel. Courtesy of the Estate of Eli Mandel.

From *August Gamble* by Linda Hall. Copyright © 1995 by Bethel Publishing, an imprint of Evangel Publishing House. Reprinted by permission of Evangel Publishing House.

From "April Fool's," by Myrna Garanis. Copyright © Myrna Garanis. Reprinted by permission of the author.

From "The Moon and the Salt Flats" from *Mimosa and Other Poems* by Mary di Michele. Copyright © 1981 by Mary di Michele. Reprinted by permission of Mosaic Press.

From "The Natural Mother" from *Poems Twice Told* by Jay Macpherson. Copyright © 1981 by Oxford University Press Canada. Reprinted by permission.

From "Annunciation" from *Here I Sit* by Rene Fumoleau. Copyright © 1999 by Novalis Publishing. Reprinted by permission of the publisher. Order toll-free 1-800-387-7164 or cservice@novalis.ca.

From *A Season in the Life of Emmanuel* by Marie-Claire Blais. Copyright © 1966 by Marie-Claire Blais.

From *A Crack in the Teacup: The Life of an Old Woman Steeped in Stories* by Joan Bodger. Used by permission, McClelland & Stewart Ltd. *The Canadian Publishers*.

From "Black Mary" by Andrea Thompson. Copyright © by Andrea Thompson. Reprinted by permission of the author.

From "Our Lady of Solitude," lyrics by Leonard Cohen. Copyright © Sony/ATV Music Publishing.

From "Song of Bernadette," lyrics by Leonard Cohen, Bill Elliott, and Jennifer Warnes. Copyright © Sony/ATV Music Publishing.

From "St. Mary Blues," by Patrick Friesen. Copyright © Patrick Friesen. Published in *Why I Sing the Blues* by Smoking Lung Press. Reprinted by permission of the author.

From "The Lost Highway," lyrics by Leon Payne. Copyright © Sony/ATV Music Publishing.

From "The Canticle of Jack Kerouac" by Lawrence Ferlinghetti. Copyright © by Lawrence Ferlinghetti.

Reprinted by permission of Limberlost Press and City Lights Books.

From "Spring Is Christ" by Jelaluddin Rumi, from *The Essential Rumi*, translated by Coleman Barks and John Moyne. Reprinted by permission of Coleman Barks.

From *Larry Gorman, The Man Who Made the Songs* by Edward D. Ives. Copyright © 1993 by Edward D. Ives. Published by Goose Lane Editions. Reprinted by permission of the author.

From *Christ Is a Native American*, translation of *Le Christ est amerindien*, by Achiel Peelman. Copyright © 1995 by Novalis Publishing. Reprinted by permission of the publisher. Order toll-free 1-800-387-7164 or cservice@novalis.ca.

From "Who is She, Then?" from *Apocrypha of Light* by Lorna Crozier. Used by permission, McClelland & Stewart Ltd. *The Canadian Publishers*.